From
To Divorce

*Five One-Act Farces
of Marital Discord*

*Georges Feydeau
translated from the French
by Laurence Senelick*

BROADWAY PLAY PUBLISHING INC
224 E 62nd St, NY, NY 10065
www.broadwayplaypub.com
info@broadwayplaypub.com

From Marriage To Divorce
© Copyright 2017 Laurence Senelick

Cover art by Leonetto Cappiello

First edition: July 2017
I S B N: 978-0-88145-715-5

Book design: Marie Donovan
Page make-up: Adobe InDesign
Typeface: Palatino
Printed and bound in the U S A

PREFACE

We think of Georges Feydeau as a nineteenth-century playwright, but some of his best work was done in the early twentieth century, as a contemporary of Shaw and Maeterlinck. In 1908, he enjoyed one of the greatest triumphs of his career, with *Occupe-toi d'Amélie* (*Keep an Eye on Amélie*) It led the poet Jean Richepin to describe him as "the mathematician, the watchmaker, the engineer, the Vaucanson[1], the Blaise Pascal, the Edison, the miracle-worker, the Demiurge who invents, dreams, combines, contrasts, mounts, sets in motion imperturbably and impeccably a machine as complicated, as miraculous, as perfect, without missing a single effect, without a single cog out of place, without a single spring working loose, without his own skull bursting into bits, exploding like a pressure cooker packed with all the explosives of laughter."

Somewhat weary of constructing his elaborate three-act bedroom farces, Feydeau was casting around for something new, and found it in his own home. He had married a famous beauty for love, but by 1908 the marriage was breaking down. His wife Marianne was constantly berating him for coming home in the wee hours of the morning and twitting him for his Sunday painting. Starting from these observed details, he wrote a one-act entitled *Feu la mère de Madame* (*Madame's Late*

1 The inventor of the mechanical chess player. (Translator's note)

Mother or in this translation *Dead Wrong*) On November
15, 1908, it opened at the Comédie-Royale, a red and
gold candy-box of a theatre, perfect for the play's
intimacy. Although third on the bill after a comedy and
a song act, as played by Feydeau's favorite actors, the
saucy Armande Cassive and the lanky Marcel Simon, it
was a huge success.

The reviewers called it "an hour of insane merriment,
inextinguishable laughter". The actor-manager
André Antoine, who had turned down the play,
visited Feydeau after the premiere and said, "I'm
an asshole." His fellow playwright Robert de Flers
correctly remarked that there is no break between
Feydeau's first and second manner: "No one should be
extremely surprised that George Feydeau has achieved
comedies—violently comic and almost realistic—yes,
realistic in the tone of the dialogue, even if they are still
sometimes fantastic, of which *Madame's Late Mother*
will remain the most perfectly achieved model."
Feydeau thought this was the only one of his works
that would last and hoped it would one day enter the
repertoire of the Comédie Française, which came to
pass in 1941.

With this play, Feydeau had launched a new genre:
the marital farce, the hell of couples. A husband and
wife stay together by force of habit, their relationship
based on nothing solid. In the course of an hour,
packed with stupid spats and trivial arguments, the
wife's aggression and bitterness and the husband's
selfishness and irresponsibility are revealed, without
disguise. This ferocious animosity, through Feydeau's
accumulation of minutiae, unleashes such powerful
comedy that it obscures the underlying darkness.
Hence the genre's originality. The plot is linear:
the complications don't go beyond standard cross-
purposes; all the comedy is in the amplified depiction

of the petty conjugal inferno. There are laughs from start to finish, but the humor is so black that Marcel Achard compared these plays to Strindberg. (Feydeau always insisted, "Farce must be played like a tragedy.")

In September 1909 Feydeau moved out, taking only his toothbrush, comb and pajamas, to sleep at the station hotel of the Gare Saint-Lazare where he would live off and on for the next ten years. "Really, I wasn't made for marriage," he later admitted. Inspired by Racine's remark that "All invention consists in making something out of nothing," he drew again on his domestic afflictions to create *On purge Bébé (Giving Baby a Purge* or in this translation *Potty Favors)* His wife had an obsession with giving the children laxatives, especially his eldest son Jacques, the model for Toto, the first *enfant terrible* on the French stage. The line about Louis XV's bastard was also Marianne's. She said she ought to get royalties.

The second great one-act *On purge Bébé* opened on 2 April 1910 at the Nouveautés, again with Cassive and Marcel Simon. "Here," noted Adolphe Brisson, "the comic effect springs only from the precise reality of the detail." Characters, inanimate objects and the stifling atmosphere have been closely observed. But Feydeau pushes this reality as far as it will go, transforming it into a kind of surreality. When it was revived two years later, Gaston Sorbets found "something classic about it." Certainly the emphasis on the bowels hearkens back to Molière and a vein of Rabelaisian earthiness. On the other hand, the pointlessness of the quarrels and the thwarting of every intention look forward to the Absurdists. Every character is despicable for his moral cowardice and egoism, providing a hopeless environment for child-rearing.

The next one-act *Mais n'te promène donc pas toute nue! ("Don't Walk Around in the Nude!"* Or *She Can't*

Bear It!) was inspired by Marianne's going around
the apartment in her nightie until lunchtime. The
episode of the wasp at the picnic also came from life.
Needing a particularly delicate profession for the
husband, Feydeau made him a legislator, opening
up the possibility for some political satire. The play
was written in three weeks and on 25 November 1911
celebrated the re-opening of the Théâtre Fémina, with
Cassive again in the lead. The politician Léon Blum
wrote in *Comoedia* "The quantity of effects of dialogue
which M. Feydeau can draw from a marital squabble,
the number of effects of situation provided him by a
woman who walks around an apartment dressed in
a nightie and a hat, are something which will always
provoke my astonished admiration. I begin to notice
besides that M. Feydeau has created a type of woman
rather close to certain types of M. Georges Courteline,
but which are entirely his own."

Whether Feydeau's heroines are named Yvonne, Julie,
Clarisse, Léonie or Marcelle, they are variations on the
same woman, drawn from the categories the poet Paul
Valéry called *"les emmerdantes," "les emmerdeuses"* and
"les emmerderesses" (Roughly, "women who are driving
you crazy," "women who drive everyone crazy" and
"women who drive you over the edge.") A woman
logical in her illogicality, she employs an apparently
reasonable dialectic which ends up in pure dementia
without anyone discerning precisely how it got there.
These elaborate arguments, fit to drive a husband to
distraction, always have so trivial a point of departure
that the irresistible comedy and the forceful impression
of everyday life come across simultaneously.

One critic noted that Feydeau, always a master builder,
had now shown himself to be a great improviser, free
to dazzle the audience at will. Gaston de Pawlowski
found him to be a moralist as well. "There is, as

in Molière, a great deal of despair, a great deal of
contained sadness, a great deal of scorn perhaps for
the public in this farce that makes us laugh as once
the characters of the Italian comedy made us laugh
with their sufferings or their blows. This theatre,
under an apparent cynical frivolity, far surpasses the
understanding of certain spectators. …M. Feydeau, like
the very great comic writers, knows how to make the
public laugh at his personal bitterness."

 On 9 December 1911, back at the Comédie-Royale,
Marcel Simon created the fourth of the great one-
acts, *Léonie est en avance ou le mal joli*, (*Léonie's Ahead
of Schedule or The Wonderful Pain*, translated here as
Blasted Event) Robert de Flers noticed how Feydeau
had pinpointed the common attitude of a number of
women; they seem to have as their mission to destroy
their husband's nerves by every possible means, while
loving them. "Spirit of contradiction, little traps, nasty
teasing, ironic compliments, irritated reproaches,
pretend merriment, then sudden silences, terrifying
endearments and menacing renunciations."

There is a general degradation in the relations
between spouses from the first to the fourth play
with increasingly dire consequences. In the first,
a husband and wife can unite against an intruder.
Then the stakes get progressively higher: we see
how the marital discord progressively results in the
destruction of an important business deal and then
a political career. By the fourth, the husband, named
Toudoux (Meekenmild), trapped in a misalliance, is
set upon by his wife, his in-laws and the midwife.
With its emphasis on birth pangs, indigestion, and
mutual recrimination, the atmosphere is exceptionally
somber and sordid. Pity the poor baby born into this
household.

Feydeau and his wife formally separated in 1913, but it was another three years before the last play in the series appeared. *Hortense a dit: "Je m'en fous!"* (*Hortense Said "I Don't Give a Damn!"* or in this translation *The Awful Tooth*) was the last new play of Feydeau to be produced in his lifetime. It opened on 14 January 1916 at the Palais-Royal, with a remarkable cast including Cassive, Firmin Gémier who had created *Ubu Roi*, and the great comic Raimu, whom Feydeau had discovered. Perhaps because of the wartime need for light entertainment, there is a return to slapstick, "speaking names" (Leboucq—Mr Ghote; Mme Dingue—Mrs Nutter) and the age-old gimmick of the dentist's chair. Feydeau may be to dentists what Molière was to doctors. Guillot de Saix asserted that the audience's enjoyment is founded on sadism, and in this last farce the conjugal aggravation leads inexorably to a divorce. Feydeau obtained his own divorce a few months later. According to Marcel Achard, it was Feydeau himself who suggested that the five one-acts eventually be collected under the title *From Marriage to Divorce*. This collection, the first time these plays have appeared together in English, honors that suggestion.

TRANSLATOR'S NOTE

I have retained all of Feydeau's prolific stage directions
because they are sure guides to staging the plays for
maximum effect. Note that they refer to the audience's
left and right. Similarly, the break-down into "French
scenes" has been kept because they are useful in
drawing up rehearsal schedules.

DEAD WRONG
(Feu la mère de Madame)

CHARACTERS & SETTING

Lucien
Yvonne, *his wife*
Annette, *their Alsatian maid*
Joseph, *a man-servant*

Yvonne's *bedroom*

*Modest interior, with a stab at elegance and comfort:
inexpensive luxury, pretty but cheap knick-knacks. On the
wall, framed modern prints, Japanese fans, etc. At back a
door opening onto the vestibule. Right of center, a double
doorway with the doors replaced by a curtain. Left of center,
on a wall panel, a door opening into* Lucien's *room. Down
left, a fireplace with a mirror above it. Down right, a double
bed; against the foot of the bed, a bench the width of the bed.
At the head of the bed, facing the audience, a little night-
table (on the table a lit night-light and a pharmacy bottle);
on the other side of the door at left, an armchair. Against
the section of wall that separates the door at back from the
door at left a little lady's writing-desk, open. Right of the
desk, against the wall, a chair. Near the fireplace, almost
downstage and back to the audience an armchair; on that
armchair, a skirt and a lady's slip. On the mantelpiece: a
clock, candle-sticks; farther right, a carafe of water topped by
a glass, on a tray; left, a box of matches and a spirit-lamp for
making herbal tea. Against the wall, right of the door at back,
a love seat. In the angle of the corner, a little table placed on*

a diagonal. Tossed on the foot of the bed, a lady's morning wrapper. On the ground, facing the audience, YVONNE's *slippers [without stiffeners or heels]; on the other side of the bed,* LUCIEN's *slippers. On the ceiling a chandelier worked by a switch left of the door at back. In the desk, writing materials and a few blank cards.*

Scene One

(YVONNE, *then* LUCIEN)

(*As the curtain rises, the stage is dim, lit only by the night-light on the little table right of the bed,* YVONNE *is sound asleep in the bed; we can hear the light, regular sound of her breathing. [Wait five seconds after the curtain rises, then the doorbell rings once.] She, not awakened by the ringing, but slightly troubled in her sleep, heaves a longer sigh and turns a bit under the covers. [Count ten after the first ring, then ring again.]*)

YVONNE: (*Lying on her left side, almost immediately after this ringing, opens her sleep-swollen eyes, lifts her head a bit, then*) What in the world is that?

(*More ringing*)

YVONNE: (*Crossly*) I bet Lucien forgot his key!... (*Throwing off the covers*) It's idiotic to give a person a heart attack! (*She jumps out of bed, in her night-gown, bare feet and legs.*)

(*Two rings in a row*)

YVONNE: (*Furious.*) Honestly! (*She grabs her wrapper abruptly and quickly puts on her slippers.*)

(*Constant ringing*)

YVONNE: Give it a rest! (*With no time to put on her wrapper, she throws it around her neck like a muffler. She reaches the vestibule, then at the front door to the landing, in a gruff voice:*) Who's there?

LUCIEN: *(Off. Pitiful like a naughty child afraid of being scolded)* Me! I forgot my key!

YVONNE: *(In the vestibule)* Ah! naturally! *(As the door is opened we hear the sound of a key in the lock.)* What fun! *(Coming back downstage)* Come on! Get in!

(Down right, she jumps into bed, on her knees, back to audience. Meanwhile, LUCIEN has closed the front door, we hear him put the safety chain on. On YVONNE's " Get in here!", he appears; he is wearing a Louis XIV costume under a raincoat buttoned up to his neck, but which doesn't come lower than his hips. A knotted kerchief round his neck. He has on drenched white gloves; his shoes are covered with mud as are his stockings up to his calves. The whole back of the raincoat is one huge water-stain. As he enters, his hands are encumbered with a lit candle in a candle-stick, a Louis XIV cane and an umbrella. His sword catches on the door when he crosses the threshold. She in bed)

YVONNE: Well? waiting for tomorrow?

LUCIEN: Here we are! ...I beg your pardon!

(As LUCIEN says this he flips the switch left of the door, and the chandelier is lit.)

YVONNE: *(Crossly)* Ah! You beg my pardon! You would have done better not to forget your key. It's no fun to be jerked awake when you're asleep.

LUCIEN: *(Embarrassed)* I woke you up!

YVONNE: *(Sharply)* Of course you woke me up! You don't think I waited up all this time?

LUCIEN: *(Very sincerely, as if relieved, as he turns to go to the fireplace and put his candle-stick down)* Ah! that's good!

(LUCIEN is about to blow out the candle but stops when YVONNE says:)

YVONNE: What you do you mean "that's good!" You're glad you woke me up?

LUCIEN: No, no! I said that's good...that you didn't wait up. *(He blows out the candle, puts it on the mantelpiece, stands his cane in its angle, then, his half-open, dripping umbrella under his arm, heads for the bed, shaking his frozen hands in his drenched gloves.)*

YVONNE: May I inquire what's the idea of coming home this time of the morning!

LUCIEN: *(Pulling off his gloves)* I couldn't find a cab. And the weather! The only street-lights were in Vaugirard or Château-d'Eau! Never any street-lights in your own neighborhood.

YVONNE: I'm sure it must be the crack of dawn...!!

LUCIEN: *(Without conviction)* Oh! no, it's barely...

(At that precise moment the clock on the mantelpiece chimes four.)

YVONNE: *(Interrupting him)* Wait!

(LUCIEN and YVONNE both lend an ear, he making a face. After it has struck four, she with a sneer.)

YVONNE: Ten after four!

LUCIEN: What do you mean "ten after"?

YVONNE: *(Sharply)* Of course! The clock is ten minutes slow!

LUCIEN: That can't be, it must be on the fritz... Just now when I was passing Saint-Lazare station...

YVONNE: Yes! yes! you're going to tell me it was midnight!

LUCIEN: Midnight, no, but...

YVONNE: Yes! yes! it's the same old story: when husbands sleep around, their wives' clocks are always on the fritz...

LUCIEN: *(Going to the bed)* Oh! you're exaggerating! Now I'm supposed to have been sleeping around! *(Sitting on the foot of the bed.)* After all, we agreed I'd come home late, since I was going to the Artists' Ball! I couldn't leave it before it started…

YVONNE: *(In an unanswerable tone)* You would have done better not to go at all! …What business is it of yours? What they must have thought of you at the Artists' Ball! …Seeing you there, a married man!

LUCIEN: *(Who, since his entrance, has held on to his umbrella, absent-mindedly doodling on the carpet as one does with a cane in sand)* Oh! I assure you they paid no attention to me!

YVONNE: *(Abruptly kneeing him in the hip through the covers)* Watch what you're doing!

LUCIEN: *(Made to leap off the bed)* What?

YVONNE: *(Shouting)* Your umbrella! You're drenching my carpet!

LUCIEN: Me! *(Instinctively he bows his head to check the damage, which makes a trickle of water drip off the brim of his hat.)*

YVONNE: *(Louder)* And your hat! …It's dripping.

LUCIEN: *(Stupefied, rushing to the door at back to put his hat and umbrella in the vestibule)* Oh! …I beg your pardon.

YVONNE: Doesn't even see how he's running!

LUCIEN: *(Exiting)* I'll go slower!

YVONNE: *(Enraged)* Oh yes! make jokes!

(LUCIEN has reappeared and stopped, pitifully, between the door and the desk. He stupidly pulls one of the ends of his kerchief to remove it from the collar of his raincoat. YVONNE, looking him over with pity.)

YVONNE: Absolutely! If you don't sell anything, you dabble. Do you sell anything?

LUCIEN: No, I don't sell anything! Of course I don't sell anything! You're so mean! I don't sell anything... because nobody buys anything! ...Otherwise!...

YVONNE: There's only one thing you've painted decently!

LUCIEN: *(Glad of this concession)* Ah!

YVONNE: My bathtub...in enamel.

LUCIEN: *(Annoyed, moving towards the fireplace)* Oh! that's funny! Oh! that's witty! *(Coming back to the bed.)* That doesn't prevent me from being more of an artist than you think! So, as an artist, it's only natural that I'd be on the lookout for artistic sensations.

YVONNE: There you are! Say you're on the lookout for sensations, true enough! But don't talk about art!

LUCIEN: *(Giving up the argument)* Ah! you're a pain in the neck! *(He reaches the fireplace and starts to remove his neckcloth in front of the mirror.)*

YVONNE: *(Throwing off the covers)* No... but...

(YVONNE leaps to the foot of the bed and, barefoot, runs to LUCIEN; then, after spinning him to face her.)

YVONNE: No, if I'm such a pain in the neck, tell me one; tell me one of your artistic sensations!

LUCIEN: Of course I will.

YVONNE: *(Incisively)* That's no answer! Tell me one! *(She comes downstage.)*

LUCIEN: *(Coming down behind her)* I only have to choose... Well, for example, when Amphitrite made an entrance. *(Looking her up and down and with a rather scornful smile.)* I don't suppose you have any idea what Amphitrite is?

YVONNE: Oh, don't I? I don't know what it is! …It's a gastric ailment!

LUCIEN: *(Startled)* What!

YVONNE: Absolutely!

LUCIEN: *(Bursting out laughing)* A gastric ailment! She's the goddess of the sea.

YVONNE: *(Nonplussed)* Ah?… *(Bitterly)* So what! I got it mixed up! …I got it mixed up with enteritis.

LUCIEN: They have nothing in common!

YVONNE: So what! A person can get mixed up.

LUCIEN: All right! Anyway, when the procession made its entrance, that was an artistic sensation! A stunning model, stark naked, in a mother-of-pearl sea-shell, carried by tritons and mermaids!

YVONNE: *(Primly)* A stark naked woman!

LUCIEN: Stark naked!

YVONNE: How indecent!

LUCIEN: *(Sedately)* That's just where you're wrong! There was nothing indecent about it!

YVONNE: Really? Why, I'd do it myself! …*(As she speaks she comes down right and jumps into bed.)*

LUCIEN: *(Lifting his arms to heaven)* Ah! sure you would…! Don't be silly.

YVONNE: *(Sitting up in bed)* Well, a thing is either indecent or it isn't.

LUCIEN: It isn't when it's artist's models! …And that one had such a figure! …And breasts, ah! …I've never seen the like. *(He crosses to the fireplace.)*

YVONNE: *(Nodding her head politely, then in a pinched tone)* Thank you very much.

LUCIEN: *(Turning around, non-plussed)* What?

YVONNE: You're so polite!

LUCIEN: *(Rolls his eyes skyward, then)* All right then! You're going to take offense. I wasn't talking about you! Of course yours are very pretty! But after all... they are not the same as the breasts of a model. *(He turns back to the fireplace to undo his neckcloth.)*

YVONNE: Oh? really?... *(Throwing off the covers and leaping to the foot of the bed to confront LUCIEN, while hurriedly untying the ribbons on her nightgown.)* And... and...

(Up against LUCIEN, making him spin around to face her.)

YVONNE: ...and what's wrong with them?

(Back to the audience, facing LUCIEN, YVONNE is planted before him, the front of her nightgown open and held apart by her hands.)

LUCIEN: *(Completely aghast at this unexpected onslaught)* Huh? Well, I don't know... Well! well, for example, here... *(He points at a spot on her breast.)*

YVONNE: *(Slapping his hand and jumping back)* Enough! I forbid you to touch them! ...Go touch that lady's, since they're better than mine!...

LUCIEN: Oh! don't be silly!

YVONNE: *(Returning to the charge)* Go on! Go on! Tell me, what's wrong with them?

(Pressed against the doorjamb right of the door at left and YVONNE literally stuck to him.)

LUCIEN: Oh! nothing much! ...They're very nice, even from underneath! There, you see, I'm being fair. But on top, well! they're a little depressed; it's...

YVONNE: *(Outraged)* Depressed!

LUCIEN: *(Drawing a picture with his hand)* So it makes them look a little bit like an overnight bag.

YVONNE: *(Quickly retying the ribbons on her nightgown)* An overnight bag! An overnight bag! That's too much!

(YVONNE quickly grabs LUCIEN by the left arm and sends him spinning center stage.)

LUCIEN: *(Not knowing what's happening)* No, what's this?

YVONNE: *(Who has immediately opened the now unimpeded door, calling)* Annette! …Annette!

ANNETTE: *(Off. Very sleepy)* Haw?

YVONNE: Annette, get up!

LUCIEN: *(Astounded)* Annette?

YVONNE: You hear what I say!

ANNETTE: *(Alsatian accent)* Matame?

YVONNE: Up and at 'em! Get up.

ANNETTE: *(Off)* Ja, matame.

LUCIEN: What's Annette got to do with it? What's Annette doing in my room?

YVONNE: *(Crossing in front of him to sit on the bench by the bed)* I'll say Annette! Yes, Annette!

LUCIEN: Really! It's unbelievable! You have the maid sleeping in my bed now?

YVONNE: I suppose you wanted me to spend all night alone in the apartment why you were gallivanting around? Oh no, no thank you! *(Leaning her left arm on the brass bar at the foot of the bed.)* I'm afraid.

LUCIEN: That's the last straw! The maid in my bed! And where am I supposed to sleep, eh?

YVONNE: Well…in there! *(She indicates the room at left.)*

LUCIEN: With the maid?

YVONNE: What? "The maid"? What? "The maid?" Now that you're home, Annette will go upstairs to her room and you can have your bed again.

LUCIEN: Not on your life! Sleep in her sheets!

YVONNE: They aren't her sheets, they're yours.

LUCIEN: But she slept in them, that's enough for me.

YVONNE: *(Rising and, as she speaks, climbing back into bed)* Oh! of course! If it were a case of sleeping in a stark naked model's sheets, you wouldn't act so disgusted…

LUCIEN: *(Mildly racy)* Highly unlikely!

YVONNE: *(Kneeling in bed, as she speaks, she shakes up the pillows, and turns to* LUCIEN *on his line.)* Just what I was saying! *(Stumping to the middle of the bed on her knees.)* You'd prefer that, wouldn't you? *(Reaching the foot of the bed.)* You'd prefer that, eh? You pig…! *(She lies down again.)*

LUCIEN: *(Exasperated)* Oh!…What a pain! *(He crosses to the fireplace.)*

Scene Two

(The same, ANNETTE*)*

*(*ANNETTE *enters left. She is in her night dress. Flannel nightgown pleated over her breast and on her back so to create a plunging neckline, two short, bell-shaped sleeves ending at her biceps. Woollen petticoat over that allowing the hem of the nightgown to show. Her legs are bare in felt, down-at-heel slippers. Her disheveled hair has a center part and is plaited behind into two tight braids which stick up in the air. She comes forward half asleep, her eyes puffy with slumber.)*

ANNETTE: Did Matame call for me?

YVONNE: *(Leaping to the foot of the bed and running to* ANNETTE*)* Yes, come over here! Do you know what the master said?

ANNETTE: *(Yawning)* No, matame.

YVONNE: He said my breasts are like an overnight bag.

ANNETTE: *(Sleepy and indifferent)* Oh? …Dot's nize, matame!

LUCIEN: *(Sarcastic)* You sent for the maid so you could tell her that?

YVONNE: Quite so, monsieur! I want her to tell you herself what she thinks of my bosom, to prove to you that not everyone is of your opinion! *(To ANNETTE)* What did you tell me the other morning concerning my bosom precisely?

ANNETTE: *(Opening her eyes with effort)* I don't know, matame.

YVONNE: *(Emphasizing each portion of her line with a little tap on ANNETTE's arm or chest)* Yes you do! I was in the middle of dressing; I said to you: "The fact is, not many women could show them as firm as this!" What did you say back to me?

ANNETTE: *(Making an effort)* Ah! ja, I zaidt to you: "Dot iss true, matame! Vhen I look at mein, from de zides, dey look like two carry-alls!"

YVONNE: There! You hear that!

LUCIEN: *(Abruptly grabbing ANNETTE's right arm and moving her out)* So what! What! What! What does that prove? I never disputed that you have an outstanding bosom; but there's a big difference between outstanding and unique.

(While ANNETTE, waiting for their argument to end, sits to snooze on the chair beside the fireplace.)

YVONNE: Oh! really? Well, from now on, you can kiss my bosom goodbye!

LUCIEN: *(Putting his hand forward to reply)* Is that so! Well…

YVONNE: *(Misjudging his gesture and slapping his hand)* Don't touch!

LUCIEN: *(Furious)* Ah! look out!…

YVONNE: I'm keeping it for others! …who know how to appreciate it. *(She has crossed down right and climbed back in bed.)*

LUCIEN: *(Furious, striding back and forth, hands in the pockets of his knee-breeches.)* Oh! fine, fine! All right then! Keep it for others! Keep it for anybody you please! For the Pope, if you like! Oh no, no, she'd try the patience of a saint!… *(Without looking he drops on to the chair by the fireplace where ANNETTE is sitting.)*

ANNETTE: *(Awakes with a start and shouting)* Ah!

LUCIEN: *(Standing up in a single bound, furious)* Ah! go to bed, Annette!

ANNETTE: *(Grumbling as she goes upstage)* Is dot vhy they made me gedt up?

LUCIEN: *(Between the bed and the back wall)* I didn't make you get up, that was your mistress.

ANNETTE: You couldt haf let me zleep!

YVONNE: That'll do, Annette, nobody's asking your opinion! …And besides

(ANNETTE who was about to exit, stops at YVONNE's voice.)

YVONNE: Since you're up, you can go back to your own room and give the master his bed back.

(ANNETTE makes to go again and stops as before at LUCIEN's voice.)

LUCIEN: *(Masterfully)* Certainly not! She took it; she can keep it! I shall sleep here.

YVONNE: With me? Oh no!

LUCIEN: *(As before)* Oh really! Did I ask you anything! *(He goes up above the bed and sits on its edge, and back to the audience starts to take off his shoes.)*

YVONNE: *(Arranging her covers)* Isn't that nice!

(Abruptly to ANNETTE *who is sleeping on her feet against the doorjamb left.)*

LUCIEN: Go to bed, you!

ANNETTE: *(Like a victim)* Yes, moussié!

LUCIEN: Go on, chuckles! Go on!

ANNETTE: Vat a choint! *(She exits, shrugging.)*

YVONNE: No! It would be too much if you go and get aroused by another woman and afterwards I'm the one…! Oh no! …I don't play stand-ins, not me!

LUCIEN: *(Exasperated)* Ah! for pity's sake! Can't you wait till tomorrow: I'm worn out.

YVONNE: *(Sinking into the covers, back to* LUCIEN*)* Oh! you're quite right! Instead of arguing, I should be sleeping.

LUCIEN: That's right! Go to sleep!

YVONNE: *(After a pause, half sitting up and over his shoulder)* Never mind! I'm just glad that the maid shut you up.

LUCIEN: *(Standing up, furious, and pointing at the door at back with the slipper in his hand)* Look here! …Do you want me to go?

YVONNE: *(Head on the pillow, in the most detached tone)* Go on if you want.

LUCIEN: *(Exasperated, crossing the stage back and forth, one foot in a slipper, the other not, so that he limps)* Oh! oh! oh!… *(Coming back to the foot of the bed.)* In the first place, what does the maid know? *(Putting on the other slipper without sitting down.)* Obviously if she's got no other standard of comparison except her own bosom, I admit that between the two…!

YVONNE: *(Leaping up to a sitting position)* Ah! you need the opinion of more competent authorities? All right! Tomorrow we're having the head of the perfume department from the department store and Monsieur Godot to dinner. I'll show my breasts to them! And they can offer their opinion.

LUCIEN: *(Shocked)* Are you crazy?

YVONNE: Why? You said yourself it wasn't indecent.

LUCIEN: *(Forcefully)* It isn't indecent when a person is stark naked!

YVONNE: *(Rapid response)* All right! I'll strip stark naked!

LUCIEN: *(Dumbfounded)* She is crazy! She is crazy as a loon!

YVONNE: *(To herself, snuggling under her covers)* Ah! mine are like overnight bags! All right! We shall see.

LUCIEN: *(Moving to the foot of the bed, hands clasped)* Oh no! Have pity on me! You're wearing me out with your constant needling! *(He crosses up to the door at back and the desk.)*

YVONNE: *(Half rising, in a scornful tone)* All right! …Go to bed! What are you waiting for? …You don't intend to be the Sun King all night long?

LUCIEN: *(In a weary voice, while rubbing his fingertips on his stomach)* No.

YVONNE: *(Observing him with pity and in an irritated tone)* What's wrong with you now?

LUCIEN: *(Wretchedly)* I have a stomach ache.

YVONNE: Here we go! That's all we needed! *(She throws off the covers and leaps out of bed.)*

LUCIEN: I want Annette to make me some camomile tea.

YVONNE: *(Putting on her slippers)* A fine thing! Have to make you camomile tea! *(So saying she heads for the door at left.)*

LUCIEN: *(Blocking her way)* Who asked you to get up? ...I can run my own errands.

YVONNE: *(Pushing him away)* Oh! no, no!... *(Returning to him.)* I don't want you to be able to say I let you drop dead! ...No! ...I know my responsibilities! ...And I carry them out! ...I do!

LUCIEN: *(In the same tone as* YVONNE*)* Fine! Perfect! Very nice indeed! *(He sits on the bench.)*

YVONNE: *(Crossing to the door at left and calling)* Annette!

ANNETTE: *(Off. Exasperated)* Oh!

YVONNE: Annette, get up!

ANNETTE: *(Off)* Huh! Again!

YVONNE: What "Again"? Yes, "again"! What do you mean by "Again"? And make some camomile tea for the master!...

*(*YVONNE *goes to the fireplace and taking the box of matches, strikes one to light the spirit-lamp; meanwhile we hear* ANNETTE's *voice grumbling offstage.)*

LUCIEN: *(After a moment, snidely)* Oh no! the way you pester that girl!

YVONNE: *(The box of matches in one hand, a match in the other, turning around at* LUCIEN's *remark)* What?... ah! honestly, that's the last straw! I'm the one who's pestering her! *(Going to* LUCIEN *and in his face.)* Tell me! ...Is the camomile tea for me? Huh? Is it for me?

LUCIEN: *(Almost shouting)* My supper didn't digest!

YVONNE: *(Same as* LUCIEN*)* Of course not! It's always the same thing! *(Turning back to the fireplace to make her preparations, light the spirit-lamp and pour some water from the carafe into the receptacle.)* It's the same old story: indigestion from his carousing away from home! …His wife isn't good enough to entertain him, but she's good enough to serve as a nurse!

LUCIEN: *(Who hasn't listened to a word of this diatribe, solely preoccupied with his stomach ache, rubbing his fingertips at the base of his sternum, —after rising, coming behind Yvonne's back.)* Say, sweetie?

YVONNE: *(Drily, not turning around)* What?

LUCIEN: *(Lamentable)* Will the camomile be ready soon?

YVONNE: Really! give it time! …It's got to boil! …You know that!

LUCIEN: *(Resigned)* Yes. *(Pause. He hiccups, then in a doleful tone.)* Ah!

YVONNE: *(Half turning)* What?

LUCIEN: *(Leaning over her and in a mournful tone)* I feel like throwing up!

YVONNE: *(Abruptly pushing him away and moving)* Oh! no! no! you're not going to throw up! That's not why I married you!

LUCIEN: No, don't worry! I said "I feel like it", I didn't say "I'm going to." You know I never can.

YVONNE: *(Scornfully)* Oh! yes, I know! …What a pity! *(She returns to her bed and climbs into it.)*

ANNETTE: *(Carrying a packet of camomile tea and a sugar bowl. She has put on a white camisole and stockings that fall over her ankles. As she puts the camomile buds into the warming water, in a grumpy tone.)* Anyzing elze vhile I am here?

YVONNE: *(In bed, arranging her covers over herself)* Ask the master, Annette! The master is the one who's sick!

LUCIEN: *(Exhausted)* I have a stomach ache!

ANNETTE: *(As before, not turning around)* Vell, if moussié vouldn't blay ze fool avay from home!

LUCIEN: *(Beside himself)* Oh! no! no! you're not going to start in as well, are you?

ANNETTE: *(Detached)* Oh, I'm chust zaying!…

LUCIEN: Well! …go to bed!

ANNETTE: *(Not waiting to be told twice)* Oh! dot's chust vhat I vant!

LUCIEN: *(To* YVONNE*)* Oh no!…

ANNETTE: *(Thinking he's addressing her)* Oh yes!

LUCIEN: *(Furious)* I'm speaking to your mistress!

ANNETTE: Ah! *(She exits.)*

LUCIEN: Oh no! …If the servants start getting involved!…

YVONNE: *(With a wry smile)* I don't see why you're so hard on the girl. She's right: if you hadn't had a late supper!…

LUCIEN: That's as may be! But it's none of her business! If I have to explain things to her as well!… *(He sits on the bench.)* I had a late supper because I was hungry, so there! …And then because I was with Monsieur Godot and the Espink twins who suggested we have a bite to eat! Is that a crime?

YVONNE: No, it's not a crime! Of course it's not a crime! But it's idiotic to eat so much it gives you indigestion! This passion for late suppers!… *(A long silent pause, then in a glacial and scornful tone)* Who paid?

LUCIEN: *(Shrugs)* Nobody!

YVONNE: What do you mean "nobody"?

LUCIEN: Well then, everybody, Dutch treat.

YVONNE: I can't believe it wasn't you! With your mania for showing off!

LUCIEN: Me!

YVONNE: Absolutely! You're stingy as can be in your own home! But the minute you're with strangers, it's delusions of grandeur!…

LUCIEN: *(Rising and crossing to the back by a circular movement)* Me! Me! I have delusions of grandeur? Unbelievable! Delusions of grandeur!

YVONNE: *(Speaking over his line)* Just look at yourself! Just look at yourself! What costume do you pick? The Sun King! I mean really! Dressing up as the Sun King… when it's raining! Ridiculous!

LUCIEN: *(Sits on the chair beside the desk)* You're the crazy one!

YVONNE: *(Not letting up)* But there you are, are you flattered to strut around like Louis XV?

LUCIEN: *(Casts a mocking and disdainful glance at her, shrugs, then in an aloof tone.)* Fourteenth!

YVONNE: "Fourteenth" what?

LUCIEN: The Sun King was Louis XIV.

YVONNE: *(Dumbfounded)* Really?… *(Getting excited.)* That's just like you! You're going to quibble with me over one Louis, but when it comes to your pleasures, you spend louis's like water.

LUCIEN: *(Rising and making a semi-circular movement to reach the bench on which he sits)* Oh! exquisite! Charming! Delightful!

YVONNE: *(After a pause and in the same glacial tone)* What did you spend on your supper?

LUCIEN: *(With a gesture of impatience)* How do I know?

YVONNE: *(With a jerk of the shoulders, then kneeling on the bed)* You don't even know how much you spent?

LUCIEN: *(Lifts his eyes skyward, then irritated)* Eleven francs seventy-five, there!

YVONNE: *(Drawing herself to her full height on her knees, hands clutching the bar at the foot of the bed, stressing each syllable.)* Eleven francs seventy-five to feed your face! ...There you have it! Just what I was saying! *(Changing her tone.)* The other day...

LUCIEN: *(Sensing the battle is about to be engaged on new terrain, nervously shakes his head, eyes skyward, and as lips move we can read the word he does not pronounce.)* Oh! sh...! *(He leaves his place and crosses up to the back.)*

YVONNE: *(Who doesn't give up, leaping to the foot of the bed, between her teeth)* What a heel!

(YVONNE has run to join LUCIEN at the back and spins him round by the arm so as to face her.)

YVONNE: The other day when I had the bad luck to buy a bottle of Rose-Coty, you told me I was ruining you; and you spend *(Stresses)* eleven francs seventy-five for your supper! At least I've still got my perfume! I can use my Rose-Coty! While you, your supper, where is it now?

LUCIEN: *(Enraged, striking his stomach)* In here! In here!

YVONNE: *(Letting him go to return to her bed and climb into it)* Ah! "in there!" "in there!" A lot better off you are! As if you wouldn't have been better off putting aside those eleven francs seventy-five! ...to pay the interior decorator, for instance!

LUCIEN: *(Who has sat down during the preceding, on the chair by the desk)* I owe him eight hundred francs; can you see me offering him eleven francs seventy-five!

YVONNE: At least you would have shown your good will! I mention him because he came round today.

LUCIEN: *(Perking up)* Huh?

YVONNE: And he insisted that he was fed up being put off...and that if you didn't fork out a hefty payment on account, well! He's made up his mind to send you a summons; and send it to the department store! You can imagine the effect that would have.

LUCIEN: *(Rising and crossing downstage)* He said that?

YVONNE: Yes.

LUCIEN: Ah! it's blackmail! *(In the direction of the door at back as if speaking to the interior decorator.)* Very well, monsieur! *(To* YVONNE*)* I was planning to make him a payment...

YVONNE: *(Implacable)* When?

LUCIEN: *(Dumbfounded)* Uh! ...When I can! But since it's like this! He can whistle for it.

YVONNE: *(Hammering each syllable, hands to heaven)* And you go and spend eleven francs seventy-five for your supper!

LUCIEN: *(Who has crossed above the bed—flying off the handle)* Ah! no, leave me the hell alone with my supper!

YVONNE: *(Not letting up)* No, really, if I were you, it would be on my stomach too!

LUCIEN: *(In his wife's face)* I've had it, damn it! I've had it up to here!

YVONNE: *(Shouting as loudly as he)* Stop shouting like that! It's true! You're driving me up the wall with your arguing!

LUCIEN: *(Crossing downstage)* Ah! no! that's torn it! I'm the one who's arguing! I'm the one driving *her* up the wall!

YVONNE: Don't you want to go to bed?

LUCIEN: *(Returning above the bed)* Yes! Oh, bed! Bed! I'm dropping with sleep!

YVONNE: *(Turning her back on him and sinking over the covers)* Well! me too! Good night!

LUCIEN: *(In the same tone)* Good night!

YVONNE: And drop dead!

LUCIEN: *(Sitting at the foot of the bed)* And drop dead!

(To LUCIEN who is both sitting on the bed and on her ankle, kicking him through the covers:)

YVONNE: My foot, watch it!

LUCIEN: *(Furious)* Hey! Your foot, watch it! *(Placing his left foot on the bar at the foot of the bed so his knee is as high as his hand to undo the garter on his breeches.)* Ah! to go to bed! *(He undoes his garter, then:)* Wild horses wouldn't drag me out of it!

(Pause. Suddenly, doorbell rings in the vestibule. A moment. LUCIEN and YVONNE are frozen in place as if petrified. —More ringing. —She slowly raises her head and sitting up looks at him with anxiety. He slowly withdraws his leg from the bar of the bed and turning fully to the left, casts a questioning glance at her.)

YVONNE: *(After this byplay, in a muffled voice)* What in the world can it be?

LUCIEN: *(In the same muffled voice)* I don't know…. It's the front door.

(More ringing which makes LUCIEN and YVONNE jump.)

YVONNE: *(Jumping while seated)* Ah! good heavens!

LUCIEN: It can't be a visitor.

YVONNE: If they're ringing at this hour, it must be something serious.

LUCIEN: *(Panicked)* Yes.

(More ringing)

YVONNE: *(Jumping out of bed and putting on her slippers)* Again! Ah! Lucien, Lucien, I'm frightened... *(She grabs her wrapper from the foot of the bed.)*

LUCIEN: *(As worried as she is)* Come, come! Show some spunk, damn it! Mustn't let ourselves be alarmed.

YVONNE: *(Panicked, moving back and forth, like someone who doesn't know what she's looking for)* Ah, it's easy for you to talk! You're a man, but I!...

(Ringing)

YVONNE: Oh!

LUCIEN: *(Turning around and around in place)* What new setback? What new setback?

YVONNE: Where is it? Where in the world is it?

LUCIEN: What?

YVONNE: *(Waving her arms around)* My wrapper! Where did I stick my wrapper?

LUCIEN: You've got it in your hand!

YVONNE: Ah! yes!

(More repeated ringing)

LUCIEN & YVONNE: Oh!

YVONNE: *(Making a vague attempt to put on her wrapper)* Ah! that ringing will drive me crazy!...

LUCIEN: *(Indicating the room at left)* And what about her, that Annette! Doesn't move a muscle!

YVONNE: *(Giving up putting on her wrapper and running to join LUCIEN)* Oh! that girl!

LUCIEN & YVONNE: *(On the threshold, he upstage of her)* Annette! Annette!

ANNETTE: *(Off)* Haw!

YVONNE: Quick, get up!

ANNETTE: *(Off)* Eh! Again!

(More ringing)

YVONNE: Hurry up, can't you!

LUCIEN: Can't you hear someone's ringing?

ANNETTE: *(Off. Tearful)* Ach! no, no, I'm goink to trop deadt.

YVONNE: *(Crossing above the bench)* I hope nothing's happened to the family!

LUCIEN: *(Near the fireplace)* No, of course not! You'll end up scaring us to death.

YVONNE: *(Quickly dropping her wrapper on the bed and tapping the bench as she speaks)* Ah! knock wood! Knock wood!

LUCIEN: You realize that if there actually…

YVONNE: Knock wood, I said!

LUCIEN: *(Startled)* Yes! you realize that if…

YVONNE: Will you knock the wood!

LUCIEN: Yes! *(Not knowing what he's doing, he knocks the marble of the fireplace three times.)*

YVONNE: Not that, that's marble!

LUCIEN: Ah! you startled me! *(He goes to knock on the desk.)*

YVONNE: With your knuckles! With your knuckles!

LUCIEN: *(Obeying mechanically)* With my knuckles.

YVONNE: Ah! you're going to bring us bad luck!

(More prolonged ringing. YVONNE bounding towards the door at left.)

YVONNE: What in the world is that Annette doing?

LUCIEN: *(Going there as well)* Ah! you'd better get cracking!

(Just at the moment ANNETTE *appears,* LUCIEN *and* YVONNE *each grab her by an arm and push her ahead of them.)*

(Coming back to them and each time pushed by LUCIEN *and* YVONNE *in the direction of the door at back, which makes* ANNETTE *keep revolving like a spinning top. With tears of rage in her voice.)*

ANNETTE: Oh, no, I haf enuff of dis! Matame vill pay me vat's owed me und denn I go.

LUCIEN & YVONNE: *(Out of patience)* Yes, yes! fine! Go on! Go on!

ANNETTE: I don't vant to trop deadt on the chob.

(Ringing)

LUCIEN: Go and open the door! You pigheaded creature!

(Overlapping one another)

YVONNE: Go on! Go on!

ANNETTE: *(Pushed into the vestibule)* Ja, but pay me vhat you owe me!

LUCIEN: Oh! this maid! This maid!

*(*ANNETTE *is off stage.* LUCIEN *to the right of the door at back and* YVONNE *to the left.)*

ANNETTE: *(In the vestibule)* Who iss de person who iss dere?

VALET: *(Off. In the distance)* Joseph! Madame's mother's new man-servant.

YVONNE: *(In a strident voice)* Mama! Something's happened to mama! Something's happened to mama!

LUCIEN: Don't scream like that! Don't scream like that!

(During this exchange, sound of the safety chain and the door opening.)

Scene Three

(The same, JOSEPH*)*

(Barely has JOSEPH *appeared when* YVONNE *lays hold of him and comes far downstage with him.* JOSEPH *is wearing a sleeved waistcoat and trousers with a lounge-suit jacket and a woolen scarf around his neck; he is holding a bowler hat in his hand.* ANNETTE, *shortly after this entrance, just long enough to close the vestibule door, will reappear on stage and come down near the fireplace.)*

YVONNE: *(Before he has time to speak)* What's happened to mama? What's happened to mama?

JOSEPH: *(Most embarrassed, head bowed)* Goodness me, madame… *(In his confusion, he turns his head towards* LUCIEN *whom he had no time to see on his entrance. His glance falls on* LUCIEN's *legs, rises in astonishment along Lucien's body, then, unable to repress a stifled cry of surprise at sight of this Louis XIV.)* Ah!

LUCIEN: *(Instinctively casting a glance at his own costume)* What? What's the matter? Answer me, instead of staring at my costume! There's nothing unusual about it.

YVONNE: *(To* JOSEPH*)* An accident?

LUCIEN: *(Head bowed, mechanically turning his hat in his hands, quickly)* Oh! no…

YVONNE: *(Exhaling)* Ah!

LUCIEN: There, you see, no accident!

JOSEPH: *(As before, but hesitant)* Only… she isn't very well…

YVONNE: *(Fearful)* Mama isn't very well? What? What's the matter with her?

JOSEPH: *(As before)* Well… she's ill.

YVONNE: *(Barely daring to ask)* Oh! my goodness! … very?

JOSEPH: *(As before)* Well… rather!

YVONNE: *(Crossing to take refuge in* LUCIEN's *arms)* Lucien! …Lucien! …Mama is ill!

LUCIEN: There, there!

YVONNE: Mama is very ill!

LUCIEN: There, there!

JOSEPH: *(As before)* And when I say very ill, it's a figure of speech; because, to tell the truth, she is rather…she is rather…

YVONNE: *(Her throat constricted)* What, what? What is she rather?…

JOSEPH: She is rather… *(Lifting his head and very wild.)* … dead!

ALL: Ah!

*(*YVONNE *falls stiffly, caught in flight by* LUCIEN.*)*

LUCIEN: *(Sitting rapidly on the ground, a fainted Yvonne in his arms.)* Ah! that's just what I was afraid of!

JOSEPH: *(Now that this business is over)* Only… I was advised to prepare madame gently so as not to upset her. *(Aside, with a long sigh of relief.)* Oof!

LUCIEN: What a tragedy! Just when we were going to bed!

ANNETTE: *(All over the place)* Matame! Matame!

LUCIEN: Ah! As if you needed to come and make that announcement, you!

JOSEPH: But, monsieur, I was told…

LUCIEN: Ah! "you were told! You were told!" All right, give me a hand.

JOSEPH: Yes, monsieur.

(JOSEPH *puts his hat on the desk, then kneels behind* YVONNE; LUCIEN *passes her to him and comes a bit downstage between* YVONNE *and the bench.)*

ANNETTE: *(Near the fireplace)* Mein Gott! Mein Gott!

LUCIEN: *(Straddling* YVONNE *to get to* ANNETTE *whom he pushes towards the door left)* And you, go get some vinegar, smelling salts, instead of yelling "Mein Gott! Mein Gott!" which is no use at all!

ANNETTE: Ja, moussié! *(Exiting)* Ach! Gott! Gott! Lieber Gott!

(JOSEPH, *who meanwhile, to hold up the fainted* YVONNE, *has passed his forearms under her armpits and has his hands cupped over her breasts.)*

JOSEPH: Let's put Madame…on the bed! *(To say "on the bed," he stresses each syllable with a shake of his fists in the direction of the bed, which shakes* YVONNE's *bosom that many times.)*

LUCIEN: *(Coming back to* JOSEPH*)* Huh? Right… *(Noticing* JOSEPH's *action and rushing toward him.)* What are you doing there, you?

JOSEPH: *(Still holding* YVONNE *in his cupped hands, shaking her slightly)* I'm holding her.

LUCIEN: *(Trying to remove* JOSEPH *to take his place)* I've got her… Can't you see she's not wearing a corset?

JOSEPH: *(Without letting go)* Oh! If monsieur thinks I give a thought to such things.

LUCIEN: *(Kneeling left of* YVONNE, *same as before)* I don't give a damn what you give a thought to! …I'm telling you to let go of her!…

(LUCIEN pushes JOSEPH upstage of him and crosses, still on his knees, to YVONNE's right.)

LUCIEN: And see if there's any ether, the bottle over there, next to the bed!

JOSEPH: *(Running to look upstage of the bed)* Yes, monsieur! Yes!

LUCIEN: *(Cursing)* How dare he paw my wife that way! *(Sees JOSEPH upstage of the bed.)* Not over there! On the table! Next to the bed!

JOSEPH: Yes, monsieur, yes! *(He jumps over the bed using his arms to get to the other side.)*

LUCIEN: Hey, the sheets! Look out for the sheets!

JOSEPH: *(Who has uncorked the bottle and smelled the contents)* There is some in here, monsieur.

LUCIEN: Good, hand it over!

(JOSEPH runs to bring it to him.)

LUCIEN: Yvonne! My Yvonne! Yvonne!... *(To JOSEPH)* A cloth now! Bring me a cloth to dab her forehead.

JOSEPH: *(Not knowing where to look and turning in place right and left like a weather-vane)* A cloth? Where is there a cloth?

LUCIEN: *(As he uncorks the bottle with his teeth)* I don't know, my good man! If I knew, I wouldn't ask you! Look around!!

JOSEPH: *(Seeing from afar YVONNE's slip on the chair left; to run there he firmly straddles YVONNE's legs.)* Ah! there! *(Taking the slip)* Maybe this'll work?

LUCIEN: *(Who, during this business, goes on gently shaking his wife with)* Yvonne! My Yvonne! ...I don't know, my good man! What is it?

JOSEPH: *(Bringing the slip to LUCIEN)* It looks like a slip!

LUCIEN: *(Cork still between his teeth)* What can you do, if there's nothing else! ...Get on your knees!

(JOSEPH obeys.)

LUCIEN: Roll it up into a plug! A plug, do you know what that is?

JOSEPH: Yes, monsieur! *(He rolls the slip into a plug.)*

LUCIEN: All right, hand it over! *(Handing the bottle of ether to JOSEPH.)* Take this!

(JOSEPH, on his knees on the other side of YVONNE, takes the bottle from LUCIEN's hands and in exchange hands him the slip. —LUCIEN, cork still between his teeth.)

LUCIEN: The cork! The cork!

(JOSEPH looks for the cork on the ground.)

LUCIEN: Here! here! in my teeth!

(JOSEPH pulls the cork from LUCIEN's mouth.)

LUCIEN: Good! Ether! Ether!

(LUCIEN hands the plug to JOSEPH who soaks it with ether, then dabbing YVONNE's face.)

LUCIEN: Yvonne! My Yvonne!

(Handing it back to JOSEPH to pour a little more ether on it; to JOSEPH.)

LUCIEN: Ah! honestly, you know, you! *(To his unconscious wife)* Yvonne, my Yvonne! *(To JOSEPH)* You could have waited until tomorrow morning to come and announce this kind of news!

JOSEPH: If Monsieur thinks I did it for my pleasure!

LUCIEN: No, but maybe for ours! *(To YVONNE.)* Yvonne, darling! *(To JOSEPH.)* What was the big hurry, I ask you? ...Of course, my poor mother-in-law, it's all very unfortunate! But, after all, now or tomorrow morning...she wouldn't have flown away! ...And then, at least, madame would not have had her rest disturbed!... *(A half-tone lower.)* nor would I!

JOSEPH: I am so sorry, monsieur! I'll know better next time.

ANNETTE: *(Runs in with coarse cut-glass salt-and-pepper shakers in a cruet stand, and, crossing in front of JOSEPH, sticks them in front of LUCIEN's nose.)* Here you are, moussié!

LUCIEN: *(Raising his head, looks at the salt shaker, looks at Annette, looks at the salt shaker, then.)* What in the world is that?

ANNETTE: The zalt-zhaker.

LUCIEN: What am I supposed to do with that?

ANNETTE: Moussié asked me to pring him de zalt.

LUCIEN: Smelling salts, you confounded mollusc! Not table salt! You think I'm going to season madame?

ANNETTE: How do I know? I'm not a toctor. *(She goes to put the salt-shaker on the mantelpiece.)*

(Seeing YVONNE coming round)

LUCIEN: That's all right! Madame is opening her eyes! Now, keep your distance ! and take this away.

(LUCIEN quickly hands the slip to JOSEPH who immediately gets up and goes to stand next to ANNETTE upstage of the fireplace. Automatically, during what follows, without the audience noticing, he will put the slip in the right pocket of his jacket. LUCIEN slides behind YVONNE's back and sits on the ground against her, his legs parallel to the footlights, his feet emerging right of YVONNE, body to the left.)

LUCIEN: Yvonne! My Yvonne!

YVONNE: *(Looks right and left like someone recovering her senses, then:)* What's happening?

LUCIEN: Nothing, darling! Nothing at all.

YVONNE: Then why am I on the floor? *(At that moment her gaze falls on* JOSEPH.*)* Ah! …Ah! Yes…yes…oh! mama! My poor mama! *(She bursts into sobs on* LUCIEN's *chest.)*

LUCIEN: *(Holding her in his arms, and gently rocking her like a baby being lulled to sleep)* There! There! Come on! …Come on! Come on! …Come on, there, there! Bloody hell! …There, there! There, come on! There, there! Come on! …Come on, there, there!

ANNETTE: Ach Gott! Gott!

LUCIEN: Come, come! Chin up, damn it! not all hope is lost!

YVONNE: *(Sobbing and almost enraged)* What more can happen since she's dead?

LUCIEN: Well, that's just it! Exactly! The worst is over! You have to accept it, damn it! tell yourself that for those who have departed it's a deliverance! … Think how much your poor mother suffered from rheumatism!

YVONNE: *(Choked with sobs)* My poor mama!

LUCIEN: *(In a sorrowfully wheedling voice)* Well! yes! Yes indeed! Well, now she isn't suffering any more! And so long as we are here to mourn her… *(With a tinge of rancor)* …out of bed! she is at rest! …She is very happy!

YVONNE: *(With a sad bobbing of the head)* Who would have thought she would go so quickly!

LUCIEN: *(With a sigh)* Ah! yes! …Just now when I was wondering how I would pay the interior decorator, I never suspected! …After all!

YVONNE: *(Sobbing)* My poor mama!

LUCIEN: Ah! yes… your poor, brave, worthy, sainted lady mother! *(Aside.)* My back is killing me! *(As he speaks, weary of his position, he first gets to his knees, then*

*bends backwards his painful loins, looks right and left to
see whether there's a chair he can pull forward, then, in a
coaxing tone.)* Listen, Yvonne dear.

YVONNE: What?

LUCIEN: Wouldn't you like to sit down, darling?

YVONNE: *(Bursts out abruptly, which makes Lucien start)*
No! "sit down! Sit down!" What difference does it
make if I'm on a chair or on the floor?

LUCIEN: *(Quickly)* Yes, yes! Fine, fine! *(He goes to sit on
the bench.)*

YVONNE: *(Lyrical in her grief)* Ah! I wish I were beneath
the sod!

ANNETTE: *(Near the fireplace, sorrowfully, to herself)* Oh! it
preaks mein heart!

YVONNE: *(Who for a moment, her body thrown somewhat
back and supported by her arms, her palms on the floor,
moves her mouth around like someone who has starch on
her face, while racked by sobs. To* LUCIEN*)* Ah! what?...
(To JOSEPH*)* Ah! What? ...What did you put on my face
that's sticky?

LUCIEN: Nothing, darling! Just ether.

YVONNE: What ether?

LUCIEN: *(Indicating the night table)* That was in the
bottle.

YVONNE: Don't be stupid! That's cough syrup! What an
idea!

JOSEPH & LUCIEN: Syrup!

JOSEPH: *(Who has pulled the bottle from his pocket, after
a glance at the label)* Oh! I didn't read the label! I just
smelled it.

*(*JOSEPH *hands the bottle to* ANNETTE *who places it on the
mantelpiece.)*

LUCIEN: Ah! you're a clever fellow!

YVONNE: *(Lyrical)* Anyway what does it matter! When your… *(Makes a face.)* heart is crucified…! *(Makes a face. —Then to* ANNETTE*)* Bring me a little water, Annette, so I can wash my face.

ANNETTE: Ja, Matame. *(She crosses to the back and exits through the door right.)*

YVONNE: *(With a mournful tenderness)* The poor dear woman! Do you remember how good she was?

LUCIEN: *(Absently, with an affirmative bob of the head, then.)* Who?

YVONNE: *(Slapping him angrily on the calf)* Mama!

LUCIEN: Ah! yes.

YVONNE: And so indulgent to you! Always making excuses for you! When I think how you used to upset her, how you would call her names…! Only the other day you went so far as to call her a "bitch."

LUCIEN: *(In a sorrowfully suppliant tone)* Yvonne!

YVONNE: *(Tearfully)* How could you have gone so far as to call her a bitch?

LUCIEN: *(With a vague gesture, then, as the best argument in the world)* I didn't think she'd die!

YVONNE: There! Well, today you're punished for it.

LUCIEN: *(Pivoting on his seat)* Ah! Lord! *(He remains back to the audience during what follows, his head in his right hand, his elbow on the bar at the foot of the bed.)*

YVONNE: What remorse when you think she passed away with the memory of your disrespect! …Bitch! My sainted mother!

*(*YVONNE, *in a slow, rhythmic, gentle tone, while* LUCIEN, *at the end of each phrase, seems to agree with a nod of the*

head, while in reality it is only the result of the lulling produced by her musical words.)

YVONNE: Well, may your conscience be at peace! I know better than anyone what treasures of forgiveness were stored in mama's heart; so, I believe I can be the interpreter of her final intention, when I say to you: "Go, Lucien! You are forgiven…!" *(Sorrowfully repeating)* You are forg…

(With no response from LUCIEN, YVONNE *lifts her head and realizing that he has gone to sleep during her speech, she vigorously slaps his thigh.)*

YVONNE: You're asleep!

LUCIEN: *(Waking with a start)* Huh? Me? Uh…! Ah! I beg your pardon! I'm so tired…!

YVONNE: *(Indignant)* Tired! Mama is no more, and he is tired. *(Rising in a single bound and grabbing Lucien sends him into Joseph's stomach)* Come on, on your feet!

LUCIEN & JOSEPH: *(Bumping into one another)* Oh!

YVONNE: Shouldn't we go over there?

LUCIEN: Ah! we're going…?

YVONNE: Of course we're going! You don't expect us to go back to bed.

LUCIEN: *(With a resigned sigh while casting a look of regret at the bed)* No!

YVONNE: *(Abruptly flinging* LUCIEN *out of her way to go to the chair on the left. Lifting her skirt from the chair and putting it down again.)* Where's my slip? Where's my slip? *(As she says the second "Where's my slip", she has pushed* JOSEPH *towards the fireplace and walked up to the chair by the desk.)*

LUCIEN: *(To* JOSEPH*)* I gave it to you!

JOSEPH: Me!

LUCIEN: Yes indeed!

JOSEPH: Ah! yes! *(Slowly pulling the slip out of his pocket.)* Here you are, madame.

YVONNE: *(Who has come down between them, to* JOSEPH*)* What! You've got my slip in your pocket?

JOSEPH: It was monsieur who used it…to smear syrup on madame's face.

YVONNE: *(Taking the slip from his hands with a rough gesture)* This is absurd! Honestly!

*(*YVONNE, *turning to* LUCIEN *and seeing him motionless, waiting for something or other:)*

YVONNE: Well! hurry up! What are you waiting for to get dressed?

LUCIEN: Oh? I have to…

YVONNE: *(Exasperated)* Of course! …you don't expect to go over there dressed as Louis XIV?

LUCIEN: No!

YVONNE: *(To* JOSEPH*)* Dressing as Louis XIV when he's lost his mother-in-law!

JOSEPH: *(Not giving it a second thought)* It's hilarious!

YVONNE: Ah! you think so, do you?

JOSEPH: Oh! sorry, no!

LUCIEN: *(To* ANNETTE *who comes out of the boudoir at that moment)* Ah! Annette! …Get me my black woollen suit, my black tie and black gloves.

*(*ANNETTE *is about to go to the room at right, but stops immediately at Yvonne's voice.)*

YVONNE: *(Making her husband spin round to face her, at the peak of exasperation)* Ah! No! No! You're not going to dress like that! You'd look like you'd ordered your mourning in advance. It isn't done! *(She crosses and puts her slip on the foot of the bed.)*

LUCIEN: You're right!

*(*LUCIEN*, going to* ANNETTE *who is near the door to the room at left:)*

LUCIEN: All right! Whatever suit you like, Annette! My…my jauntiest!

ANNETTE: Ja, moussié. *(She exits.)*

YVONNE: *(Muttering, while undoing the ribbons on her nightgown which she is about to take off to put on her slip)* No, honestly!

*(*YVONNE *is facing the foot of the bed, back to* JOSEPH *who stares at her actions indifferently and absent-mindedly.)*

LUCIEN: *(Crossing to* JOSEPH*)* As for you… *(Halted by* JOSEPH's *position, looking at what he's looking at and immediately leaping on his wife and pulling up around her neck her nightie which is already off her shoulder)* Ah! what are you doing? Have you lost your mind?

YVONNE: *(Startled by the missile hitting her shoulders)* What?

LUCIEN: You're changing your slip here now?

YVONNE: *(Nerves on edge)* Oh! for pity's sake, listen…! *(She flings back the collar of her nightie so she can pull out her arms.)*

LUCIEN: *(Pulling her collar up again)* Not on your life! You're not going to strip naked in front of this servant!

JOSEPH: *(With a profoundly aloof air)* Oh! don't mind me, monsieur…!

LUCIEN: *(Furious, in* JOSEPH's *face)* Well I do mind you!

YVONNE: *(To* JOSEPH *with* LUCIEN *between them)* No! I lose my mother and all he cares about is if I'm wearing my nightie or not! *(She moves away to the bed.)*

LUCIEN: *(Furious)* A person can lose her mother and still be decent!

YVONNE: Oh! yes, oh! shut up!

(ANNETTE appears at left, carrying Lucien's suit and holding in her right hand his shoes, with his bowler hat hanging from the toes. Lucien's suspenders, held by the back buttons, dangle from his trousers. —To ANNETTE:)

YVONNE: Come here, Annette! Come and help me! *(She exits right carrying off her wrapper and her slip.)*

(While ANNETTE places his suit on the chair at left, his shoes on the floor and his hat on one of the candles on the mantelpiece:)

LUCIEN: Oh! what a night, good grief! What a night!

JOSEPH: Fortunately, monsieur, it doesn't happen every day!

LUCIEN: Ah! if you think this is a picnic!… *(To* ANNETTE*)* Listen, my girl! I don't know what you're up to? You're always under foot!

ANNETTE: *(In a weepy voice, as she exits.)* I'm chust doink mein chob, moussié!

LUCIEN: Get out, my girl! Get out! Oh!

(As ANNETTE exits right, to JOSEPH, laying his right hand on his right shoulder:)

LUCIEN: Listen, my good man, you're going to help me.

JOSEPH: Very good, monsieur!

LUCIEN: Are you intelligent?

JOSEPH: Yes, monsieur!

LUCIEN: Good! Then, look here…uh! You…you're going, uh!…

(JOSEPH crosses upstage.)

LUCIEN: Where are you going? Where are you going?

JOSEPH: *(Startled)* I don't know, monsieur!

LUCIEN: Ah! you're a clever fellow, friend! With all this, I've forgotten what I wanted to say! *(Suddenly)* Ah! yes!

(LUCIEN crosses upstage in the direction of the desk; JOSEPH, eagerly, not knowing why, crosses up at the same time.)

LUCIEN: What's this, friend? I'm going to write something. I don't need you!

JOSEPH: Oh! sorry!

LUCIEN: That's all right! *(He takes the chair at back, puts it in front of the desk and, sitting down, starts to write.)*

(After a pause, moving up left of the desk, next to LUCIEN who is writing:)

JOSEPH: I weren't all that happy myself, y'see, monsieur, to come here! ...It's the first time I've had the honor of meeting monsieur and madame, but, to tell the truth, I'd rather have to announce that they'd won the jackpot on the million franc lottery than this kind of news!

(LUCIEN, still writing, signals with his left hand to JOSEPH to be silent. He pays no attention.)

JOSEPH: Anyway I'm glad to have got that off my chest! Honest to goodness! I wouldn't want to have to do that again!

LUCIEN: *(Still writing)* You're keeping me from writing, friend.

JOSEPH: Sorry! *(Hands behind his back, hat in hands, he crosses down to the foot of the bed.)*

LUCIEN: Annette!... *(He moistens the edges of one of the letter-cards he's just written)* Annette!

JOSEPH: *(Casts a glance at LUCIEN, then, to oblige, goes to the door through which the women exited, and pulls the curtain all the way aside.)* Mademoiselle, monsieur is calling for you!

ANNETTE: *(Off)* I'm tressink matame, monsieur.

YVONNE: *(Off)* You can wait a minute !

LUCIEN: *(Sealing the second letter-card)* All right! All right!

JOSEPH: *(Still holding the curtain aside, his eyes fixed on the interior of the boudoir)* It won't be long now, monsieur! Madame has already put on her slip.

(LUCIEN, *slamming his fist on the desk pad and hurling himself at* JOSEPH *whom he spins around so as to send him center stage:)*

LUCIEN: That's too much, honestly! Why do you have to stick your nose in!

JOSEPH: *(Startled by this way of acknowledging his assistance)* It was to oblige monsieur!

LUCIEN: Ah! Keep your mouth shut! "oblige me! Oblige me!" In that case, hand me my clothes!

(A startled JOSEPH *turns right and left.)*

LUCIEN: My clothes! Over there! There!

(Sending JOSEPH *to his left.)*

LUCIEN: Go on! Get out of it!

(LUCIEN *goes to get his suit himself. Turning around, he bumps into* JOSEPH *who had hurried to help him get his clothes.)*

LUCIEN: Will you get out of there!

(LUCIEN *sends* JOSEPH *to his right, near the fireplace, and heads for the foot of the bed. To a completely bewildered* JOSEPH:)

LUCIEN: Well! come over here!

JOSEPH: *(On the run)* Yes, monsieur!

LUCIEN: And help me!

JOSEPH: Yes, monsieur!

(During what ensues, JOSEPH removes LUCIEN's mantle, then unhooks his jerkin. Underneath LUCIEN has on his shirt and his tie beneath a turned-down collar. This business is done at the foot of the bed, near the bench.)

LUCIEN: *(Letting himself be undressed)* Say! have you got a cab downstairs?

JOSEPH: Yes, monsieur.

LUCIEN: Then there's no time to lose.

JOSEPH: Especially since the meter's running. *(Finished unhooking LUCIEN, he moves left.)*

LUCIEN: *(Crossing above the bed)* Ah! that's a pity! What can you do? Not every day's a holiday!...

JOSEPH: *(Shocked)* Holiday?

LUCIEN: Huh?...Uh! no! What? Anyway... you understand! *(He has taken his trousers and unconsciously puts them on over his Louis XIV knee-breeches.)*

(ANNETTE, coming out of the boudoir and moving in front of LUCIEN who is getting dressed back to the audience, immediately stops left of him:)

ANNETTE: Moussié needts me?

LUCIEN: *(Getting dressed)* Is your mistress dressed?

ANNETTE: Zoon!

LUCIEN: What were you asking me?

ANNETTE: Does moussié needt me?

LUCIEN: No!

(ANNETTE is about to leave.)

LUCIEN: Yes!

(ANNETTE stops.)

LUCIEN: *(Still dressing, chopping up his words like someone doing two things at once)* Look, my girl, there are two… two letters on the…

(LUCIEN, to JOSEPH, who he sees is heading for the desk, to make himself useful.)

LUCIEN: …not you! *(To ANNETTE)* You, you damned mollusc! Don't you understand? On the desk pad! Take them downstairs and put them in the post.

ANNETTE: *(With a negative reaction)* Now!

LUCIEN: Of course, now! They have to be delivered tomorrow as soon as possible!

ANNETTE: *(Surly)* Vhat fun! *(She heads for the door left.)*

LUCIEN: *(Putting on his waistcoat and his jacket without noticing that his suspenders are hanging from the back buttons of his trousers)* Hey! Where are you off to? Where are you going?

ANNETTE: I'm goink to put on a shkirt!

LUCIEN: "A shkirt! A shkirt!" as if anyone would pay any attention to you! At five in the morning!

ANNETTE: I gan't go oudt mitoudt a shkirt! It ain't decent.

LUCIEN: All right! Put on a raincoat.

ANNETTE: I ain't godt a raingoat.

LUCIEN: Well, then take my overcoat that's hanging in the hall.

ANNETTE: Ah! it's de zame ding! It ain't decent!

LUCIEN: All right, all right, go on, go on!

ANNETTE: Vhat vouldt I look like? A vooman of ill dispute!

LUCIEN: All right, if anyone kidnaps you, you come and tell me.

ANNETTE: A loozie floozie! *(She exits at the back.)*

LUCIEN: *(Dressed, his suspenders hanging down behind; to* JOSEPH*)* There! Hand me my...hand me my...

*(*LUCIEN, *seeing* JOSEPH *who doesn't understand what he wants, turns right, left, finally looks upwards.)*

LUCIEN: ...my shoes! They're not on the ceiling! *(Taking his shoes himself and sitting on the bench to put them on.)* Ah! you're not the brightest bulb, friend.

JOSEPH: Monsieur didn't explain!

LUCIEN: Well, come here!

*(*JOSEPH *hurries over and kneels before* LUCIEN *to help him; he takes the shoe* LUCIEN *hasn't yet taken;* LUCIEN *snatches the shoe from his hand:)*

LUCIEN: Get the hell out of it! *(Putting on his shoes.)* Tell me! What make of car is it?

JOSEPH: A Renault.

LUCIEN: A little red cab? Better and better! It's quicker and cheaper.

JOSEPH: It was a stroke of luck to find it at this hour.

LUCIEN: Yes, a real stroke of luck! What can you say, we're just so lucky.

YVONNE: *(Leaving the boudoir, in a big cloak over her wrap and her head enswathed in a muslin scarf)* Well! are you ready?

LUCIEN: *(Finishing putting on his shoes)* Right away.

*(*YVONNE, *to* JOSEPH *who is near the desk:)*

YVONNE: You have a car?

JOSEPH: Yes, madame, downstairs.

LUCIEN: *(Going to the fireplace to get his hat)* A Renault! A little red cab; it'll be quicker and cheaper. *(Putting on his hat without noticing that he is still wearing his wig and joining his wife at back.)* There! I am ready!

YVONNE: *(Spinning him round and sending him downstage)* What about your wig! You're not going out with your wig on!

LUCIEN: Huh! My wi… You're confusing me, what do you expect! You're confusing me. *(He takes off his wig and puts it on the mantelpiece.)*

YVONNE: Oh goodness! Now that we're departing, so is my courage.

LUCIEN: *(Crossing up to the exit)* Yes, yes! It's no fun for me either, but life is full of cruel responsibilities! *(He moves between the two of them and exits at back.)*

(YVONNE, taking JOSEPH by the arm and coming far downstage. LUCIEN, already in the vestibule, stops at hearing his wife's voice and follows them.)

YVONNE: Tell me, my good man!

JOSEPH: Madame?

YVONNE: Did she change much at the end?

JOSEPH: Oh no, not at all.

YVONNE: Poor mama! Tell me she didn't suffer too much.

(LUCIEN, seeing this might go on for a while, sits on the chair next to the fireplace.)

JOSEPH: *(Glad to give YVONNE this consolation)* Not for a minute! …In fact she was in very good health…she ate her dinner with a good appetite: two slices of roast lamb…

YVONNE: *(Emotionally, eyes heavenward)* Two slices of roast lamb!

LUCIEN: *(Broken-hearted)* Two slices of roast lamb!

JOSEPH: *(With a sigh)* Two slices of roast lamb, yes!
(Proceeding with his narrative.) After dinner, she played
two or three hands of solitaire; then she went to bed…
with monsieur.

YVONNE: *(Prostrate in her grief, in a very faint voice)* My
poor mam… *(Only at that moment do* JOSEPH's *last words
enter her brain, she slowly lifts her head like someone who
has a question, then turning it to* JOSEPH.*)* Monsieur?

LUCIEN: *(At the same time as his wife)* Monsieur?

YVONNE: Mama went to bed with a monsieur?

LUCIEN: What monsieur?

JOSEPH: *(With a tinge of anxiety in his voice)* Why…
Monsieur Fajolet! …Madame's father!

YVONNE: My father!

LUCIEN: *(Who has risen and, with teeth clenched, chin
jutting out, advances towards* JOSEPH, *making him spin
towards him with a brisk tap on his arm)* What father?
Whose father? My mother-in-law is a widow!

JOSEPH: *(Spinning around and back to the audience,
retreats far downstage)* Ah! good grief! Then you're not
Monsieur and Madame Pinnevinnette!

YVONNE: Pinnevinnette!

LUCIEN: *(Furious, marching on him like a wild beast about
to leap on his prey)* No, monsieur, no, we are not the
Pinnevinnettes!

(JOSEPH *has retreated in step with* LUCIEN's *and* YVONNE's
advance on him, and ends up backed against the night table.)

YVONNE: *(Who has followed her husband in a scissors
movement, which puts her at the right).* Do we look like
Pinnevinnettes?

LUCIEN: The Pinnevinnettes are on the right side of the
landing!

JOSEPH: *(Choking)* Ah! so this ain't the right side of the landing?

LUCIEN: No, monsieur, this is the left side! It's on the right when you get out of the elevator, but on the left when you take the stairs.

YVONNE: If you had taken the stairs like everybody else!…

JOSEPH: *(Suddenly)* Oh my God!

YVONNE & LUCIEN: What?

JOSEPH: Why then…I have to make the announcement all over again?

LUCIEN: *(Taking him by the arm and sending him center stage)* No, you don't think I'm going to do it for you?

JOSEPH: Oh! all over again! I was so glad to be done with it.

LUCIEN: Have you ever seen such an idiot!

YVONNE: *(Also marching on him)* Coming here and stirring up emotions by announcing that your mother is dead when she isn't!

JOSEPH: Madame, I'm ever so sorry.

YVONNE: *(Shrugging)* Oh! keep your mouth shut. *(She comes down right.)*

(LUCIEN, making JOSEPH spin round and sending him to the back of the stage:)

LUCIEN: Go on, get the hell out of here! You bloody imbecile!

YVONNE: *(Downstage at the foot of the bed)* Blunderer!

LUCIEN: *(Downstage, near the fireplace)* Moron!

JOSEPH: *(At back)* But, monsieur, it ain't my fault! …You should be pleased!

LUCIEN & YVONNE: *(Leaping in place)* Pleased!

LUCIEN: Brute!

YVONNE: Idiot!

LUCIEN: Sonuvabitch!

JOSEPH: *(In the doorway)* That's going too far, honestly! You chew me out because your mother isn't dead! I can't do anything about that!

LUCIEN & YVONNE: *(Leaping at JOSEPH)* What did you say?

LUCIEN: *(Left of the door, to JOSEPH)* Will you get the hell out! Damn it all!

YVONNE: *(Pushing Joseph out)* Will you get out of here!

JOSEPH: *(While being expelled)* Oh! no, no, I'll never forget this.

YVONNE: Oh! neither will I!

(YVONNE follows JOSEPH out, chasing him into the hall.)

LUCIEN: *(Who remains on the threshold, continuing to insult JOSEPH, through the audience can see neither him nor YVONNE. There should a two-second interval between each "Get the hell out!")* Get the hell out!...

YVONNE: *(Indignant)* Oh!

LUCIEN: Get the hell out!..

YVONNE: Oh!

LUCIEN: Get the hell out!..

YVONNE: Oh!

LUCIEN: Get the hell out!...

YVONNE: Oh!

(This is all mixed with JOSEPH's protests, the sound of the front door opening, then slammed shut on someone's back. LUCIEN, coming downstage, and as a last snarl, addressed to no one in particular:)

LUCIEN: Get the hell out!

YVONNE: *(Very enervated, coming down to the foot of the bed and throwing her kerchief and her cloak on it.)* Oh!

LUCIEN: Oh!

YVONNE: Oh!

LUCIEN: Oh! what a brute! What a brute!

YVONNE: Clobbering us like that! *(Sits, very shaken, on the bench)*

LUCIEN: *(Indignant)* Oh! *(After a pause, happy to take the opportunity for reprisals)* Well! that's your mother for you! That's what YOUR mother does to us!

YVONNE: *(Startled)* Oh really! What's wrong with you? What's come over you?

LUCIEN: Yes! Now what am I going to tell the interior decorator? …Once he learns that your mother isn't dead? that it was all a gag?

YVONNE: What do you mean, once he learns it? But you haven't told him.

LUCIEN: *(Almost shouting)* I wrote to him!

YVONNE: *(Standing up indignantly)* Already!

LUCIEN: *(As before)* Of course! Since the fellow was pestering us!

YVONNE: Oh!

LUCIEN: I let him know that I would be able to settle the bill since I had…the sad occasion to lose my mother-in-law.

YVONNE: That's going too far! You were cashing in on mama!

LUCIEN: How could I suspect that it was a gag! *(Shaking his fist at the door at back.)* Oh! the bitch! the bitch!

YVONNE: *(Leaping on him like a tigress)* How dare you call mama a bitch! How dare you call mama a bitch?

LUCIEN: I do! I do! Bitch! Bitch!

YVONNE: *(With her nails in his face)* Wretch! Wretch!

(At that moment, a distant ringing, different from that of their front doorbell, is heard, stopping their altercation short. YVONNE, suddenly imperative:)

YVONNE: Ssh! shut up!

LUCIEN: *(Impressed)* What is it?

YVONNE: The servant just rang next door.

LUCIEN: *(Coming downstage)* What the hell do I care?

YVONNE: *(Jumping for joy)* The neighbors lost their mother! The neighbors lost their mother!

LUCIEN: There you go, rejoicing at other people's misfortune.

YVONNE: *(Joyously coming down right and bounding to sit on the bed)* Well! when I think it was almost me!

LUCIEN: No such luck! *(Coming upstage.)* Ah! we're so well off!

Scene Four

(The same, ANNETTE)

ANNETTE: *(Entering dressed in LUCIEN's long, loose overcoat)* Dere! It's done!

LUCIEN: *(Springs toward her and grabs her wrists)* Ah! ... the letters! What did you do with the letters!

ANNETTE: *(Recoiling into the space between the back wall and the bed)* I pudt zem in de post.

LUCIEN: There we go! She put them in the post!

ANNETTE: Vell! Ja, zince moussié...

LUCIEN: That was a neat trick! Why did you have to be in such a hurry about it?

ANNETTE: Budt moussié toldt me to…!

LUCIEN: I did, I did …! But that was before, when madame's mother was dead. *(He comes downstage.)*

YVONNE: *(Beaming, to Annette who is close to her on the other side of the bed)* Yes, and now… she isn't.

ANNETTE: *(Above the bed)* Lieber Gott! …zey been grazy!

YVONNE: *(Very excited)* It isn't mama; it's the neighbors' mother! The servant mixed up the doors!

ANNETTE: No! iss dot true?

LUCIEN: *(Furious)* Yes it is!

ANNETTE: *(Jumping for joy)* Ah! how clad I been!

LUCIEN: *(Furious)* There you are, she's clad! She's clad!

ANNETTE: Ja wohl!

YVONNE: *(Pointing a finger at Lucien who is down left)* No, but monsieur is sorry for it!

LUCIEN: *(Shrugs)* Come on now!

YVONNE: He would have been overjoyed to bury mama!

LUCIEN: *(As before)* Oh! "bury her"…! *(Suddenly.)* Ah! damn it to hell!

YVONNE: What!

LUCIEN: My letter to Borniol!

YVONNE: What about "your letter to Borniol"?

LUCIEN: *(Quickly and in a despondent voice)* I wrote to the Borniol undertakers to show up at your mother's tomorrow and arrange for the funeral!

YVONNE: *(Jumping on her knees on to the bed)* You did what!

LUCIEN: Oh well! That'll be nice!

YVONNE: *(Advancing on her knees to the foot of the bed)* You want to kill her! You want her head!

LUCIEN: Oh well! It's no big deal! I'll send a telegram tomorrow morning!

YVONNE: *(Shaking her fist at him)* Wretch! He wants to kill mama! He wants to kill mama!

LUCIEN: *(Going to the foot of the bed, in a commanding tone)* That's enough! It's time to go to sleep!

(All this should be almost simultaneous until the end.)

YVONNE: *(Not listening)* Cutthroat! Assassin! Jack the Ripper!

LUCIEN: *(Half standing on the bench)* Will you shut up! Will you shut up!

ANNETTE: *(Standing on the edge of the bed, trying to interpose between them)* Come now, matame! Moussié!

YVONNE: He wants to kill mama! He wants to kill mama!

LUCIEN: *(Abandoning his place and facing the audience)* Oh! no! no! I'd rather sleep in the maid's sheets!

YVONNE: *(As the curtain falls)* And he said my breasts were like an overnight bag.

ANNETTE: Matame! Matame!

LUCIEN: *(Reaching the door at left)* Oh! What a pain! Damn and blast!

YVONNE: He said my breasts were like an overnight bag.

LUCIEN: Damn and blast! *(He exits furiously.)*

(Curtain)

END OF PLAY

POTTY FAVORS

(On purge Bébé!)

CHARACTERS & SETTING

FOLLAVOINE, *a porcelain manufacturer*
JULIE FOLLAVOINE, *his wife*
TOTO, *age 7, their son*
ADHÉAUME CHOUILLOUX, *a government official*
CLÉMENCE CHOUILLOUX, *his wife*
HORACE TRUCHET, *her cousin*
ROSE, *the maid*

FOLLAVOINE's *Study*

*A box set. Down left, door opening into Madame
Follavoine's rooms. Center back, door opening to the
vestibule. On either side of this door, a bookcase, with
latticed glass doors, each door hung with pleated taffeta
to conceal the interior (The left door of the bookcase must
be fixed; the two chamber pots will be placed behind this
door, so that they cannot be seen by the audience when the
bookcase is opened) Right, filling up almost the entirety
of that wall of the set, a big window with four hinged
panes (Short lace curtains and full curtains) Center right,
a big desk facing the audience; on it, file folders, books, a
dictionary, scattered papers, and a box of rubber bands.
In the drawer on the actor's right, a box of mints. Beneath
the desk, a waste basket. Behind the desk, an office chair on
wheels. Before the desk at its far right an armchair. Left,
a divan somewhat on a diagonal. Left of the divan, a low
pedestal table. Up right of the divan, a straight chair.*

Note: Behind the backdrop of the vestibule, set up a perpendicular board in some kind of stage frame, and insert between the backdrop and the board cast-iron plates to create a hard surface to make the chamber pots break when they are thrown.

Scene One

(FOLLAVOINE, *then* ROSE)

(*As the curtain rises, FOLLLAVOINE, bent over his desk, left leg kneeling on the seat of his desk chair, his butt on the chair-arm, is leafing through the dictionary.*)

FOLLAVOINE: (*His dictionary open before him on the table*) Let's see: "Philippine Islands?" ...Philippine Islands? ...Philippine Islands?... (*Knock at the door. —Without raising his head, annoyed*) Drat! Come in!

(FOLLAVOINE, *to* ROSE *who appears:*)

FOLLAVOINE: What? What do you want?

ROSE: (*Coming through the door left*) Madame is asking for Monsieur.

FOLLAVOINE: (*Diving back into his dictionary, gruffly*) Well, have her come here! ...If she wants to talk to me, she knows where I am.

ROSE: (*Who has crossed down center*) Madame is busy in her boudoir; she can't be disturbed.

FOLLAVOINE: Really!! Well, neither can I! Sorry! I'm working.

(ROSE *is about to go back upstage.*)

FOLLAVOINE: (*Raising his head, but still holding the dictionary. —In the same gruff tone.*) Anyway, what is it? What does she want?

ROSE: (*Who has stopped at* FOLLAVOINE's *question*) I don't know, monsieur.

FOLLAVOINE: Well, go and ask her!

ROSE: Yes, monsieur. *(She heads upstage.)*

FOLLAVOINE: Honestly! …

(FOLLAVOINE, calling ROSE back just as she is about to exit:)

FOLLAVOINE: By the way, you there!…

ROSE: *(Crossing downstage)* Monsieur?

FOLLAVOINE: By the way, the…the Philippines…?

ROSE: *(Not understanding)* What?

FOLLAVOINE: The Philippines? …Do you know where they are?

ROSE: *(Startled)* The Philippines?

FOLLAVOINE: Yes.

ROSE: Ah! No! …No!… *(As if to justify herself.)* I'm not the one who straightens up in here! …That's the mistress.

FOLLAVOINE: *(Straightening up as he closes the dictionary on his index finger, to keep his place)* What! What! "who straightens up"! The Philippines! …Islands! You blasted ignoramus! …Land surrounded by water… don't you know what that is?

ROSE: *(Eyes wide open)* Land surrounded by water?

FOLLAVOINE: Yes! land surrounded by water, what is that called?

ROSE: Mud?

FOLLAVOINE: *(Shrugs)* No, not mud! It's mud when there's not a lot of land and not a lot of water! but, when there is a lot of land and a lot of water, it's called islands!

ROSE: *(Stunned)* Ah!

FOLLAVOINE: Well, that's the Philippines! Islands! Consequently they are not located in this apartment.

ROSE: *(Trying to understand)* Ah! right! …They're outside!

FOLLAVOINE: *(Shrugs)* Of course, they're outside.

ROSE: Ah! well, no! I haven't seen them.

FOLLAVOINE: *(Leaving his desk and unceremoniously ushering her to the door she entered by)* Yes, thanks, that'll do!

ROSE: *(As if to justify herself)* I ain't been in Paris long, see…?

FOLLAVOINE: Yes! …Yes, yes!

ROSE: And I don't go out very often!

FOLLAVOINE: Yes! all right! Get along with you! …Go and get your mistress.

ROSE: Yes, monsieur! *(She exits.)*

FOLLAVOINE: That girl doesn't know a thing! What do they teach them at school? *(Coming down to the front of desk and leaning against it)* "She's not the one who clears up the Philippines!" I should think not! *(Diving back into his dictionary)* "The Philippines…the Philippines…" *(To the audience)* This is incredible! I can find "Theban," "theft", "theism," "thematic," but not "the Philippines"! If they were there, they'd be between "Theban" and "theft." You can't find anything in this dictionary! *(To make sure, he runs his eyes over the column he just read.)*

Scene Two

(FOLLAVOINE, JULIE)

JULIE: *(Bursting like a whirlwind through the door to her room. Dressed like a slattern: a terry-cloth dressing-gown, whose unattached cord trails behind her: a little silk petticoat, over her nightgown which is showing at the bottom; curlers in her hair; stockings drooping over her heelless slippers. —She is holding a covered slop bucket full of water.)* Well? So you can't be disturbed? Is that it?

FOLLAVOINE: *(Leaping up)* Ah! please, don't always burst into a room like a bomb! ...Ah!...

JULIE: *(Sarcastically apologizing)* Oh! excuse me! *(Pursed mouth, in a saccharine tone.)* You can't be disturbed? Is that it?

FOLLAVOINE: *(Crossly)* Well? what about you? Why should I be disturbed more than you?

JULIE: *(With a sarcastic smile)* That's fair! That's fair! We're married, aren't we!...

FOLLAVOINE: What? What? What's the connection?...

JULIE: *(As before)* Ah! if I were somebody else's wife, it'd be another story!...

FOLLAVOINE: Ah! leave me alone! I'm busy, that's all!

JULIE: *(Putting down the slop bucket center stage, and crossing left)* Busy! Monsieur is busy! That's incredible!

FOLLAVOINE: Yes, busy! *(Noticing the bucket.)* Ah!

JULIE: *(Turning around at FOLLAVOINE's exclamation)* What?

FOLLAVOINE: There! Are you crazy? You and your pail go everywhere together now?

JULIE: Who's "pale"? Do I look "pale"?

FOLLAVOINE: *(Pointing to it)* That!

JULIE: Oh! that! That's nothing. *(The most naturally in the world)* That's my slops.

FOLLAVOINE: What am I'm supposed to do with them?

JULIE: They're not for you! It's to empty them out.

FOLLAVOINE: Here?

JULIE: No, not here! What a stupid thing to say! I am not in the habit of emptying my slops in your study: Give me credit for tact.

FOLLAVOINE: Then, why did you bring them in?

JULIE: No reason! Because I had the bucket in my hand to go and empty it when Rose came and brought me your charming reply; so, lest I keep you waiting...

FOLLAVOINE: You couldn't leave it at the door?

JULIE: Ah! you're such a fussbudget! If it annoys you that much, you only had to let yourself be disturbed when I asked you to come; but Monsieur was busy! With what? I ask you. *(She has crossed far upstage.)*

FOLLAVOINE: *(Grousing)* With things, most likely!

JULIE: Which ones?

FOLLAVOINE: *(As before)* Well, things! ...I was looking for "The Philippine Islands" in the dictionary.

JULIE: The Philippine Islands! Are you crazy? Are you planning to go there?

FOLLAVOINE: *(As before)* No, I am not!

JULIE: *(Scornfully, while sitting on the divan)* Then, what do you care? Why should a manufacturer of porcelain care where the Philippines are?

FOLLAVOINE: *(Still in a grouchy tone)* I don't care! Far from it! ...Believe me, it's not on my account! ...It's for Junior. He has such questions! The things kids come up with, honestly! They think parents know everything!... *(Imitating his son)* "Papa, where are the Philippines?"

(Resuming his grumpy tone to imitate himself.) "What?"
(His son's voice.) "Where are the Philippines, papa?"
Oh! I heard him all right! I made him repeat it
anyway... *(Cursing)* "Where are the Philippines"! How
do I know! Do *you* know?

JULIE: Why, yes, they're... I've seen it somewhere, on
the map; I don't remember where.

FOLLAVOINE: *(Going upstage to sit at the desk on which he
puts his dictionary, open to the page he had been inspecting)*
Ah! neither do I! But I couldn't give the kid that
answer! What would he have thought! I tried to avoid
it by a diversion: "Ssh! it's none of your business! The
Philippines are not for children!"

JULIE: What an idea! That's idiotic.

FOLLAVOINE: It was a bad idea; his governess had set
him geography questions.

JULIE: *(Shrugs)* Well, of course!

FOLLAVOINE: Eh! Should they still be teaching children
geography nowadays! ...What with trains and boats
that can take you right there! ...And the street signs up
everywhere!

JULIE: What's the connection?

FOLLAVOINE: I mean it! When you need a city, do you
go and look it up in geography? No, you look in the
railway time-table! Well then!...

JULIE: But what about the child? *(Rising and picking up
her bucket on the way.)* You didn't help him! You left
him in the lurch!

FOLLAVOINE: I'll say! What else could I do? I mean I put
on a serious,well- informed look; that of a gentleman
who could answer but who doesn't want to, and I said,
"My child, if I were to show it to you, you would not

have the benefit of working it out for yourself; try to find it, and if you can't, then I shall point it out to you."

JULIE: *(Near* FOLLAVOINE, *left of the desk)* In other words, get lost!

FOLLAVOINE: I left his room as dignified as I could; and as soon as the door closed, I rushed to this dictionary convinced that I would find it! Ah! well, take it from me! Zilch.

JULIE: *(Doesn't understand)* Zilch?

FOLLAVOINE: Nothing!

JULIE: *(Incredulous)* In the dictionary?

(JULIE *puts her bucket on the ground left of the desk and, pushing away* FOLLAVOINE *to examine the dictionary in his place)*

JULIE: Let me have a look! Let me have a look!…

FOLLAVOINE: *(Coming down far right)* Oh! you can look! …No! Really, you should tell his governess not to stuff the kid's head with things that grown-ups don't know about… and can't even find in the dictionary.

JULIE: *(Who has sat down and for a moment with her eyes fixed on the open page of the dictionary)* Aha! But! …But!…

FOLLAVOINE: What?

JULIE: You've been looking for it under T?

FOLLAVOINE: *(Somewhat at a loss)* Huh? …well… yes…

JULIE: *(With a condescending shrug)* The Philippines, under T? Well, of course you didn't find it.

FOLLAVOINE: What? They're not under T? *(He goes around the table and crosses up to* JULIE.*)*

JULIE: *(Rapidly leafing through the dictionary)* He asks if they're under T!

FOLLAVOINE: Under what then?

JULIE: *(Stopping on a page of the dictionary)* Call yourself a porcelain maker! ...Looking for them under T. *(Running down the column of words)* Uh! ..."Filibuster, filigree, filing" It's under F! "Fillet, fillip, film.." *(Astonished)* What! How can that be?

FOLLAVOINE: What?

JULIE: It's not there!

FOLLAVOINE: *(Crossing left, triumphantly)* Aha! I'm not surprised! ...You always have to know better than anybody else!

JULIE: *(Discountenanced)* I don't understand. It ought to be between "fillip" and "film".

FOLLAVOINE: *(Enraged)* Didn't I tell you you wouldn't find anything in this dictionary! You can look for words under any letter you please, it makes no difference! You only find words you don't need!

JULIE: *(Staring at the dictionary)* It's peculiar!

FOLLAVOINE: *(Sitting on the divan, in a prim tone)* Anyway, I see that "porcelain maker's wife" can't do any better than the "porcelain maker."

JULIE: *(Drily)* Anyway I looked under F, and that's more logical than under T.

FOLLAVOINE: *(Shrugs)* Indeed! "more logical than under T"! Why not under P?

JULIE: *(Annoyed)* "Under P... under P!" What do you mean "under P"? *(Gradually changing her tone.)* Why... as a matter of fact...under P...why not? ...Of course: "Philippines...Philippines", I do believe...? Why yes! *(She rushes to the dictionary and leafs through it feverishly.)* P! ...P! ...P!...

FOLLAVOINE: *(Imitating her)* "Peepeepee!"

JULIE: *(Rapidly runs down the column of words)* "Philately, Philharmonic, Philippines!" *(In triumph.)* There they are!: "The Philippines!"

FOLLAVOINE: *(Rushing to his wife)* You found them? *(As he crosses, he bumps his foot against the bucket. Enraged.)* Ah! look at that! *(He picks up the bucket and not knowing where to put it, sets it on the left corner of the desk. Both his forearms are leaning on the lid of the bucket.)*

JULIE: In full: "The Philippines, islands in the western Pacific Ocean. Capital Manila."

FOLLAVOINE: *(Heading left, beaming, as if he had found them himself)* Good, now we have it!

JULIE: Wait! There's more: "They are comprised of three islands, Luzon, Visayas and Mindanao."

FOLLAVOINE: *(As before)* "Luzon, Visayas and Mindanao!" That's right! A minute ago we didn't have any Philippines at all, and now we've got more than we need! The same old story! What a life!

JULIE: Yes, but which ones does the child need now?

FOLLAVOINE: *("I could care less")* Oh! never mind! He can pick the ones he wants! He needed the Philippines, he's got them, that's the main thing! If he has too many, he can drop some!

JULIE: And to think we were looking under T and F...

FOLLAVOINE: *(Dropping on to the divan)* We'd be a long time looking.

JULIE: *(Rising and slipping her arm into the handle of the bucket to take it away)* And it was under P!

FOLLAVOINE: *(Casual to the point of unconsciousness)* Just what I was saying!

JULIE: *(Startled by his gall, turns towards him, then:)* What do you mean, just what you were saying!

FOLLAVOINE: *(As calm as can be)* Well, yes, what about it? Wasn't I the one who said, "Why not under P"?

JULIE: Excuse me! You said it! …You said it… sarcastically.

FOLLAVOINE: *(Rising and crossing to her)* Sarcastically! What do you mean, sarcastically?

JULIE: Positively! To make fun of me: *(Imitating his voice.)* "Ah! why not under P?" *(She crosses left.)*

FOLLAVOINE: Oh no, really!…

JULIE: I was the one who suddenly had a sort of vision of the word.

FOLLAVOINE: *(Crossing right above the desk)* "A sort of vision of the word!" Incredible! "A sort of vision of the word!" The way women make things up! I say to you: "Why not under P?" Then you jump up, you go "As a matter of fact, under P, why not?" And you call that "having a vision of the word"? How convenient!

JULIE: *(Furious, crossing to the left corner of the desk on which she places her bucket)* Oh! that's going too far! When I was the one who picked up the dictionary! When I was the one who looked it up!

FOLLAVOINE: *(Crossing down right of the desk. In a teasing tone.)* Yes, under F!

JULIE: Under F…under F, first! Just as you did, under T! but then under P.

FOLLAVOINE: *(Sitting in the armchair at right, in front of the desk. Aloof, staring at the ceiling.)* Pretty dodgy, since I had said, "Why not under P?" Under P!

JULIE: *(Crossing left)* You're getting on my nerves with your constant P-ing!

FOLLAVOINE: Oh! no, my love, no! if you're going to be obscene!…

JULIE: *(Turns around, startled, nonplussed for a moment; then:)* What do you mean? Obscene?

FOLLAVOINE: I admit I'm no match for you!...

JULIE: *(Crosses left of the table)* What's so obscene? Because I don't give up? Because I tell it like it is! *(Angrily shaking her slop bucket over the table as she speaks.)* Well, I found it! Yes, I'm the one who found it!

FOLLAVOINE: *(Rushing to take the bucket out of her hands)* Yes, yes! ...all right, all right! *(He looks around to figure out where to put the bucket.)*

JULIE: *(Watching him)* What? What are you looking for?

FOLLAVOINE: *(Enraged)* I'm looking...I'm looking...I'm looking for somewhere to put this thing.

JULIE: Well, put it on the floor.

FOLLAVOINE: *(Placing it center stage)* Right.

JULIE: *(Returning to the charge)* No, really, to have the gall to pretend!...

FOLLAVOINE: *(Exasperated)* Oh! ...All right! I give up! You are the one who found it!

JULIE: Of course I did! You don't have to act as if you were making me concessions.

FOLLAVOINE: Ah! please, that's enough, eh! With your Fs and your Ts, your Ps and your P-P's! Honestly! Go on, get dressed instead!

JULIE: *(Grumbling)* Telling me I didn't have a vision!... *(She sits on the arm of the divan.)*

FOLLAVOINE: All right, all right! ...It's almost eleven o'clock and you're still running around like a slob...

JULIE: *(Instinctively adjusting her dressing-gown)* Oh yes! change the subject! ...Change it!

FOLLAVOINE: ...with your dirty wrapper, your curlers and your stockings falling down around your ankles!

JULIE: *(Roughly pulling up her stockings)* Well, whose ankles do you want them to fall over?

FOLLAVOINE: Nobody's ankles!

JULIE: There! They're up!

FOLLAVOINE: If you think that's going to stop them from falling down again. Can't you keep them in place?

JULIE: With what? I'm not wearing garters.

FOLLAVOINE: Well, put some on!

JULIE: And what am I supposed to attach them to? I'm not wearing a corset.

FOLLAVOINE: *(Crossing right near the armchair in front of the desk)* Well, put on a corset, damn it!

JULIE: Ah! Sure! Why not tell me to put on a ball gown when I'm cleaning my boudoir! *(As she speaks, she has picked up her bucket, with her right arm through the handle, and goes back up to her room.)*

FOLLAVOINE: For Chrissake! Who's asking you to clean your boudoir? Somebody would think you don't have a servant! You've got a maid, for heaven's sake!

JULIE: *(Who was already on the threshold, turning around as if stung to the core by her husband's remark, dashing at him like a wild beast, and, after placing her bucket at FOLLAVOINE's feet—arms crossed, right in his face)* Have my maid clean my boudoir!

FOLLAVOINE: *(To avoid a fresh argument, passing in front of his wife and crossing left)* Oh!…

JULIE: *(Holding tight and keeping in step behind him)* No thank you very much! so everything will get broken and smashed! No, no! I can do that myself. *(She leaves her husband and crossing far right, sits in the armchair in front of the desk.)*

FOLLAVOINE: Then there's no point in keeping a maid if she's no use to you.

JULIE: *(Resting her half-bare right leg on the bucket as if it were a footstool)* I beg your pardon, she is of use to me: she's around!

FOLLAVOINE: Yeah! And what's she up to while you do her work?

JULIE: *(A bit at a loss)* Well, she...she watches me.

FOLLAVOINE: There we have it! She watches you! I pay a girl four hundred francs a month so that she can watch you!

JULIE: Oh please! Stop talking about how much you pay all the time! You sound so mercenary.

FOLLAVOINE: Mercenary or not! I think that when I pay a woman four hundred francs a month!...

JULIE: *(Rising, without taking the trouble to lift her leg off the bucket, but simply letting it slip in front of the bucket, which is how she gets to her feet; crossing to* FOLLAVOINE*)* No, tell me! I don't ask you for a salary, do I? Well, so long as it doesn't cost you any more, what difference does it make who does the work?

FOLLAVOINE: The difference...the difference...is that I have a maid to do my wife's work; and not a wife to do the maid's work...; or, if that's the case, I'll get rid of the maid.

JULIE: *(With sweeping gestures of indignation)* There you go! There you go! I knew that's what you were driving at! He's begrudges me a maid! *(She crosses far right.)*

FOLLAVOINE: *(Same as her, crossing far left)* Now I'm begrudging you a maid!

JULIE: *(Turning around to him)* Absolutely.

FOLLAVOINE: *(At the end of his rope)* Ah! why don't you pull up your stockings!

JULIE: *(Abruptly pulling up her stockings)* Oh! *(Resuming)* All this because I prefer to clean my boudoir myself! *(Going up right as she speaks, as far as the desk.)* Ah! you must be the first husband to scold his wife for doing housework.

FOLLAVOINE: Excuse me! Excuse me, but between doing housework and…

JULIE: *(Nervous, automatically arranging the papers on her husband's desk)* You'd prefer me to behave like all those ladies I call on, wouldn't you,? …No thought except to rig themselves out, and run up bills?…

FOLLAVOINE: *(Noticing Julie's actions and trembling for his papers)* Oh dear!…oh dear!

(He hurries to protect them.)

JULIE: *(As before)* Always out of the house: in the park, at the races, in the department stores…

FOLLAVOINE: *(Protecting his papers as best he can)* No, please! …Please!…

JULIE: *(Not stopping)* The skating rink in the morning, the skating rink in the afternoon!

FOLLAVOINE: *(As before)* Please, will you…?

JULIE: *(As before)* What a lovely aim in life!

FOLLAVOINE: *(As before)* No! Don't do that! Leave it! leave it!

(FOLLAVOINE moves JULIE to the right.)

JULIE: Leave what?

FOLLAVOINE: *(Trying to put his papers back in order)* My papers, damn it! I didn't ask you to organize them!

JULIE: I can't stand a messy desk.

FOLLAVOINE: Well, it's none of your business! leave them alone.

JULIE: *(Coming down right)* Ah! I don't care a fig for your desk. *(As she passes by, she picks up her bucket.)*

FOLLAVOINE: Well, prove it! and go organize your own stuff! *(Muttering under his breath.)* This obsession with tidying everything up! *(He sits at his desk.)*

JULIE: *(Who has moved around the desk to reach its left corner. Returning to the charge.)* Well, anyway! That's the way you'd like me to be, eh!

FOLLAVOINE: *(At the end of his tether, almost shouting)* What do you mean "like you to be"? Like what? What are you talking about?

JULIE: Like those other women!

FOLLAVOINE: *(Exasperated, while arranging his papers)* How do I know? I only ask you not to rummage around in my papers; that's not much to ask!

JULIE: *(Not letting go; crossing left with mincing minuet movements, which makes the bucket she is still holding swing back and forth like a censer, putting the carpet in jeopardy)* ...Like a social butterfly! A Madame Flibbertigibbet! *(Changing her tone.)* Ever so sorry, my dear! But I was not brought up that way.

FOLLAVOINE: *(Who has had it up to here)* Yes, fine! And a good thing too!

(JULIE, coming back to him—left corner of the table—and as she speaks putting her bucket on FOLLAVOINE's papers just as he's about to pick them up:)

JULIE: You should know that my family...

FOLLAVOINE: *(Prevented by the bucket from taking his papers)* Oh! ...Look at that!

JULIE: *(Lifting the bucket to free the papers)* ...that my family...

FOLLAVOINE: *(Eyes skyward)* Oh!

JULIE: …when it came to my upbringing, they had only one thing in mind: to make me a good housekeeper! … And a good manager!

FOLLAVOINE: Listen, I assure you, this is very interesting, but it's eleven o'clock and…

JULIE: *(Interrupting)* I don't care! …That's why I was taught to do everything for myself! …And to count on nobody but me! Because you never know in life if you'll always have people to serve you. *(She crosses left with dignity.)*

FOLLAVOINE: *(Shrugs, eyes skyward, then)* Your stockings!

JULIE: Oh! tush! *(Without bothering to sit down, she quickly pulls up her stockings one at a time, then resuming:)* I was trained that way even when I was a girl! So it's become second nature to me. *(Sitting in the armchair right of the desk.)* Now is that an asset? Or a liability? *(Leaning on the edge of the desk, head leaning on her hand.)* All I can say is: I got it from my mother.

FOLLAVOINE: *(Busy leafing through his papers and without any ulterior motive)* Ah! …My mother-in-law.

JULIE: *(Head half turned to FOLLAVOINE and in an irritated tone)* No! …"my mother"!

FOLLAVOINE: *(As before)* It's the same thing.

JULIE: *(As before)* That may be! But "my mother" is loving, it's affectionate, it's polite; whereas "my mother-in-law" is something cold, harsh, an unforgivable discourtesy.

FOLLAVOINE: *(As before)* Oh! if you say so.

JULIE: I said "my mother"; well, she's "my mother." There's no point in correcting me to say "my mother-in-law."

FOLLAVOINE: I assure you that if I said "my mother-in-law" it was in regard to myself…

JULIE: *(Springing up and, back to the audience, hands clutching the edge of the desk, body leaning forward to annihilate her husband)* What? Hasn't she always been good to you? Do you have something to complain about?

FOLLAVOINE: *(Body thrown back as far as possible to the back of his armchair, to put himself out of her reach)* No! no! What are you getting at? Only, , that doesn't mean in regard to myself your mother…

JULIE: *(Who has crossed center, turning around, haughtily and trenchant)* Ah! Please! That'll be enough about mother!

FOLLAVOINE: *(Startled)* What?

JULIE: I mean it! The way you are always attacking the poor woman! …Taunting her at every opportunity!…

FOLLAVOINE: Me?

JULIE: All that, because I had the bad luck to bring my slop bucket into your study!

FOLLAVOINE: Ah! no, really…!

JULIE: *(Slipping an arm under the handle of the bucket which is still on her husband's desk)* Well, I'm going to take my bucket away! See, I'm picking it up! No more need for all this fuss! I'm taking it away!

FOLLAVOINE: *(Grumbling, while pretending to dive into his papers)* All right! …About time too.

JULIE: *(Grousing, as she goes upstage to her room)* No! All this carry-on over a miserable slop bucket, really, as if I'd committed a crime!… *(On the threshold, she stops. A thought has crossed her mind, she spins around, comes back down to the desk, puts her bucket on it in the same place as before, then:)* Only, you know! The next time you want to find fault with me…

FOLLAVOINE: *(Interrupting her)* No, sorry! …Sorry!…

JULIE: *(Startled)* What?

FOLLAVOINE: The bucket's back again!

JULIE: *(Teeth clenched)* Idiot! *(Resuming.)* The next time you want to find fault with me, you should say so straight to my face! …and not take it out on mama! *(She comes a bit downstage, leaving her bucket on the table.)*

FOLLAVOINE: *(Beside himself, crossing to* JULIE*)* Ye gods and little fishes! What the hell did I say?

JULIE: Oh, nothing, nothing. It's obvious! Now you can play the hypocrite!

FOLLAVOINE: *(Exasperated, unable to fight back)* Oh! *(He crosses up left to the back.)*

JULIE: *(Moving above the desk on which she automatically begins to organize his papers as she speaks)* As if I didn't always understand exactly what you mean…when you don't say anything!

FOLLAVOINE: *(Turning around)* No! that's the last straw! What! I say… *(Rushing forward when he sees his wife rummaging in his papers.)* Ah! No! no! leave my papers alone, won't you!…

*(*FOLLAVOINE *takes* JULIE*'s place and moves her left of the table.)*

FOLLAVOINE: What is this obsession you have…?

JULIE: *(Peremptorily)* I love everything in its place.

FOLLAVOINE: *(Shrugs)* Ah, "you love everything in its place! You love everything in its place!" *(Indicating the bucket on the table and holding it out to her.)* Look at that.

JULIE: *(Taking the bucket)* What now?

FOLLAVOINE: *(Muttering)* "You love everything in its place!" It would be a good idea if you applied that to the way you dress! *(Rising)* I'm begging you! You were on the right track a minute ago; you and your bucket were almost out the door! Did you have to bring it back...

JULIE: *(Interrupting, peremptorily)* I have to talk to you.

FOLLAVOINE: *(Gently pushing her in the direction of her room)* Yes, well, later!

JULIE: No, not later. I really have to talk to you about...

FOLLAVOINE: *(Near the divan, as is* JULIE*)* For pity's sake, it's eleven o'clock; you haven't even started to get dressed. We have Monsieur and Madame Chouilloux to lunch...

JULIE: "Chouilloux! Chouilloux!" I don't give a rap for Monsieur and Madame Chouilloux.

FOLLAVOINE: Well, I do! Chouilloux is a man whom I have the greatest interest in treating with respect...

JULIE: That may well be! but he can wait. It's about Baby, and if I had to choose between Baby and Chouilloux, I wouldn't hesitate!

FOLLAVOINE: *(Beside himself)* Oh! What? What about Baby?

JULIE: *(Crossing in front of him and reaching the right)* Or perhaps you prefer Chouilloux! *(She sits in the armchair in front of the desk, with the bucket in her lap.)*

FOLLAVOINE: *(Almost shouting)* No, no! That's not the point! I am not putting Baby and Chouilloux on a par; that doesn't mean that when you invite a stranger of some importance into your home, you shouldn't take some pains over him; it doesn't imply that you prefer him to your family! Chouilloux is to arrive shortly before lunch to confer with me about an important piece of business I have in mind…

JULIE: Well, go ahead and confer! What do I care?

FOLLAVOINE: But he may show up at any minute! You can't receive him with your dirty wrapper, and curlers, and slop buckets on your lap and your stockings drooping over your heels!

JULIE: (*Angrily placing her bucket in front of her*) Oh! you're a pain about my stockings! (*Standing, one foot on her bucket, bending over to pull up her stockings.*) So what? Your Chouilloux never saw stockings fall down? Really? When Madame Chouilloux gets up in the morning, she's wearing a ball gown?

(FOLLAVOINE, *while* JULIE *nervously pulls up her stockings:*)

FOLLAVOINE: I don't know what Madame Chouilloux is like when she gets up, but I do say that your outfit is not an outfit in which to receive people we're having to lunch for the first time. (*He crosses up to the back.*)

JULIE: (*Rummaging on* FOLLAVOINE's *desk to find a particular object*) Well! you're wearing a frock coat, that makes up for it.

FOLLAVOINE: (*Turning around at that remark*) I am properly dressed! (*Seeing his wife's actions.*) What are you looking for? What are you looking for?

JULIE: (*Taking rubber bands from a box*) Your rubber bands.

FOLLAVOINE: (*Above the table*) What? What for?

JULIE: (*Putting the box back on the desk and sitting in her armchair*) So you'll shut up about my stockings!

FOLLAVOINE: But those are rubber bands for my documents! They're not garters!

JULIE: *(Finishing putting on the rubber bands, stressing "garters" each time)* They're not garters, because nobody made them into garters; but since I've made them into garters, they are now garters.

FOLLAVOINE: *(Crossing left in dismay)* Ah! no! this mess!...

JULIE: *(Shrugs)* "You are properly dressed!" If this isn't grotesque: putting on a frock coat at eleven in the morning! ...For Monsieur Chouilloux! ...That cuckold!...

FOLLAVOINE: *(Astonished, stares at his wife; then)* "That cuckold"? What do you mean "that cuckold?" What do you know about it?

JULIE: *(Pleased to put her husband in the wrong)* Ah! ... you're the one who told me!

FOLLAVOINE: Me?

JULIE: I didn't make it up, did I? I don't know Chouilloux. He's no friend of mine; I have no reason to badmouth him. *(She crosses in front of FOLLAVOINE and moves left.)*

FOLLAVOINE: *(Backed against a corner of the desk)* Chouilloux a cuckold! How can a person say such a thing!

JULIE: *(Coming down to him)* Of course a person can, since you said it to me.

FOLLAVOINE: I said it to you, I said it to you... when I didn't need him! But now that I need him...

JULIE: *(Tit for tat, face to face with FOLLAVOINE)* What? He's stopped being a cuckold?

FOLLAVOINE: No! ...Yes! ...Anyway, how do we know! ...That's not how we've going to treat him. *(He crosses far right.)*

JULIE: Do tell!

FOLLAVOINE: *(Crossing up far right above the desk)* He's a man who, at the present moment, can be very useful to me…

JULIE: How so?

FOLLAVOINE: In a big deal I'm brewing up; it would take too long to explain.

JULIE: *(Crossing right)* Yes. Oh! I know, you're very broad-minded when your interests are at stake!

FOLLAVOINE: So what? Do you care that he's a cuckold?

JULIE: Certainly not! His wife can cheat on him dozens of times! But what I do care about is that you invited her to lunch; yes indeed!

FOLLAVOINE: *(Left side of the desk)* I couldn't invite the gentleman without his wife; it isn't done.

JULIE: Really? How about her lover, Monsieur Horace Truchet? You were obliged to invite her lover!

FOLLAVOINE: Naturally! it's customary, my love! They're invited everywhere like that. I mean, if I hadn't invited Monsieur Truchet, it would have been undiplomatic! Chouilloux might even have wondered what I meant by it! It simply isn't done!

JULIE: *(Leaning against the table, arms crossed)* Incredible! So we're going to have all three! The complete *menage à trois*! How moral! *(Picking up her bucket and crossing left.)* A nice contact for your wife! And a fine example for Toto.

FOLLAVOINE: *(Coming downstage)* Oh! Toto…he's seven.

JULIE: He won't always be.

FOLLAVOINE: Yes, but in the meantime he is.

JULIE: Oh! Of course! Of course! Whether it's his moral well-being or his physical well-being: you don't give a rap for either!

FOLLAVOINE: *(Arms to heaven while crossing above the desk)* What does that mean? What do you mean by that?

(JULIE, putting down her bucket center stage and immediately crossing up to join FOLLAVOINE *who sits at his desk:)*

JULIE: Why…why, it's obvious: for an hour now I've been trying to talk to you about Baby; to discuss his health with you; and can't get a word in edgewise! Every time I open my mouth and say "Baby", you go "Chouilloux"; it's all about "Chouilloux!" "Chouilloux, Chouilloux" and more "Chouilloux"!

FOLLAVOINE: *(Out of patience)* Well then, what about it? What's the matter? What do want to tell me?

JULIE: *(Peremptory)* I have to talk to you.

FOLLAVOINE: Well, go on, talk!

JULIE: Ah? …it's about time! *(She crosses down to sit on her bucket as on a footstool.)*

FOLLAVOINE: *(Jumping out of his seat and slamming his fist on the desk when he sees his wife on her slop bucket)* Ah! no! no!

JULIE: *(Startled)* What?

FOLLAVOINE: Can't you settle somewhere other than your bucket? Is a slop bucket the only place you can sit?

JULIE: It doesn't matter! I'm comfortable.

FOLLAVOINE: The point is not whether you're comfortable! A slop bucket is not a seat; please sit on a chair.

JULIE: *(Looking him up and down, then disdainfully turning away her head as she rises)* Ah! …You are such a snob!

FOLLAVOINE: It's nothing to do with snobbery: you might make a wrong move, spill your bucket on the floor, I don't feel like having your dirty water on my carpet.

JULIE: What a disaster! It would wash it.

FOLLAVOINE: Thank you, how thoughtful! I'd rather not. Anyway, what about "baby"? What's the matter with "baby"?

JULIE: *(Scornfully submissive)* Ah! ...May I?

FOLLAVOINE: *(His nerves on edge)* Yes you may!

JULIE: *(Who gets the chair next to the divan, brings it to the desk on her husband's side, and sits down)* Well, here it is: I am very worried.

FOLLAVOINE: Ah!

JULIE: I am worried about Toto.

FOLLAVOINE: All right! ...What has he done?

JULIE: He didn't go this morning.

FOLLAVOINE: *(Echoing, without comprehending)* He didn't go?

JULIE: No.

FOLLAVOINE: He didn't go...where?

JULIE: *(Immediately boiling over)* What! "Where?" Nowhere! "He didn't go", that's the point, that's all. It seems clear to me.

FOLLAVOINE: *(Understanding)* Ah! yes, to the...

JULIE: *(Brutally)* Yes, yes!... *(Changing her tone.)* We tried...! Four separate times! No results! ...Once, yes! Oh! ...Nothing! *(Holding out her little finger with the thumb nail against the next-to-last joint.)* No bigger than that!

FOLLAVOINE: Ah!

JULIE: *(Eyes skyward)* And hard!

FOLLAVOINE: *(Shaking his head)* Yes...constipation.

JULIE: *(Despondent)* Constipation.

FOLLAVOINE: Yes! ...Well? ...What do you want me to do about it?

JULIE: *(Shocked)* What do you mean, "What do you want me to do?"

FOLLAVOINE: For heaven's sake! I can't go for him.

JULIE: *(Rising)* Oh! aren't you clever! Such a clever remark. Of course you can't go for him!

FOLLAVOINE: So?...

JULIE: A lot of good it would do me if you went for him! But just because a person can't go for a person doesn't mean you should let them die. *(Coming down left)* Really, you are so heartless!

FOLLAVOINE: *(Rising in turn and joining his wife. Good-naturedly.)* You can't expect me to burst into tears because the kid is a bit constipated.

JULIE: Why not? Constipation is no laughing matter!...

FOLLAVOINE: *(Incredulous)* Oh!

JULIE: *(Pompously)* I read in a book called *The Backside of History* that a bastard of Louis XV almost died at the age of seven as the result of a stubborn constipation.

FOLLAVOINE: All right! But it was stubborn and he was a bastard, which is not the case with Toto either way.

JULIE: Yes, but Toto is seven same as him! and he's constipated same as him!

FOLLAVOINE: For heaven's sake! He just needs a purge.

JULIE: *(Pitying* FOLLAVOINE*)* Oh! ...obviously.

FOLLAVOINE: Well, give him one! *(He crosses right.)*

JULIE: Thank you! I wasn't asking for your permission! What are we going to purge him with? There are mineral laxatives and vegetable laxatives.

FOLLAVOINE: *(Who has returned to his wife)* Give him castor oil; it's easy to take and has guaranteed results.

JULIE: *(With an instinctive horror)* Oh! no! no! No castor oil! I can't stand it! I immediately throw it up.

FOLLAVOINE: But…it's not you taking it, it's your son!

JULIE: Yes, but it's the same thing! Just seeing it, just talking about it…! *(She retches.)* Oh! no! …Besides, I don't see why you make things so complicated! Just next door, in the medicine cabinet, we have a bottle of milk of magnesia, I don't see why we can't use that, just because you prefer castor oil!

FOLLAVOINE: *(Startled)* Me!

JULIE: *(In a tone that brooks no reply)* The milk of magnesia is there. Baby will take milk of magnesia.

FOLLAVOINE: *(Crossing far right)* All right, give him milk of magnesia! …Only, I don't see why you bother to consult me. *(He goes up far right to his desk.)*

JULIE: To find out what I ought to do.

FOLLAVOINE: I never would have guessed. *(He sits at the desk.)*

JULIE: It's no fun having to give the child a purge! But it never fails! Every time I leave him with his grandmother…

FOLLAVOINE: *(Absently, busy scanning a paper)* What grandmother?

JULIE: *(Trenchant and drily)* Well…*his* grandmother! … He doesn't have thirty-six of them. Your mother lives in Düsseldorf, so it has to be mama. *(She sits on the divan.)*

FOLLAVOINE: Ah yes! ...*Your* mother.

JULIE: Yes, my mother. *(Imitating him)* "*Your* mother!
Your mother!" I know she's *my* mother! The way you
say "*Your* mother." You always seem to be scolding
me.

FOLLAVOINE: *(Startled)* Me!

JULIE: *(Going back to her old theme)* Anyway: every time
she takes Baby for the day, it never fails: she stuffs him
with cakes and candy...!

FOLLAVOINE: *(Writing a few notes)* Oh! ...All
grandmothers are like that.

JULIE: That may be so! but it's wrong of her to do it!
Especially since I asked her not to.

FOLLAVOINE: Oh! she wasn't thinking, poor woman...

JULIE: *(Coming upstage)* "She wasn't thinking, she
wasn't thinking," of course! But she was wrong to do it
all the same.

FOLLAVOINE: *(Indulgently)* Oh! well...!

JULIE: *(Getting excited)* Yes indeed! Yes indeed! Don't go
"Oh well"! ...It's a funny thing, this pose you have of
always agreeing with mama! ...taking her side against
me! I tell you she was wrong: so she was wrong.

FOLLAVOINE: *(For the sake of peace)* Fine! ...Fine!

JULIE: Result: Baby doesn't go and we have to give him
a purge.

FOLLAVOINE: Yes, well, it's a nuisance; but it won't kill
him.

JULIE: *(At that word, draws herself up in revulsion)* I hope
not! I hope it won't kill him! Thank you very much!
(Dashing at her husband and shaking him) What you said
is monstrous! ..."It won't kill him" about your own

son! For he is your child, you know! You don't seem to realize: he's yours!

FOLLAVOINE: I should hope so!

JULIE: I'm not the same as Madame Chouilloux! I don't get my little cousins to do your job for you!

FOLLAVOINE: Oh! leave me alone!

JULIE: *(Crossing down and to the right)* When I have a child, it's by my husband!

FOLLAVOINE: Whoever said it wasn't?

JULIE: *(Sitting in the armchair facing the desk)* Ah! there's not much father in the way you behave! You don't deserve to have him as your son!

FOLLAVOINE: *(Shrugs)* Oh! don't be silly!

JULIE: You deserve that he be a bastard too! ...And that I had him with *(Unable to find a name to suggest.)* with Louis XV!

FOLLAVOINE: *(Laughing up his sleeve)* Louis XV!

JULIE: Yes, monsieur!

FOLLAVOINE: Well, for heaven's sake, that just about takes the cake!

JULIE: Oh! I dare you to laugh! I dare you to laugh!

FOLLAVOINE: *(Exasperated)* Ah! now listen here! I'd had enough! The incident is closed! It's been decided that Baby will have to take a laxative! All right, go give it to him!

JULIE: *(Heartbroken)* Ah! he's going to make a scene!

FOLLAVOINE: *(Rising)* Well, then there'll be a scene! Too bad! Now, please, leave me alone! I have to compose myself before Chouilloux gets here and figure out how to position my troops. Go on! go on! ...Go get dressed! *(He heads up towards the bookcase.)*

JULIE: *(Rising effortfully and crossing up to her room, muttering broken phrases in a desolate voice)* Ah! that poor child! ...When I think that he has to take a laxative... it makes me sick just thinking about it...

FOLLAVOINE: *(Who has already opened the right door of the bookcase, turning around, noticing the bucket abandoned by JULIE center stage)* Julie! Julie!

JULIE: *(In the same grief-stricken voice)* What?

FOLLAVOINE: *(Pointing to the bucket)* Your bucket, please! ...I assure you I've seen enough of it.

JULIE: *(Furious, coming down to get her bucket)* "My bucket, my bucket"! Always "my bucket!"... "Chouilloux, my bucket! ...my bucket, Chouilloux!" that's all you hear around here!

FOLLAVOINE: But, for heaven's sake, a study is no place to parade slop buckets! *(As he speaks, he has pulled from the bookcase a chamber pot which he reveals at just these last words.)*

JULIE: *(Immediately calm and in a mocking tone)* Well, you've got a nerve! You make a scene over my bucket and then you waltz around with a chamber pot!

FOLLAVOINE: *(In a vexed tone)* A chamber pot!

JULIE: Well, unless you're launching some sort of fashion in hats.

FOLLAVOINE: A chamber pot! You dare compare your slop bucket... to this! Your slop bucket is nothing but... your slop bucket! in other words, a vile, low object which is not to be displayed, but rather concealed!... *(With the admiration one has for a work of art, holding out his vessel, making a pedestal of his five fingertips.)* While this is...

JULIE: *(Interrupting and coming down right)* "This is, this is" …a chamber pot! In other words, a vile, low object which is not to be displayed, but rather concealed.

FOLLAVOINE: *(Crossing down near his wife, lyrically)* Yes, for you, for anybody, for the profane; but for me it is something so noble, so great that I do not blush to bring it in here! It is the product of my labors! a specimen of my industry! my creation! my…bread-and-butter!

JULIE: *(With a mocking little curtsey)* Well! eat it, my dear! Eat it! *(She crosses right.)*

FOLLAVOINE: *(Going to place his pot on the little pedestal table left of the divan)* Yes! Laugh! Laugh! You won't always be laughing! When we're making three hundred thousand livres a year…!

JULIE: *(Backed against the desk on the right and passing her bucket from her weary right arm to her left arm)* Three hundred thousand livres a year from chamber pots?

FOLLAVOINE: *(Going to join his wife)* Chamber pots, exactly! It may surprise you and yet, God…and Chouilloux willing! it can be done!

JULIE: What? What? What in the world is this fairy tale?

FOLLAVOINE: It's no fairy tale! I didn't bring it up before so I could surprise you if it works out; but since it's like this…! What you don't know…is that today the government's one aim is to improve the soldier's lot! He's cared for, he's coddled, he wrapped in cotton wool; lately they've gone so far as to issue him slippers!

JULIE: Slippers on a soldier!

FOLLAVOINE: And naturally they don't want to stop there. So they have just decided, lest the men be exposed to catching cold when they have to go outside at night in wind and rain, that every soldier in the French army will have his own chamber pot!

JULIE: *(Astounded)* No!

FOLLAVOINE: Personalized with his initials.

JULIE: *(Agog)* Ah! ...I can hardly believe it!

FOLLAVOINE: Consequently: an upcoming award of the contract for this new...piece of military equipment; and, as a manufacturer of porcelain, I decided to enter the competition. And here's where Chouilloux turns out to be a *deus ex machina!*...

JULIE: What does that mean?

FOLLAVOINE: *(Nonplussed)* What?

JULIE: Whatmacallit! ..."max ina"?

FOLLAVOINE: *(With an indulgent smile)* Not "maxina"! *(Correcting.)* "machina"!

JULIE: *(Gruffly)* Well, suppose I did say "maxina"! I'm asking what it means.

FOLLAVOINE: What it...?

JULIE: Yes!...

FOLLAVOINE: Well, uh...!

JULIE: Well, go on!

FOLLAVOINE: Ah! it's not so easy to explain.

JULIE: Why? Is it dirty?

FOLLAVOINE: *(Laughing)* No, it's not dirty! *Deus ex machina* is...is an expression, on its own! The Greeks... the Greeks used the phrase to designate somebody big!

JULIE: *(Summing up)* A fat man!

FOLLAVOINE: No, a big shot, a man of considerable influence.

JULIE: Ah! ...So figuratively!

FOLLAVOINE: Figuratively. Well, Chouilloux is one of those! Chouilloux is the chairman of the inspection committee, charged by the State to choose the model to be imposed as the standard to the selection committee. Now do you understand the interest I have in making an impression on him? I hold the patent for unbreakable porcelain, don't I? Through Chouilloux's influence the committee will adopt unbreakable porcelain and there we are! The deal is in the bag and my fortune is made!

JULIE: *(Thoughtful for a moment, nodding her head, then)* Yes! ...and what comes next?

FOLLAVOINE: *(Excited)* What? Why, if I succeed, next will come a gold-mine! Overnight I'll be the exclusive purveyor to the French army.

JULIE: The purveyor to the French army of chamber pots?

FOLLAVOINE: *(Proudly)* Every chamber pot in the French army!

JULIE: *(Frowning)* And...people will know?

FOLLAVOINE: *(As before)* Of course people will know.

JULIE: Oh no! ...Oh, no, no, no, no, no, no! ...I don't want to be the wife of a gentleman who sells chamber pots.

FOLLAVOINE: Huh! ...What an idea! Don't you realize it'll make us a fortune!

JULIE: I don't care! It's disgusting! *(She crosses far right.)*

FOLLAVOINE: But, good grief! What else do I do now? I sell chamber pots! I sell them every day! ...not on that scale, but I do sell them!

JULIE: *(Returning to the desk)* Oh! "you sell them, you sell them"...just like you sell other things; you manufacture porcelain, it's quite natural that you sell articles associated with your industry; it's normal, it's fine! But to specialize! To become the gentleman who sells chamber pots exclusively! Oh no, no! even if it's for the government, no!

FOLLAVOINE: *(Disconcerted and worried)* But you must be crazy! Think about it!

JULIE: *(Back against the desk, arms crossed)* Oh! I've thought about it! It's kind of you, but I have no wish to go through life crowned with a chamber pot! I have no wish to hear every time I enter a drawing-room, "Who is that lady?" "That's Madame Follavoine, the wife of the chamber pot salesman." Oh no! no!

FOLLAVOINE: *(More and more worried by the prospect of seeing his whole structure collapse)* Ah! really! I never expected... Oh! for pity's sake! At least don't go and say such things to Chouilloux. That's would be terrible!

JULIE: *(Scornfully)* Oh! I have nothing to say to Chouilloux!

FOLLAVOINE: Listen! I'll look into it...there may be a way to arrange things so as...so as to install a middleman, I don't know! But don't make me blow this deal, I entreat you! And when Chouilloux is here, do be nice to him! Be polite!

JULIE: No, tell me: am I in the habit of being impolite! I know how to behave! *(She crosses to him.)*

FOLLAVOINE: I don't doubt it, but...

JULIE: My father was visited by the President of the Republic!

FOLLAVOINE: Yes, well...you weren't even born then.

JULIE: That's as may be, but my father was visited all the same! So, doesn't that mean something? *(She crosses.)*

FOLLAVOINE: Really? Fine! That'll do! (*Pushing her gently towards her room.*) Go give Baby his laxative! Get dressed, and get rid of this bucket, eh? Will you?

JULIE: (*Heading towards her room, accompanied by* FOLLAVOINE) I've got my bucket, haven't I! Please, I don't need you to keep telling me what to do. (*Doorbell.*)

FOLLAVOINE: There! Someone's ringing! It's bound to be Chouilloux. Please, hurry up! If they show him in...!

JULIE: (*On the threshold*) So what? He'll see me!

FOLLAVOINE: (*Making her leave*) That's the point! With you looking like that I'd rather he didn't! (*Closing the door and crossing down far left.*) Oh! women, women! What a complication!... (*Crossing, he picks up the chamber pot.*) Well, why are they so slow showing in Chouilloux? (*Going to the door at back and through the half-open door, risking a look, then opening it fully.*) Nobody?... (*Calling into the wings*) What the! ...Rose! ... Rose!...

Scene Three

(*The same,* ROSE, *then* JULIE)

ROSE: (*In the doorway*) Monsieur?

FOLLAVOINE: (*Standing at his desk, the chamber pot in his left hand*) What was that about? Who was at the door?

ROSE: A lady came to have a tooth pulled.

FOLLAVOINE: What's that got to do with me? You should send her to the dentist.

ROSE: That's what I did. She's gone upstairs.

FOLLAVOINE: (*Moving the chamber pot from his left hand to his right*) This is intolerable! Always the same thing!

ROSE: *(Who from this moment has her eyes fixed on the chamber pot)* Oh! …Is Monsieur aware?

FOLLAVOINE: What?

ROSE: That he has his chamber pot in his hand?

FOLLAVOINE: I'm well aware! I know! Thanks.

ROSE: Ah! …I thought it was an oversight! …sorry!

FOLLAVOINE: Anyway, it's not a chamber pot! It's an article of military equipment… *(He places the pot on his right, on the pile of file folders to the left of the table.)*

ROSE: Well, it's really funny how much it looks like a chamber pot!

FOLLAVOINE: *(Sending her away)* That'll do, my girl! … Go away! Go away!

(ROSE exits at the back. —FOLLAVOINE sits at his desk and calculates.)

FOLLAVOINE: Let' see, figuring that in peacetime the French army comprises about three hundred thousand men, with one crockery vessel per man, if the crockery vessel costs…

JULIE: *(Still in the same outfit, abruptly thrusting half her body into the opening of the door in the wall)* Bastien! Come here a minute!

FOLLAVOINE: *(Deep in his calculations. Drily, without raising his head.)* Ssh! …I don't have the time!

JULIE: *(Coming downstage with her bucket in her right hand)* I tell you to come! Baby won't take his laxative.

FOLLAVOINE: *(As before, raising his head)* Well, make him! You're in charge…! *(Noticing the bucket in his wife's hand.)* Ah!…

JULIE: What?

FOLLAVOINE: *(Drawing himself up, indignantly)* You've brought me back your bucket!

JULIE: I haven't had time to empty it. Please come! I…

FOLLAVOINE: *(Exploding)* Ah! no! no! I've had enough of that! …Take it away! Take it away!

JULIE: All right! …But please: Baby is…

FOLLAVOINE: Go on! Go on! take it away!

JULIE: But I repeat…

FOLLAVOINE: I don't give a damn, take it away!

JULIE: But I…

FOLLAVOINE: Take it away! Take it away!

JULIE: *(Unyielding and coming down to deposit her bucket center stage)* Ah! You're getting on my nerves with my bucket!

FOLLAVOINE: *(Startled)* What?

JULIE: *(In front of the divan)* "Take it away! Take it away!" I'm not your servant!

FOLLAVOINE: *(Can't believe his ears)* What did you say?

JULIE: It's true! I'm always the one who does everything around here! My bucket bothers you? Well, all you have to do is take it away.

FOLLAVOINE: Me!

JULIE: I brought it in, so you can take it out.

FOLLAVOINE: *(Crossing down to JULIE)* But, for heaven's sake! It's your slops, not mine!

JULIE: *(Passing in front of him)* So? …Well, I make you a present of it! Then you don't have to have any misgivings about it! *(She slips away by crossing up center towards her room.)*

FOLLAVOINE: *(Running after his wife and trying to catch her by the skirt of her wrapper)* Julie! …Julie! Don't be crazy!

JULIE: It's my gift to you, I tell you! It's a gift! *(She disappears into her room.)*

FOLLAVOINE: *(On the threshold, speaking into the doorway)* Julie! Will you take this away! …Julie!

Scene Four

(FOLLAVOINE, ROSE, CHOUILLOUX)

(ROSE, entering at back and introducing CHOUILLOUX:)

ROSE: Monsieur Chouilloux!

FOLLAVOINE: Will you please take…!

CHOUILLOUX: *(Comes quietly on stage. He wears a frock coat, a rosette of the Legion of Honor in his button-hole)* Good morning, my dear Monsieur Follavoine!

FOLLAVOINE: *(Without turning around)* Ah! will you leave me the hell in p…!

(FOLLAVOINE, turning around the moment when ROSE exits and recognizing CHOUILLOUX:)

FOLLAVOINE: Huh! Monsieur Chouilloux! Already!

CHOUILLOUX: Am I too early?

FOLLAVOINE: Not at all! not at all! Only I was chatting with Madame Follavoine; so I didn't hear the bell.

CHOUILLOUX: But I did ring, and I was let in through the door. *(Jocular)* I don't yet have the gift of passing through walls!

FOLLAVOINE: *(Flattering)* Ah! charming! Charming!

CHOUILLOUX: *(Modestly)* Oh! not at all…!

FOLLAVOINE: *(Taking his hat from his hands)* If you will allow me!

CHOUILLOUX: Too kind! *(Crossing downstage and stopping stupefied when he sees the slop bucket.)* Goodness!

FOLLAVOINE: *(Who has placed* CHOUILLOUX'*s hat on the edge of the bookcase left, quickly crossing down to place himself between the bucket and* CHOUILLOUX*)* Oh! sorry! Excuse me! If you don't mind! My wife put it there just now; she was holding it in her hand and then, absent-mindedly… *(So saying, he has crossed up to the door at back. Opening it and calling in a gruff voice.)* Rose! … Rose!

ROSE: *(Off)* Monsieur!

FOLLAVOINE: Come in here! *(To* CHOUILLOUX, *while crossing back down to him so that the bucket is between them)* I am really embarrassed! Especially on a day when I have the honor…!

CHOUILLOUX: *(Bowing several times)* Oh! don't mention it! don't mention it!

FOLLAVOINE: *(Lots of bowing and scraping)* I speak my mind, Monsieur Chouilloux! I speak my mind!

CHOUILLOUX: *(As before)* Too kind! …Yes, really!

ROSE: *(Appearing at the back)* Monsieur called?

FOLLAVOINE: Yes. Take away Madame's bucket.

ROSE: *(Stunned)* Ah! …What in the world is it doing there?

FOLLAVOINE: The mistress left it there… accidentally.

ROSE: Ah! …Madame must surely be looking for it! *(She picks it up.)*

FOLLAVOINE: Yes, all right, go on!

*(*FOLLAVOINE, *crossing upstage behind* ROSE *and pushing her towards* JULIE's *room:)*

FOLLAVOINE: Take it! go and tell your mistress that Monsieur Chouilloux is here!

ROSE: Yes, monsieur. *(She exits left.)*

CHOUILLOUX: *(Quickly, crossing up to* FOLLAVOINE*)* Oh! Please! Don't disturb the lady.

FOLLAVOINE: Never mind! Never mind! If I don't insist a bit...! Women are never ready!

CHOUILLOUX: Ah well! I can't say the same for my wife! ...Every morning she's the first one out of the house! She's been prescribed jogging; I'm too old for that, but she has her cousin... who jogs with her.

FOLLAVOINE: *(Casually amiable)* Yes! yes! of course! So... so I've been told!...

CHOUILLOUX: It suits me to a T.

FOLLAVOINE: Yes, it...it keeps it in the family.

CHOUILLOUX: It keeps it in the family... and doesn't wear me out! ...

(They laugh. —Pivoting to come downstage, CHOUILLOUX *notices the chamber pot on the desk.)*

CHOUILLOUX: Ah! I see you've been busy with our little affair!

FOLLAVOINE: *(Who has also come down)* Ah! yes...yes!

CHOUILLOUX: *(Firm in his conviction. Pointing to the crockery)* This must be the chamber pot.

FOLLAVOINE: It is the...yes! ...Yes! ...Ah! you recognized it?

CHOUILLOUX: *(Modestly)* Oh yes!... *(So saying he has crossed right in front of the desk. Turning around and contemplating the pot.)* Well, it doesn't look half bad! ... well constructed!...

FOLLAVOINE: Oh! when it comes to construction!...

CHOUILLOUX: So it's made of unbreakable porcelain? *(He taps the pot with his bent finger.)*

FOLLAVOINE: *(Crossing above the table)* Perfectly unbreakable.

CHOUILLOUX: *(In front of the pot, contemplating it)*
Imagine that! *(Abruptly, sitting in the armchair right of the desk.)* No, I asked because that was the feature that caught our attention, the under-secretary of State and myself.

FOLLAVOINE: Aha!

CHOUILLOUX: Because ordinary porcelain is something which, upon mature consideration, we do not desire.

FOLLAVOINE: Oh, I understand!

CHOUILLOUX: The least little thing and it breaks!

FOLLAVOINE: Ah! …Right away!

CHOUILLOUX: It's a waste of government money.

FOLLAVOINE: Absolutely! *(Pointing to his pot)* While this one: bravo! It's solid! It will last a lifetime! *(Coming downstage)* No, hold it, take it in your hand, you're the expert!

CHOUILLOUX: Oh! …Not so much!

FOLLAVOINE: Yes! yes! See how light it is!

CHOUILLOUX: *(Taking the pot and weighing it)* Oh! how interesting! It doesn't feel its weight!

FOLLAVOINE: *(Taking CHOUILLOUX's wrist and moving it to make the pot move like a frying pan).* And how comfortable in the hand? …Eh? I mean, it becomes a pleasure. *(Changing his tone.)* Of course, we can make them in white and in color; if you like, for the army, striped like sentry-boxes, for example…in the national colors?…

CHOUILLOUX: Oh no! That would be pretentious.

FOLLAVOINE: I agree absolutely; and actually a pointless increase in cost.

CHOUILLOUX: Well, that remains to be seen! *(He puts the pot on the desk and comes back to FOLLAVOINE.)* We have also been offered pots in enameled cast-iron, which isn't bad either.

FOLLAVOINE: Oh! Monsieur Chouilloux! No... you can't be serious! ...You can't accept enameled cast-iron?

CHOUILLOUX: Why not?

FOLLAVOINE: Why, because! ...This has to do with more than my personal interest, I put that aside! But enameled cast-iron, Monsieur Chouilloux! Why, it smells bad from the start; and you don't have the cleanliness of porcelain! *(Pointing to his pot)* This is the genuine article!

CHOUILLOUX: Obviously there are pros and cons.

FOLLAVOINE: Not to mention the issue of hygiene! ... You must know that it is acknowledged that most cases of appendicitis are due to the use of enameled utensils.

CHOUILLOUX: *(Half laughing, half serious)* Well, given the intended use, I can't imagine that...

FOLLAVOINE: You never know, Monsieur Chouilloux! Young men are so thoughtless! They want to break in the brand-new receptacle: they brew an ultra-strong punch in it; the heat cracks the enamel; a few fragments fall in; they drink it, they swallow it... Anyway, I'm sure you know all about it?

CHOUILLOUX: Me? No! ...No, I swear I never happened to drink punch out of a...

FOLLAVOINE: No! but you were a soldier.

CHOUILLOUX: Not really! I went in for the physical examination; they made me strip naked and said, "Your vision's poor!" That decided my military career! I spent the whole of it in the War Office.

FOLLAVOINE: Ah? ...Ah? Well, believe me, monsieur! No enameled cast-iron! Take, if you like, vulcanized rubber! Celluloid! Whatever you please! Although in the long run nothing is as good as porcelain! It's only fault is fragility; well, now we've done away with that inconvenience! Now, you're going to see. (*Trying to get to the desk but* CHOUILLOUX *is in the way.*) Sorry!

CHOUILLOUX: (*Not understanding where he wants to go and moving in* FOLLAVOINE'*s direction*) Sorry!

FOLLAVOINE: (*Indicating his pot on the desk*) No, I was going to...

CHOUILLOUX: (*Moving aside to let him pass*) Ah! sorry!

FOLLAVOINE: (*Taking the pot from the desk*) You are going to see how solid it is. (*He raises the pot into the air as if to throw it on the ground, then changes his mind.*) No, on the carpet, that's no proof! ...But there, in the hall on the wooden floor... You'll see! (*As he speaks, he goes to open wide the door at back and comes back down to the prompter's box with his pot, next to* CHOUILLOUX. *—Indicating to Chouilloux the point he is to look at.*) Over there, Monsieur Chouilloux!

(CHOUILLOUX *starts to head there,* FOLLAVOINE *holds him back.*)

FOLLAVOINE: No, stay here, but look over there! (*About to fling his pot*) Keep your eyes peeled! (*Balancing it to give it some "english."*) One! ...Two! ...Three!... (*Flinging the pot, during its trajectory*) Bingo! There you have it!

(*Just as he says "There you have it!" the pot falls and breaks; they both stand for a moment, mouths agape, as if stupefied.*)

(*Note: In case, as sometimes happens, the pot does not break as it falls, the actor playing* FOLLAVOINE *should simply say, "You see! Unbreakable! And you know, you can throw it as many times as you like... So, if you want proof: one, two, three...bingo! There you have it!" etc.*)

CHOUILLOUX: (*Half-circling around a petrified* FOLLAVOINE, *to find himself facing him and the audience, somewhat up right*) It broke!

FOLLAVOINE: Huh?

CHOUILLOUX: It broke.

FOLLAVOINE: Ah! yes, it…it broke.

CHOUILLOUX: *(Who has gone up to the door)* It didn't make it! …It's not an optical illusion.

FOLLAVOINE: *(Who has also gone up)* No! no! it really broke! That's odd! I can't understand it! I swear it's the first time that's ever happened.

CHOUILLOUX: *(Coming downstage)* Maybe there was a flaw in it.

FOLLAVOINE: *(Also coming down)* Yes, maybe! … Anyway, to tell the truth, I'm glad of this experience; it proves exactly that…that… Anyway, as the saying goes, "the exception proves the rule". Because it never, never breaks!

CHOUILLOUX: Never?

FOLLAVOINE: Never! Or, I don't know, one in a thousand!

CHOUILLOUX: Ah! One in a thousand.

FOLLAVOINE: Yes, and…and more! Anyway, you'll see! *(Going up to the bookcase)* I've got another specimen: we will be able to throw it again and again… *(Coming down with a second pot which he has taken from the bookcase.)* Don't concern yourself with the other one: the firing was bad.

CHOUILLOUX: Yes, someone should have been fired.

FOLLAVOINE: Here we go. *(Placing himself in front of the prompter's box, next to* CHOUILLOUX *who is already there.)* Take a good look: one… two… *(Changing his mind.)* No, wait! Throw it yourself! *(He puts the pot in his hand.)*

CHOUILLOUX: Me?

FOLLAVOINE: Yes! That way you'll get a better feeling for it.

CHOUILLOUX: Ah?

(FOLLAVOINE *steps aside a bit to the right;* CHOUILLOUX *takes his place, on the same level.*)

FOLLAVOINE: Go ahead!

CHOUILLOUX: All right! *(Balancing the pot)* One…two… *(He stops, very moved.)*

FOLLAVOINE: Well! Go ahead! What's stopping you?

CHOUILLOUX: I just realized it's the very first time I've gone bowling with a…

FOLLAVOINE: Go on! go on! Don't be afraid! *(To calm him)* I tell you: one in a thousand!

CHOUILLOUX: One! two! And three! *(He tosses the pot.)*

FOLLAVOINE: *(During the trajectory)* Bingo! *(Just as the pot hits the ground.)* There you have it!

(The pot breaks in smithereens. Same business as before; they both stand dumbfounded.)

CHOUILLOUX: *(After a pause, going up to the door to inspect the breakage)* It broke!

FOLLAVOINE: *(Who has also gone up)* It broke, yes! It broke…

CHOUILLOUX: Two in a thousand!…

FOLLAVOINE: Two in a thousand, yes! Listen! I don't understand it. I can't figure it out! Obviously it must have to do with how we threw the pot; I know that when my foreman flings it, it never, absolutely never…!

CHOUILLOUX: Ah! never?

FOLLAVOINE: Never.

(CHOUILLOUX, *going to sit on the divan, while*
FOLLAVOINE *closes the door at back:*)

CHOUILLOUX: It's most interesting.

FOLLAVOINE: Yes, oh! but no! …That's not it! …Of
course you should have been able to tell the difference
between breakable porcelain and…

CHOUILLOUX: *(Finishing his sentence)* …unbreakable
porcelain.

FOLLAVOINE: Yes! …But all the same these experiments
are not conclusive enough to make up your mind.

CHOUILLOUX: Yes indeed, yes indeed, I've reached a
conclusion… They're the very same pots! Only, instead
of breaking, they don't break!

FOLLAVOINE: There you have it!

CHOUILLOUX: Most interesting!

Scene Five

(The same, JULIE*)*

JULIE: *(Abruptly storming out of her room: she is in the
same outfit as before, but without the bucket)* Bastien,
please, come in here! The boy is driving me crazy! I
can't get it done!

(At JULIE's *voice,* CHOUILLOUX *has risen.)*

FOLLAVOINE: *(Leaping towards his wife and quickly, in
an undertone)* Ah! have you lost your mind! You come
in here like this! Look at yourself, for heaven's sake!
(Indicating CHOUILLOUX.*)* Monsieur Chouilloux!

JULIE: *(Without even turning towards* CHOUILLOUX*)* What
do I care about Monsieur Chouilloux!

CHOUILLOUX: Huh!

FOLLAVOINE: *(Panicked)* No! no! for heaven's sake! *(Making introductions at random)* Monsieur Chouilloux! My wife!

CHOUILLOUX: *(Bowing)* Madame!

JULIE: *(Very rapidly)* Yes! good morning, monsieur! You must excuse me, won't you, for appearing like this…!

CHOUILLOUX: *(Very chivalrously)* Not at all, madame! A pretty woman looks good whatever she wears!

JULIE: *(Not listening)* Too kind! Thanks! *(To her husband)* Please, there's no way to get the boy to do it! The minute you say laxative…

FOLLAVOINE: Well, too bad! I'm sorry! I'm here having a serious talk with Monsieur Chouilloux! I have other things to do than worry about your son's laxatives.

JULIE: *(Indignant, to* CHOUILLOUX*)* Oh! there's a father for you, monsieur! There's a father! *(She crosses right.)*

CHOUILLOUX: *(Not knowing what to reply)* Yes indeed, madame! Yes!

FOLLAVOINE: *(Imperiously)* I insist that you get dressed! I'm ashamed to see you in your present state of undress! You really must have no concern for your dignity…

JULIE: Well, if you think I care about my appearance at a time like this!

CHOUILLOUX: *(Wants to appear interested)* You have a sick child, madame?

JULIE: *(In a doleful tone)* Yes, monsieur, yes!

FOLLAVOINE: *(Shrugs)* It's nothing, Monsieur Chouilloux! It's nothing!

JULIE: *(As an unanswerable argument)* He didn't go this morning.

CHOUILLOUX: Ah? Ah?

FOLLAVOINE: Well, yes! his bowels are a little sluggish.

JULIE: He calls that nothing, he does! He calls that nothing! You can see it doesn't matter to him!

FOLLAVOINE: What then? All he needs is a laxative!

JULIE: Oh! oh! I know! Well, you give him a laxative if you can. That's why I asked you to come. Only, no fear of that! All the hard chores fall to me!

FOLLAVOINE: Really, you'd think it was something serious!

CHOUILLOUX: *(Shaking his head, seriously)* It isn't serious, true; but all the same you mustn't joke about such things!

JULIE: Ah! you see what the gentleman says... and he ought to know.

FOLLAVOINE: *(Flattering)* Ah! is that so, Monsieur Chouilloux...?

CHOUILLOUX: Of course it is! ...Of course!... *(To JULIE)* Is the child subject to—excuse the word—constipation?

JULIE: He does have a tendency, yes.

CHOUILLOUX: Really? Well...you'd better keep an eye on that! Because one fine day, it will turn into enteritis, and it's the devil to get rid of that.

JULIE: *(To FOLLAVOINE)* There! There! You see?

CHOUILLOUX: I can speak from personal experience: I had it once and it lasted for five years!

JULIE: *(Instinctively turning her head to the room where her son is)* Ah! *(As she turns her head back to CHOUILLOUX.)* Poor baby!

CHOUILLOUX: *(Bowing)* Thank you!

JULIE: What?

CHOUILLOUX: Ah, sorry, I thought you were referring to me…

JULIE: No! …No!

CHOUILLOUX: Yes, madame, five years! I caught it at the war.

JULIE: 1870?

CHOUILLOUX: No, 1898.

JULIE: *(Staring at him, somewhat disoriented)* 1898? But… there was no war in 1898?

CHOUILLOUX: "at the war, at the war"! at the War Office! …Where I am a functionary.

JULIE: Ah! that's nice!

FOLLAVOINE: Yes, because Monsieur Chouilloux is…

JULIE: Yes, yes, I know.

CHOUILLOUX: I would get awfully thirsty… I used to drink the water that came there from god knows where…I was the fellow who used to say, "Germs! …Microbes! …Tap water's good enough for me!…" Yes, well, on that diet, I caught a stubborn case of enteritis! And the result: I had to go to the hot springs at Plombières three years in a row!

JULIE: *(Leaping upstage)* Ah! Then, you think that, for Baby, Plombières…?

CHOUILLOUX: Ah! No! …No, his enteritis would have to be the constipated kind: the thermal baths at Châtel-Guyon would suit him better. The sort of enteritis I had… But suppose we sit down!

(FOLLAVOINE, *as* CHOUILLOUX *and* JULIE *sit on the divan)*

FOLLAVOINE: Really, Monsieur Chouilloux! This is all so interesting! *(He has gone to his desk to take the chair on wheels which he brings next to the divan and sits.)*

CHOUILLOUX: The sort of enteritis I had—excuse me for being so intimate—was loose bowels…

JULIE: Aha?

FOLLAVOINE: *(Flattering)* Oh! how interesting, Monsieur Chouilloux!

CHOUILLOUX: So Plombières was the right place. Ah! what a treatment!

JULIE: *(Back to what interests her)* And… what do they have you do at Châtel-Guyon?

CHOUILLOUX: *(Somewhat at a loss)* Huh? Uh…? I don't know, madame. I've never been there. *(Returning to what interests him.)* But at Plombières…! Every morning a high colonic: two, two and a half pints.

JULIE: Yes, I don't care! But do you know if at Châtel-Guyon…?

CHOUILLOUX: No, Madame, I'm telling you I was never there… *(Returning to his obsessions.)* Once the colonic is over, I would take a bath…a bath lasting an hour; after that a massage…

JULIE: *(In a hurry to get back to what interests her)* Yes! … yes…

CHOUILLOUX: After that, the meal: nothing but bland food: mashes, purees, pasta, noodles; rice cakes, tapioca…

JULIE: Yes, but… at Châtel-Guyon…?

FOLLAVOINE: *(Rising, annoyed)* Oh! didn't Monsieur Chouilloux tell you he wasn't there!

CHOUILLOUX: Yes, I've very sorry, but…

FOLLAVOINE: He can only tell you about his treatment at Plombières.

JULIE: *(As innocently as possible)* But I don't care about his treatment at Plombières

CHOUILLOUX: *(Out of countenance)* Ah? …Excuse me!

JULIE: Why should I be interested in Monsieur Chouilloux's treatment at Plombières, since it's Châtel-Guyon for Baby! *(Rising)* Monsieur Chouilloux, who is an intelligent man, understands me very well.

*(*CHOUILLOUX, *while* JULIE *crosses left:)*

CHOUILLOUX: Of course! Of course!

JULIE: He might just as well tell me about cod fishing in Newfoundland; it would be very interesting but it would have nothing to do with Toto's health.

CHOUILLOUX: *(Conciliating)* Indeed! Indeed!

JULIE: I'm not here to listen to anecdotes; I have to give Baby a laxative!

FOLLAVOINE: *(Totally fed up)* Fine! Great! All right! Go and give Baby a laxative!

JULIE: *(Very amiably, to* CHOUILLOUX*)* You will excuse me, won't you, monsieur?

CHOUILLOUX: *(Rising)* By all means, madame.

JULIE: *(Flatly, to* FOLLAVOINE*)* So, you don't intend to come?

FOLLAVOINE: No! No!

JULIE: What a father! What a father!

FOLLAVOINE: We know! Fine! And get dressed!

JULIE: All right! Oh! …What a father! *(She exits.)*

Scene Six

(The same, minus JULIE*)*

FOLLAVOINE: *(At the back, turned towards the door his wife came from)* Showing herself off in a get-up like that! She has no idea…!

CHOUILLOUX: *(Crossing up right)* Madame Follavoine strikes me as a very charming woman.

FOLLAVOINE: Huh! ...Delightful, delightful, Monsieur Chouilloux! She is sometimes a bit...! But otherwise delightful. You haven't seen her at her best; I'm sorry that you met her that way, undressed...

CHOUILLOUX: Oh! but I can imagine that when she is wearing... *(He ends his thought with mime that suggests frills and furbelows.)*

FOLLAVOINE: Oh yes! but no! ...That way, her hair uncombed...with her curlers...! Why, her hair is her best feature! ...Gorgeous hair! ...Naturally curly!

CHOUILLOUX: Ah? ...Ah?

FOLLAVOINE: Why, when you see her like that...! She doesn't care about making an impression! ...And then, on top of that, she imagines there's something wrong with her son...!

CHOUILLOUX: *(Coming downstage and sitting on the armchair before the desk)* So, after all, nothing's wrong with the child!

FOLLAVOINE: *(Following him down and leaning against the desk)* Nothing at all! ...But try and tell her that! Look: you mentioned Châtel-Guyon? There we have it: from now on we'll never hear the end of Châtel-Guyon!

CHOUILLOUX: Oh! I'm very sorry if it's my fault...!

FOLLAVOINE: Not at all, not at all! Only, when after that, you started to tell her about your treatment at Plombières, I couldn't help laughing to myself. *(He laughs.)*

CHOUILLOUX: *(Chiming in)* It didn't interest her at all.

FOLLAVOINE: *(Laughing)* Not a bit!

CHOUILLOUX: Oh! Poor Madame Follavoine! And I was going on and on...! Oh!

(CHOUILLOUX *laughs. While both are guffawing, the door left suddenly opens:* JULIE *appears dragging* TOTO *by the right hand; she has a large wine glass in her left hand and is pressing against her chest a bottle of milk of magnesia.)*

Scene Seven

(The same, JULIE, TOTO *wears a pinafore over his clothes.)*

JULIE: Yes! well, we'll see what your father has to say! *(She lets go of* TOTO *in order to close the door; after that, she takes him by the hand again and drags him towards his father as she speaks:)* Your papa is very mad at you! *(Crosses to* FOLLAVOINE.*)* Will you tell your son…

*(*JULIE, *noticing that* FOLLAVOINE *is laughing with* CHOUILLOUX, *kicks him in the shin, and sotto voce on account of* TOTO, *whom she moves away so he can't hear:)*

JULIE: Will you please!

FOLLAVOINE: *(Rearing up in pain)* See here!

JULIE: I told Toto that you are very mad at him; if he sees you having a laugh with Monsieur Chouilloux…!

FOLLAVOINE: What? What? Now what is it?

*(*JULIE, *handing* TOTO *over to* FOLLAVOINE*:)*

JULIE: I only want you to make your son mind! …Do me the pleasure of giving him a laxative! *(She crosses left.)*

FOLLAVOINE: Me?

JULIE: Yes, you! *(Putting down the bottle, then the glass, on the little pedestal table next to the divan)* Here's the bottle! Here's the glass! I wash my hands of it! *(She sits on the divan.)*

FOLLAVOINE: But that's not my job! What's it got to do with me?

JULIE: I beg your pardon! You are his father! You have to show a little authority.

FOLLAVOINE: *(His eyes skyward, then, to* CHOUILLOUX, *with a sigh of resignation)* I beg your pardon, Monsieur Chouilloux...!

CHOUILLOUX: By all means!

FOLLAVOINE: *(Severely to* TOTO) What is this I hear, sir? I am very displeased!

TOTO: *(Stamping his foot and moving, as he does so, between his father and* CHOUILLOUX) I don't care! I don't wanna laxative!

FOLLAVOINE: What?

JULIE: *(Nervously)* There! That's all I've been hearing for the last half-hour!

CHOUILLOUX: *(Putting his hand amiably on his shoulder)* What's that, my little friend? ...A big boy like you...

(TOTO pulls his shoulder away in annoyance.)

FOLLAVOINE: *(Who has seen his gesture)* What do you call that? ...First of all, say good morning to the gentleman!

TOTO: *(Pigheaded, stamping his foot)* I don't care! I don't wanna laxative!

FOLLAVOINE: *(Shaking him)* Nobody's asking you what you want! ...Speak up, you little brat, do you think...

JULIE: *(Seeing him mistreat the child, leaping at Follavoine and roughly pushing him away)* Ah! don't you start, you!

FOLLAVOINE: Ah! Drat! *(He goes upstage angrily, and then comes down to his desk, but without sitting at it.)*

JULIE: *(To* CHOUILLOUX) But he has to have his laxative! ...His tongue is all white!... *(To* TOTO) Show your tongue to the gentleman!

CHOUILLOUX: *(Complacently)* Hold on! sorry! *(He kneels on the ground to be at Toto's level, pulls from his pocket a pince-nez which he adjusts on his nose above his regular eyeglasses, then to* TOTO*)* Let's see!

JULIE: There! Show him your tongue!

*(*TOTO *sticks out his tongue black with ink.)*

CHOUILLOUX: Goodness me! To me it looks… black.

JULIE: *(With a certain pride)* Ah! it's because he's been doing his homework in pen and ink!… *(Changing her tone)* But it's easy to tell that his breath is affected. *(To* TOTO, *moving him towards* CHOUILLOUX*'s face.)* Go on, go "hhah" in the gentleman's face!

CHOUILLOUX: *(Instinctively shielding himself with his hand)* No thank you! No!

JULIE: What? You're disgusted by a child's breath?

CHOUILLOUX: Not at all! but…

JULIE: What then?… *(To* TOTO, *pushing his head as before towards* CHOUILLOUX*'s face)* Go on! go "hhah" in the gentleman's face!

CHOUILLOUX: No! no! I assure you, I don't need to; I am well aware…! *(Sitting back down and to* TOTO*)* What's the matter, my little friend? Is that any way to behave? …What's your name?

(Surly gesture from TOTO *who doesn't answer.)*

FOLLAVOINE: *(Leaning over the desk to speak to* TOTO*)* Go on, answer him! What's your name?

TOTO: *(Obstinate)* I don't wanna laxative!

FOLLAVOINE: *(Just about had it)* Oh! *(Amiably, to* CHOUILLOUX.*)* His name is Toto!

CHOUILLOUX: Ah!

FOLLAVOINE: It's short for Hervé.

CHOUILLOUX: Really! Ah? …That's odd! …And…how old are you? Six!

JULIE: *(Proudly)* Seven, monsieur!

CHOUILLOUX: There, you see! Seven years old! And your name is Toto! But, if your name is Toto and you're seven years old, there's no reason to make a fuss about a laxative!

TOTO: I don't care, I don't wanna laxative!

CHOUILLOUX: That's very naughty! What will you say later on when you go to war?

JULIE: *(Quickly drawing* TOTO *to her to protect him, while knocking the wood of the desk two or three times superstitiously)* Ah! Be quiet!

TOTO: *(In his mother's skirts)* I don't care! I won't go to war!

CHOUILLOUX: "You won't go! You won't go!" If there is one, though, you'll have to...!

TOTO: I don't care! I'll go to Switzerland!

CHOUILLOUX: Huh?

JULIE: *(Smothering him with kisses)* Ah! darling! ...Isn't he intelligent?

CHOUILLOUX: *(To* FOLLAVOINE*)* My compliments! ... Bringing him up with such ideas!

FOLLAVOINE: *(Quickly)* No, no, no! *(To* TOTO.*)* It's very naughty to say things like that! You hear me...Hervé!

JULIE: *(Taking* TOTO *to the divan)* Leave the child alone! You don't want to bother him with things that are too grown-up for him! *(Sitting on the divan with* TOTO *between her knees.)* He's a good boy, very well-behaved; he's going to make his mother happy and take his nice laxative. *(So saying, she has filled the glass with milk of magnesia and, on the last word, offers it to* TOTO.*)*

TOTO: *(Leaving his mother's knees)* I don't wanna laxative!

JULIE: But you have to!

FOLLAVOINE: *(Coming to sit on the chair next to the divan)* Look, Toto! If you had obeyed right away, it would be all over. You'd be done with it.

TOTO: I don't care, I don't wanna!

FOLLAVOINE: Will you be sensible or not!

TOTO: *(Pulling loose and moving center)* No, I don't wanna!

CHOUILLOUX: *(Who has risen during the preceding. Intervening.)* My little friend, when I was your age... when I was very little, when my parents told me to do something, well!...

TOTO: *(In* CHOUILLOUX's *face)* Shut your trap!

FOLLAVOINE & JULIE: Oh!

CHOUILLOUX: *(Nonplussed)* What!...

FOLLAVOINE: *(Leaping on* TOTO *and putting him behind him)* Nothing! Nothing!

CHOUILLOUX: *(Giving up)* Ah! sorry I said anything! *(He goes to sit in the armchair right of the desk.)*

FOLLAVOINE: *(Furious, shaking* TOTO*)* Ah! That'll be enough of that! You are going to do me the pleasure of obeying, eh! I won't let a runt like you...

JULIE: *(Interposing and snatching the child from his hands)* Are you crazy! You're not going to bully the child, now?

FOLLAVOINE: But didn't you hear him? He said "Shut your trap!"

JULIE: So what if he said "shut your trap"? It's good grammar!

FOLLAVOINE: *(Indignant)* Oh!

JULIE: *(To Toto, embracing him)* My poor darling! *(She brings him to the divan on which she sits.)*

FOLLAVOINE: *(Crossing up to his desk)* Ah! no, drat! Drat! Drat! *(He sits down angrily.)*

JULIE: *(To TOTO whom she holds tight in her right arm. Caressing his cheek with her hand.)* Your father is a bad man! Luckily, your mother is here!

FOLLAVOINE: *(Furious)* There we have it! Putting ideas like that into his head!

JULIE: *(Taking in her right hand the full glass from the table and moving it to her left hand)* Certainly! …Picking on the child when he isn't well!

FOLLAVOINE: *(Turning his chair almost back to the desk, like a man who affects to be aloof from what is going on)* From now on, you know, you can address your remarks to whomever you please!

JULIE: *(Rudely)* Oh! *(To TOTO, suddenly sweet while offering the glass to his lips).* Take your laxative, darling!

TOTO: *(Pressing his lips together and moving his head away)* No, I don't wanna!

JULIE: *(Her nostrils dilated, her lips compressed, throws a look of rage at her husband, then controlling herself, turning to TOTO, supplicating)* Yes you do! …To make me happy.

TOTO: *(Stubborn)* No, I don't wanna!

JULIE: *(Same look at FOLLAVOINE; same change to TOTO)* Pretty please, darling, take your laxative.

TOTO: No…

JULIE: *(Clenching her teeth)* Oh! *(Casting a look of hate at FOLLAVOINE.)* Ah! once you start meddling!

FOLLAVOINE: *(Startled)* Me!

JULIE: Of course, you! *(To* TOTO) Listen, Toto! If you take all your laxative, well, mama will give you a mint!

TOTO: No! I want the mint first!

JULIE: No, after!

TOTO: No, before.

JULIE: Oh! ...Well, all right! We'll give you the mint before; only, afterwards, will you take the laxative?

TOTO: Yes.

JULIE: You promise?

TOTO: Yes.

JULIE: You give me your word of honor?

TOTO: *(A long drawn-out "yes")* Yes!

JULIE: All right! I trust you.

(JULIE, *to* FOLLAVOINE *who is seated at his desk, back almost turned and eyes on the ceiling in a resigned attitude:)*

JULIE: Papa!...

(JULIE, *seeing that* FOLLAVOINE, *distracted, doesn't answer. Drily:)*

JULIE: Bastien!...

CHOUILLOUX: *(Automatically)* Bastien!

FOLLAVOINE: *(As if coming out of a dream)* Huh?

JULIE: *(Drily)* The box of mints!

CHOUILLOUX: *(Passing on the request)* The box of mints!

FOLLAVOINE: *(With the sigh of a victim)* Here! *(He has opened a drawer and extracted the box. Rising and to* CHOUILLOUX *just as he hands the box to* JULIE.) I'm really sorry for involving you in this family drama.

CHOUILLOUX: Not at all! It's very interesting! ...For a man who has no children.

FOLLAVOINE: *(Offering the open box to* JULIE*)* Here's the box of mints!

JULIE: *(Taking a mint)* Thank you. *(To* TOTO*)* Open your little beak, darling! *(Putting a mint in his mouth)* There!

FOLLAVOINE: *(Going to put the box back in the drawer. To* CHOUILLOUX*)* This isn't why I invited you to lunch!

CHOUILLOUX: *(Carelessly)* Oh! well!...

JULIE: *(To* TOTO*)* Was it good?

TOTO: Yes!

JULIE: *(Holding out the glass to him)* There! Now, drink it, darling! Drink your laxative.

TOTO: *(Running away)* No, I don't wanna laxative!

JULIE: *(Startled)* What?

FOLLAVOINE: *(His nerves on edge)* Good grief! Here we go again!

JULIE: But you can't be serious, Toto? I gave you a sweetie!

TOTO: *(Going upstage to the back)* I don't care, I don't wanna laxative!

FOLLAVOINE: *(Barely able to contain himself)* Oh! That kid! That kid!

JULIE: *(Furious, to* FOLLAVOINE, *while going after* TOTO*)* "That kid!" Why do you keep repeating "That kid! That kid!" instead of helping me! Can't you see I'm at my wit's end? *(She lifts* TOTO *under the armpits and carries him to the divan where she sits.)*

FOLLAVOINE: *(Beside himself)* So what? What do you expect me to do?

JULIE: *(Crossing up center)* Oh! nothing! Nothing! Naturally! *(Bitterly)* Ah! for heaven's sake! *(So saying, she heads for her room.)*

FOLLAVOINE: What? What is it? Where are you going?

JULIE: Where do you think? I'm going to try something else!... *(On the threshold, turning around and indicating* CHOUILLOUX *with a gesture.)* Oh! ...And today would be the day you picked to invite people to lunch! *(She exits slamming the door.)*

FOLLAVOINE: *(Leaping up and to himself)* Oh!

CHOUILLOUX: *(Who has also risen. To* FOLLAVOINE*)* What did she say?

FOLLAVOINE: *(Playing the innocent)* What?

CHOUILLOUX: What did Madame Follavoine say?

FOLLAVOINE: Nothing! Nothing! ...She said "I really don't know...at what time we can have lunch."

CHOUILLOUX: *(Indifferent, sitting down again)* Ah? ... Well, what can you expect?

FOLLAVOINE: *(Going to* TOTO *and pulling him by the hand off the divan)* This is a disgrace, Toto, going back on your word! ...Isn't it, Monsieur Chouilloux?

CHOUILLOUX: *(Cautiously)* Oh, I've nothing to say! I've nothing to say!

FOLLAVOINE: *(Squatting before* TOTO *to be at his level)* See here, Toto! You are seven! You're a little man! You haven't the right to act like a child any more! Well, if you take the laxative like a good boy, I'll give you a surprise. *(He stands up.)*

TOTO: *(Curious)* What?

FOLLAVOINE: Well, I'll tell you where the Philippine Islands are.

TOTO: Oh, I don't care, I don't wanna know.

FOLLAVOINE: *(Tit for tat)* You're wrong!... *(To himself)* Especially after all the trouble I took to find them! *(To* TOTO*)* They're in the Pacific Ocean.

TOTO: *(Indifferent)* Ah?

FOLLAVOINE: And besides that, the capital is Manual...
Melanin...Melanesia... Anyway, they're in the Pacific
Ocean, that should be enough for you! *(He leaves* TOTO,
and pivoting on his heel, crosses right.)

TOTO: *(Catching him by the tail of his frockcoat)* And what
about Lake Michigan?

FOLLAVOINE: *(Frowning)* What?

TOTO: Where is Lake Michigan?

FOLLAVOINE: *(Repeating mechanically)* "Where is Lake
Michigan?"

TOTO: Yes?

FOLLAVOINE: Oh! I heard you all right!... *(Aside)*
What a nuisance this kid is, with his questions! *(To*
CHOUILLOUX*)* Tell me! ...Suppose I asked you about
Lake Michigan... Do you remember by any chance
where it is?

CHOUILLOUX: Lake Michigan?

FOLLAVOINE: Yes!

CHOUILLOUX: Why...it's in America! ...In the United
States!

FOLLAVOINE: Boy, am I dumb! Of course!

CHOUILLOUX: In the state of Michigan!

FOLLAVOINE: Michigan! That's it! it was the name of the
state I couldn't recall!

CHOUILLOUX: Lake Michigan! In 1877 I bathed in it!

FOLLAVOINE: No! you did! *(To* TOTO, *bending over and
indicating* CHOUILLOUX.*)* There, you see, Toto! You
were asking about Lake Michigan, well, this gentleman
here...who doesn't look like much, eh? Well, he took a
bath in it! *(Without transition)* I hope, after this, that you

are going to be sensible and a good boy and take your laxative!

TOTO: *(Running away and climbing on the divan)* No! I don't wanna!

FOLLAVOINE: *(Eyes skyward)* Oh!

CHOUILLOUX: This child has a good deal of will power!

FOLLAVOINE: *(Unimpressed)* Yes he does!

JULIE: *(Entering with a second glass identical to the first and coming far down left to the pedestal table)* There! I'm bringing another glass!... *(While filling the glass with milk of magnesia.)* ...And so that Baby will be a good boy and take his milk of magnesia... *(Putting down the bottle, taking* TOTO *along the way and going with him to her husband's right.)* Well! papa will take a big glass with him!

FOLLAVOINE: *(With a start)* What?

JULIE: *(To* FOLLAVOINE, *holding out the glass under his nose)* Won't you?

FOLLAVOINE: *(Taking refuge at his desk)* Not on your life! I won't, thank you very much!

JULIE: *(Drily, in an undertone)* Ah! for heaven's sake! You can't say no!

FOLLAVOINE: Absolutely not! I have no desire to take a laxative! Drink it yourself, if it makes you happy!

JULIE: Oh! ...You can't do even that for your son?

FOLLAVOINE: *(Pushing away the glass that Julie obstinately offers to his lips)* "For my son! For my son!" He's yours too!

JULIE: There you go! All the unpleasant chores, right? *(Placing the glass on the corner of the desk)* All the unpleasant chores! You don't think I've done enough for him since he was born? ...And especially before?

…You don't think it's enough to have carried him for nine months in my insides!… *(She crosses in front of* TOTO, *and comes down left a bit.)*

FOLLAVOINE: *(Exasperated)* "In your insides"? What's "in your insides" supposed to mean? *(He sits at his desk.)*

TOTO: Mama!

JULIE: What?

TOTO: Why did you carry me in your insides? Why didn't papa?

JULIE: *(Lifting up* TOTO *and setting him on the divan where she sits too)* Ah! why…because your father! …If I had to count on him! …But since he knew it had to be me… well then!

FOLLAVOINE: *(To* CHOUILLOUX*)* I ask you if that's the sort of thing to tell a child!

TOTO: You could have took another man.

FOLLAVOINE: *(Furious)* There: "you could have took another man!" Charming!

JULIE: Oh, you know, one man is much like another!…

TOTO: I wouldn't be like that!

JULIE: *(Embracing him)* Darling! At least you have a heart!

FOLLAVOINE: *(To* CHOUILLOUX*)* This is ridiculous, Monsieur Chouilloux! Ridiculous!

CHOUILLOUX: Not at all, it's charming! *(Rising, observing* TOTO *from a distance)* Children say the darnedest things!

JULIE: *(To* TOTO*)* You see the difference between a father and a mother! Your father won't even take a laxative for you!

TOTO: I don't care! I don't wan'im to take a laxative!

FOLLAVOINE: *(Coming down to the divan)* Aha! …You hear that! He has more sense than you do.

CHOUILLOUX: *(Also coming down towards* TOTO*)* Aha! … he doesn't want to make his papa drink it!

TOTO: *(Pointing at* CHOUILLOUX*)* I want that man to drink it!

FOLLAVOINE: Huh?

CHOUILLOUX: *(Instinctively recoiling)* What?

JULIE: *(Glad to seize this opportunity to please her son)* You want this man to drink it? Well then, this man will drink it! *(She takes the full glass from the pedestal table and, with* TOTO *beside her, heads for* CHOUILLOUX.*)*

FOLLAVOINE: *(Interposing)* You can't think such a thing!

JULIE: *(Moving him away and crossing with* TOTO*)* Ssh! Leave me alone!

CHOUILLOUX: *(In front of the prompter's box, muttering to himself)* Really, this is the most badly brought-up child! Oh!

JULIE: *(Glass in hand)* Here, dear Monsieur Chouilloux!… *(She puts the glass to his lips just as he is saying, "…badly brought-up child! Oh!" so that in exclaiming "Oh!" he involuntarily gulps some down.)*

CHOUILLOUX: Ah! Pooh!

JULIE: *(Accompanied by* TOTO, *marching on* CHOUILLOUX *with the glass held out)* Be so kind, drink a little to make Toto happy! *(Once again she brings the glass to his lips.)*

CHOUILLOUX: *(Spitting)* Ah! pfutt!

*(*CHOUILLOUX, *recoiling right as* JULIE *marches on him:)*

CHOUILLOUX: Oh no, madame! No thank you!

FOLLAVOINE: Have you gone out of your mind?

JULIE: *(To* CHOUILLOUX*)* Oh, it's such a little thing! Half the glass would be enough!

(Same business with the glass, while CHOUILLOUX *tries to defend himself.)*

CHOUILLOUX: No, no, madame! For pity' sake! ...I'm very sorry!...

FOLLAVOINE: You can't mean it! Monsieur Chouilloux didn't come here to take a laxative!

JULIE: What! There's no need to make such a fuss over a little milk of magnesia!

CHOUILLOUX: *(Backed up against the armchair right)* I'm not saying that, but...

JULIE: I can understand it from a child, but from a grown-up!... *(Wheedling)* Come on, Monsieur Chouilloux. *(She puts the glass under his nose.)*

FOLLAVOINE: Julie, see here!

CHOUILLOUX: Absolutely not, Madame! I am very sorry, but a laxative! I've already told you in detail that the state of my bowels will not allow it!...

FOLLAVOINE: Certainly not!

JULIE: Yes, but half a glass of milk of magnesia isn't going to do your bowels any harm!

FOLLAVOINE: Julie! Julie!

JULIE: And, honestly, if I have to choose between Toto's health and your bowels, I'd choose!...

FOLLAVOINE: For pity's sake, Julie!

CHOUILLOUX: Besides, madame, I assure you! ...I'm not sure how good a laxative would be for your son...

JULIE: *(Quickly moving* TOTO *to her other side, sotto voce to* CHOUILLOUX*)* Ah! no, for goodness sake! ...If you're going to say things like that in front of the child! Ah! that's the limit!

FOLLAVOINE: *(Moving* TOTO *to his other side)* Julie! …
Julie!

CHOUILLOUX: I beg your pardon, madame! If I may say
so!…

JULIE: *(To* CHOUILLOUX'*s face)* You see the trouble I'm
having with Baby! All the tactics I have to employ!…

FOLLAVOINE: Julie! Julie!

JULIE: *(Not letting go)* If on top of that you're going to
persuade him that he doesn't have to take his laxative!

CHOUILLOUX: Not at all! Not at all! …However I do
believe…

JULIE: *(Right up in his face)* Ah! "You believe ! you
believe!"

FOLLAVOINE: Julie! Julie!

JULIE: What do you know about it? Where did you
learn about it? During your treatment at Plombières?
But your treatment at Plombières was the opposite! It
was the opposite!

CHOUILLOUX: Listen, madame, I'll take it back!

FOLLAVOINE: For heaven's sake, Julie! That's enough!

JULIE: *(Crossing far left followed by* TOTO*)* It's true! Do
I interfere if his wife cuckolds him with her cousin
Truchet? *(She puts the glass on the pedestal table.)*

CHOUILLOUX: *(Jumping up)* Cuckold!

FOLLAVOINE: *(To himself)* Oh! bloody hell!

(Ignoring CHOUILLOUX, JULIE *has lifted* TOTO *and made
him sit on the divan; after which she sits on his left.)*

CHOUILLOUX: What did you say? …Cuckold! …My
wife! …Truchet!…

FOLLAVOINE: That's not true, Monsieur Chouilloux! It's
not true!

CHOUILLOUX: *(Pushing* FOLLAVOINE *away)* Leave me alone! Leave me alone! Ah! ...Ah! I'm choking! *(He notices the glass originally left by* JULIE *on the table, rushes to it and greedily swallows the contents.)*

FOLLAVOINE: Ah!

TOTO: *(Delighted to see this, pointing out* CHOUILLOUX *to his mother)* Mama! Mama! *(Skipping about, he goes above the desk and crawls on his knees on to his father's chair.)*

JULIE: *(To* CHOUILLOUX, *as he swallows the laxative)* Well! Why couldn't you have done that before? ...instead of making such a fuss!

FOLLAVOINE: *(Panicked)* Monsieur Chouilloux, for heaven's sake!

*(*CHOUILLOUX's *expression abruptly contracts; his eyes look wild; the laxative is working on his insides; he casts desperate glances right and left. Then, suddenly, remembering where Follavoine found his pots, he dashes like a madman to the bookcase back right. Follavoine, reads his thoughts and running after him.)*

FOLLAVOINE: No! not in there! There aren't any more! There aren't any more! *(Pushing him towards the door down left.)* Over there, look! Over there!

*(*CHOUILLOUX *rushes into the next room.)*

Scene Eight

*(*JULIE, FOLLAVOINE, TOTO*)*

FOLLAVOINE: *(Turns to his wife, after closing the door)* Ah! congratulations! That's just fine and dandy! What do you think you're doing? *(He nervously crosses upstage.)*

JULIE: *(Rising and crossing right)* Well, he shouldn't have interfered in what doesn't concern him!

FOLLAVOINE: *(Reaching center stage)* Telling that poor man he's a cuckold!

TOTO: Mama!

JULIE: What is it, darling? You want a laxative?

TOTO: No! …What's a cuckold?

JULIE: *(With a sarcastic sneer)* Ah?… *(Indicating the door Chouilloux left through.)* It's the gentleman who just left.

FOLLAVOINE: *(Who has not stopped pacing the stage, suddenly spinning round)* No! no! …What a thing to say to a child!

JULIE: If he had drunk it right away, the way he was asked!

FOLLAVOINE: You are a wonder, you are: a laxative! *(He crosses upstage.)*

JULIE: Well! … When you are invited into someone's home, you take what you're offered! He has no manners, your Chouilloux! A man who comes here for the very first time and talks to us about his loose bowels! …Where was he brought up?

FOLLAVOINE: *(Coming back down center stage)* But you asked him to take the laxative!

JULIE: *(Rising and crossing to her husband)* I asked him to take the laxative, did I? I don't care a rap if he takes a laxative! I asked him to drink a glass of milk of magnesia! I didn't ask him to take a laxative! *(She crosses above the desk, takes her son on the way and comes down with him far right.)*

FOLLAVOINE: But it was a laxative all the same!

JULIE: *(Sitting in the armchair right of the table with* TOTO *between her knees)* Ah! well, that's his business. After all! he swallowed it all the same, his laxative? Besides, what's he bothering us for?

(Doorbell)

FOLLAVOINE: Yes! that puts me in a pretty position... over the contract for military chamber pots!

JULIE: There! ...you have a one-track mind!...

FOLLAVOINE: *(Above the divan)* How am I going to fix things now?

Scene Nine

(The same, ROSE, MADAME CHOUILLOUX, TRUCHET)

ROSE: *(Announcing)* Madame Chouilloux! Monsieur Truchet!

FOLLAVOINE: Ah! no! no! You greet them! After all this, I don't want to see them. *(He heads for the door down left.)*

JULIE: *(Rising)* Huh? No! No! Bastien! ...I don't know them!

FOLLAVOINE: I don't care, work it out! *(He exits.)*

(MADAME CHOUILLOUX, breezing in followed by TRUCHET:)

MADAME CHOUILLOUX: Madame Follavoine, I presume?

JULIE: *(At a loss)* Huh? No! ...Yes!...

(JULIE is against the left corner of the table. TOTO hides behind his mother's back, pulling the hem of her wrapper in front of him.)

MADAME CHOUILLOUX: Ah! madame! Delighted! *(Alluding to JULIE's get-up.)* I was afraid that we would be late, but I see it's quite the contrary.

JULIE: *(Very flustered)* No! ...No! ...Excuse me, I...I haven't had time to dress...

MADAME CHOUILLOUX: Well, never mind! Please! If you're going to stand on ceremony…! *(Introducing)* Monsieur Truchet, my cousin, whom you had the great kindness to…

TRUCHET: Madame, I hope I don't intrude! …The first time I've had the honor…!

JULIE: Don't mention it!…

MADAME CHOUILLOUX: *(Noticing* TOTO's *head sticking out of his mother's wrapper)* And is this charming little girl yours, madame?

JULIE: *(Extricating* TOTO) Yes! …yes! …only he's a little boy.

MADAME CHOUILLOUX: *(Amazed)* Ah? *(As an excuse)* At that age, of course? …There's no way to tell them apart.

JULIE: That's so true…

TRUCHET: And Monsieur Follavoine isn't here?

JULIE: *(Indicating the door down left)* Yes, he is! In there! …In there!

TOTO: *(Innocently putting his foot in his mouth)* With the cuckold!

JULIE: *(Quickly pulling Toto behind her)* Oh!

MADAME CHOUILLOUX: *(Wondering if she has heard right)* What?

JULIE: *(Quickly)* Nothing! Nothing! He's…he's an employee of my husband.

MADAME CHOUILLOUX: *(Delighted)* Whose name is Dekocolt? How embarrassing!

JULIE: *(With a curt forced laugh)* Isn't it? …Isn't it?

TRUCHET: And hard to bear! Very hard!

JULIE: Yes! …Yes!…

MADAME CHOUILLOUX: *(As before)* What an idea: "Dekocolt"! *(Without transition)* Oh! which reminds me: my husband must be here!

JULIE: Yes! ...Yes, quite so! he is here.

MADAME CHOUILLOUX: Aha! ...With both of them?

JULIE: Both of them? Which "both"?

MADAME CHOUILLOUX: Why, Monsieur Follavoine and Monsieur Dekocolt.

JULIE: Ah! ...Yes! ...Yes, yes... Do sit down, please! Do sit down!

*(*MADAME CHOUILLOUX *crosses left to sit on the sofa, while* TRUCHET *goes a bit upstage to the desk chair. At that moment the door left opens and* CHOUILLOUX *bursts in followed by* FOLLAVOINE. *They are both speaking at once.)*

Scene Ten

(The same, CHOUILLOUX, FOLLAVOINE*)*

FOLLAVOINE: Monsieur Chouilloux! I swear to you...!

CHOUILLOUX: No, leave me alone! Leave me alone!

MADAME CHOUILLOUX: *(Crossing towards her husband)* Ah! Adhéaume!

CHOUILLOUX: You wretched creature!

TRUCHET & MADAME CHOUILLOUX: *(Startled)* What?

FOLLAVOINE: *(Above the sofa)* Oh my God!

CHOUILLOUX: *(Pointing to his wife)* There she is! The woman taken in adultery!

MADAME CHOUILLOUX: Me?

CHOUILLOUX: *(Going to* TRUCHET *and pointing at him)* There he is! The treacherous friend!

TRUCHET: My friend!

CHOUILLOUX: *(Center stage, removing his frockcoat and puffing out his chest)* Here he is! The cuckold! Behold!

FOLLAVOINE: *(Who has moved behind the other characters to join* CHOUILLOUX *center stage)* Good grief! Good grief!

MADAME CHOUILLOUX: Why, this is insane, my love, insane!

TRUCHET: Who in the world told you...?

CHOUILLOUX: Who told me? He did! *(Pointing at* FOLLAVOINE *on his right.)* Ask that gentleman! *(Pointing to* JULIE *on his left.)* Ask madame!

FOLLAVOINE: It's not true, monsieur Chouilloux! It's not true!

MADAME CHOUILLOUX: *(Going to* CHOUILLOUX*)* My love...!

CHOUILLOUX: *(Waving her away with a gesture)* Get back, madame! I do not wish to see you any more. *(Crossing to* TRUCHET*)* As for you, monsieur, you will receive my seconds! *(He crosses upstage to get his hat.)*

MADAME CHOUILLOUX: *(Dashing after him)* My love, for pity's sake, listen to me!...

TRUCHET: *(Also crossing up)* Chouilloux, my friend...

CHOUILLOUX: No!

*(*CHOUILLOUX *exits followed by* MADAME CHOUILLOUX*.)*

TRUCHET: *(Coming downstage directly to* FOLLAVOINE*)* Did you tell him that?

FOLLAVOINE: Of course not! It was a misunderstanding!

TRUCHET: Very well, you shall give me satisfaction. *(He slaps him.)*

FOLLAVOINE: *(Seeing stars)* Bloody hell!

TRUCHET: I shall expect your seconds! *(He exits furiously.)*

FOLLAVOINE: *(Rubbing his cheek)* Oh! damn and blast!

JULIE: *(After a pause, hands on her hips, scornfully looking her husband up and down)* Well, I hope you're satisfied! That's where you've got us with all your fussing!

FOLLAVOINE: *(Startled)* Me! ...Me! ...You dare say that it was me!...

JULIE: *(Shrugs)* Naturally it was you! If you hadn't invited all those people to lunch!

FOLLAVOINE: Me! Me!

JULIE: Oh! leave me in peace! It's not the worst thing you've done! *(She exits furiously through the door to her room.)*

FOLLAVOINE: It's all my fault! My fault! I have a duel on account of her and it's all my fault! *(Collapsing on to the divan)* Oh! no, no, that woman will drive me crazy! *(Choking with indignation, he notices beside him on the pedestal table the other glass of milk of magnesia. He rushes up to it and swallows it in one gulp.)*

TOTO: *(Watching him swallow the laxative. —Aside, delighted.)* Oh!

FOLLAVOINE: Ah! pooh! *(He rushes like a madman into his room down left.)*

Scene Eleven

(TOTO, then JULIE, then FOLLAVOINE)

TOTO: *(Once his father is gone, joyfully snapping his fingers)* Goody! Goody! *(He goes to the pedestal table, takes the glass his father emptied, turns it over shaking it like a bell to make sure it's really empty; then snapping his fingers again.)* Goody! Goody! *(Running far left, with the glass in hand, half opens the door to his mother's room and calls.)* Mama! ...Mama!

JULIE: *(Off)* What? What's the matter?

TOTO: Mama! Come here! *(He comes down center.)*

JULIE: *(Appearing and joining* TOTO*)* What do you want, darling?

TOTO: *(With disconcerting aplomb)* Here! …I drank it! *(He holds out the glass.)*

JULIE: *(Kneeling beside him)* You drank it! Ah! darling, isn't that sweet! There, you see: it wasn't so awful!

TOTO: *(With a malicious smile)* Oh! no!

FOLLAVOINE: *(Erupting into the room, in an overcoat and hat)* No! no! I'd rather leave! I'd rather leave home! *(He goes up to the desk, from which he takes papers and nervously stuffs them into a folder before he exits.)*

JULIE: *(Without even noticing what he's doing)* Bastien! Baby took his laxative.

FOLLAVOINE: I don't give a damn! *(He leaves furiously.)*

JULIE: *(Indignant)* He doesn't give a damn! …He doesn't give a damn! *(To* TOTO*)* Well, that's your father for you! He doesn't give a damn! Ah! fortunately, you have your mother! Love her to bits, darling! Love her to bits! *(She smothers* TOTO *with kisses.)*

(Curtain)

END OF PLAY

SHE CAN'T BARE IT!

(Mais n'te promène pas toute nue!)

CHARACTERS & SETTING

JULIEN VENTROUX, *a legislator*
CLARISSE, *his wife*
VICTOR, *their servant*
HOCHEPAIX, *a provincial mayor*
DE JAIVAL, *a journalist*

The drawing-room of the VENTROUX *apartment. Up center at back a double door leading to the hallway. The right panel of the door is held open by an offstage hook. It leads to a vestibule, at the far side of which, opposite the door, is the main entrance to the apartment. It opens on to the landing (The right panel is stationary) Right of the drawing-room door, in the back wall, a folding door that opens to the offstage area, supposedly leading to* CLARISSE's *room. Down left, a wall panel, with a stand of some kind leaning against it. Center, forming a canted panel, a double door leading to* VENTROUX's *study. Down right, a fireplace with its implements and a mirror above it. Farther upstage right, a large window with a fan-light. Between the curtains and the window, a lace window shade that can be pulled all the way down and that slides along its rod from the forestage into the distance. Pull-cord for the shade is to the left of the window. Facing front, a big sofa with a high back, its right end nearly touching the upstage side of the fireplace. In front of the sofa, at right, on a low coffee-table, a cup of coffee, a small coffee pot, and a sugar bowl, all on a little tray. Far downstage, near the fireplace, back to the audience, a deep easy chair.*

Left, a big library table set perpendicular to the audience, a chair on either side of it. Chairs right and left of the double-door entry. Electric bell at the window corner of the fireplace. On the table, a note pad. Chandelier, fire screen, andirons, etc. The rest of the furniture ad lib.

Scene One

(VICTOR, *then* VENTROUX)

(*As the curtain rises,* VICTOR, *on a stepladder, is fixing the pull-cord of the window shade. The left panel of the hallway door is open. From offstage in* CLARISSE's *room come snatches of conversation in which* VENTROUX's *voice and his son's are loudest,* CLARISSE's *somewhat fainter, as if from a more distant room. After a moment, we can make out:*)

VENTROUX: (*Off*) What? What did you say, Clarisse?

CLARISSE: (*Off. Too distant and indistinct to make out.*) ????

VENTROUX: (*Off*) Oh. Well, I don't know. As soon as this term is over, we'll leave for the seashore.

VENTROUX JR: (*Off*) Oh great, Papa! Yay, seashore!

VENTROUX: (*Off*) Yes, well, eh? Wait till the Chamber adjourns for the vacation.

CLARISSE: (*Off*) (*Now as clear as the others*) Wait, darlings, wait till I get my nightie.

VENTROUX: (*Off*) (*Indignant*) Clarisse, really! Have you lost your mind?

CLARISSE: (*Off*) Why?

VENTROUX: (*Off*) Well, I ask you! Look, look at yourself! And there's your son!

CLARISSE: (*Off*) Oh yes, yes of course, just a second while I get out of my slip, and...

VENTROUX: *(Off)* No, no! For pity's sake! You're out of your mind! Everybody can see you! Go back in!

CLARISSE: *(Off)* Oh, you are tiresome. If you're going to make a big scene…

VENTROUX: *(Off)* No, really! I'd rather go myself than see things that… And you, you, Auguste, what are you hanging around your mother's room for?

VICTOR: *(Who has stopped working to listen for a moment, nods)*: Here they go again!

VENTROUX: *(Off)* Get out, beat it!

VENTROUX JR: *(Off)* All right, Papa.

VENTROUX: *(Enters, slamming the door behind him)* None! No modesty at all!… *(To VICTOR)* Well, what are you doing there, eh?

VICTOR: *(Still on his ladder)* I'm adjusting the pull-cords.

VENTROUX: Can't you make yourself scarce when you hear I'm… I'm conversing with Madame?

VICTOR: I wanted to finish up, monsieur.

VENTROUX: Yes! So you can listen better at the doors!

VICTOR: Doors? …I'm at the window.

VENTROUX: Fine. Get out!

VICTOR: *(Leaving the window shade wide open as he comes off the ladder)* Yes, monsieur. *(He folds up the ladder.)*

VENTROUX: And take your ladder with you!

VICTOR: Yes, monsieur. *(He exits, taking the ladder with him.)*

VENTROUX: *(Testily closing the door behind him)* That fellow's always under foot! *(He crosses downstage and peevishly sits right of the table.)*

Scene Two

(VENTROUX, CLARISSE)

CLARISSE: *(Bursts in from her room. She is wearing her nightgown, a Merry Widow hat, and high-button shoes)* Well, really! You want to tell me what's come over you? Who are you so mad at?

VENTROUX: *(Chin in hand, elbow on table, not turning around)* Obviously, anyone who asks me that. *(Turning to her, he sees how she's dressed)* Oh no! No! You're not going to parade around the apartment in your nightie! ...with your hat on!

CLARISSE: Yes well, but first I wish you'd explain. I'll take off my hat in a minute.

VENTROUX: Your hat? I don't give a hoot for your hat! I've got nothing against your hat!

CLARISSE: Well then, now what have I done wrong?

VENTROUX: Oh, nothing, nothing! You've never done anything wrong!

CLARISSE: *(Crosses up to the sofa)* Well, I don't understand...

VENTROUX: *(Standing)* Too bad, then! Because it's even worse if you aren't aware of the full implications of your actions.

CLARISSE: *(Sitting on the sofa)* If you'd care to explain yourself!...

VENTROUX: So you consider it proper behavior for a mother to go and change her slip in front of her son?

CLARISSE: That's what all this fuss is about?

VENTROUX: Obviously, that's what.

CLARISSE: Well, really! I thought I'd committed a crime or something.

VENTROUX: Oh, you find it perfectly normal?

CLARISSE: *(Casually)* Pooh! What difference does it make? Auguste is a child… If you think he even looks, poor dear! Anyway, mothers don't count.

VENTROUX: *(Sharply)* It's not a matter of what counts; it isn't done… *(Goes above the sofa.)*

CLARISSE: Twelve years old!

VENTROUX: *(Behind her)* Excuse me, thirteen.

CLARISSE: He's twelve.

VENTROUX: Thirteen, I tell you! He's been thirteen for three days now.

CLARISSE: Oh well, yes, three days, that doesn't count.

VENTROUX: *(Crossing down center)* Oh yes! Nothing counts, according to you.

CLARISSE: He doesn't even know what a woman is!

VENTROUX: Even so, it's not your job to teach him! Look here, what is this mania you've got for parading around stark naked?

CLARISSE: Oh come on! Stark naked! I had my nightie on.

VENTROUX: That's even more indecent. You can see through it like tracing paper.

CLARISSE: *(Rising and crossing to him)* Aha! There! There we have it: admit it! That's what you're driving at! You want me to wear flannel nightgowns!

VENTROUX: *(Flabbergasted)* What? What flannel nightgowns? Who said anything about flannel nightgowns?

CLARISSE: I'm awfully sorry, my dear, but all the women in our set wear linen nighties, and I don't see why I should have to wear burlap ones. *(As she speaks she crosses far left.)*

VENTROUX: *(Crossing down right)* Ah! Fine! Now we're down to burlap.

CLARISSE: Thanks but no thanks! What would people say?

VENTROUX: *(Turning around)* People? What people? Are you planning to show off your undergarments to "people"?

CLARISSE: *(Turning abruptly and moving towards her husband)* Me? Me? I'm planning to show people my undergarments? You accuse me of showing people my undergarments? So that's what you're driving at!

VENTROUX: *(Stressing every denial)* No! No! Don't keep twisting the conversation to put me on the defensive! I am not accusing you of anything at all! I do not insist on your nighties being flannel or burlap! I am simply requesting that when your son is in your bedroom, you have the modesty not to undress in front of him!

CLARISSE: *(With disconcerting calm)* Oh my, you have got a nerve! That's exactly what I did!

VENTROUX: *(Dumbfounded by her impudence, holds his head as if to prevent it exploding, then stalks upstage, waving his hands over his head)* Ah! No! No, you...you know, really, talk about nerve!

CLARISSE: *(Crossing up towards him)* Absolutely! It's one more proof of your never-ending unfairness! *(Coming down.)* Just try to please people...! *(She sits in the chair by the fireplace.)* Just because I know your narrow-minded ideas and because you were both in my bedroom, I took particular care to undress in my boudoir.

VENTROUX: *(Sitting on the sofa)* Yes, only as soon as you put on your slip, you march back into your bedroom! If I had my choice, I'd have preferred the reverse order.

CLARISSE: But that was only to get my nightie!

VENTROUX: Yes! Oh, you've always got compelling reasons. But, in the first place, why do you have to put on your nightie at four o'clock in the afternoon?

CLARISSE: Well! You are a fine one, you are! It's plain to see *you* weren't collapsing from the heat at the Duchomier girl's wedding. *(Getting up.)* And furthermore, who insisted that I go? Hm? It was for your sake, not mine, that's for sure! *(She reaches center stage while speaking.)* To save you the trouble! As usual! Remember, *I'm* not the bride's father's fellow deputy! I'm not a delegate, not me! You're the one. You've got a lovely way of thanking me!

VENTROUX: *(Shrugging)* Thanking you has nothing to do with it!…

CLARISSE: *(Interrupting)* Oh I know, it's only what you're due. I'm still waiting for a word of thanks out of you. *(Crossing up to him)* No matter that when I got home all in a sweat, I felt like getting comfortable. That's still allowed, isn't it?

VENTROUX: Oh yes, of course…I grant you!

CLARISSE: *(Going above the sofa)* Thank goodness for that! Heavens, you're in a nice cool spot here! You'd never guess it's at least eighty or ninety degrees… latitude outside.

VENTROUX: *(Ironical)* Ninety degrees latitude!

CLARISSE: *(Missing the irony)* Ninety degrees, that's right!

VENTROUX: What do you mean, "latitude"? What's "latitude" got to do with it?

CLARISSE: *(Mildly scornful)* You don't know what "latitude" means? *(Coming down)* Well! That's pathetic, at your age! *(At the right of the table, turns to her husband, crushing him with her superior knowledge.)* "Latitude" is the thermometer.

VENTROUX: *(Mocking)* Oh? ...I beg your pardon! I had no idea.

CLARISSE: It wasn't much use going to school. *(Sitting on the chair right of the table.)* When I think that at ninety degrees...latitude you force us to stay in Paris! And all because you're a deputy and can't leave town before the Chamber adjourns! ...I ask you! As if the Chamber of Deputies couldn't get along without you!

VENTROUX: *(Jumping up like a shot and shouting)* I do not know whether the Chamber can get along without me or not. What I do know is, when one accepts an office, one serves one's term! Wouldn't it be jolly if all the delegates started to take off, on the theory that the government has no specific need of any of us individually! They'd have to close down the government! *(He heads upstage.)*

CLARISSE: Oh, pooh, is that all? It wouldn't matter a fig! The country is always at its most peaceful when the Chamber's on vacation, so!...

VENTROUX: *(Who has come down left of the table. Stressing each word)* But, my dearest love, we are not in office to keep the country peaceful! That's not what we were elected for! Besides, and once and for all, we're getting off the track! I ask you why you walk around in your nightie and you reply by attacking representative government. It's got nothing to do with the case. *(He sits down to face his wife.)*

CLARISSE: I beg your pardon, I'm sure! It's on account of your parliament we're still in Paris at ninety degrees...latitude...

VENTROUX: *(Jeering)* A one-track mind.

CLARISSE: Exactly! Because it's ninety degrees... latitude, I perspire. Because when I perspire I feel like changing my slip. And then because I *did* change, you felt you had to criticize me!

VENTROUX: I did not criticize you for changing your undergarments. I criticized you for strolling around in front of your son in a see-through nightie.

CLARISSE: *(Almost shouting)* Is it my fault it's see-through?

VENTROUX: No! But it's your fault if you come into your room in it.

CLARISSE: Ah no, that's the limit! I haven't the right to come into my own room now?

VENTROUX: I never said any such thing! Don't put words in my mouth!

CLARISSE: *(Not listening)* Where do you want me to undress? In the kitchen? The pantry? In front of the servants? Oh! if I did, you'd howl like a polecat.

VENTROUX: Stick to the point!…

CLARISSE: *(Rising and crossing up to the sofa)* I *am* sticking to the point! I was in my own house, in my own room! You're the one who had no business being there. Did I ask you to come in? Did I? *(Sits on the sofa)* Well, if my outfit bothered you, you could just have left.

VENTROUX: *(Rising)* Wonderful! Brilliant logic!

CLARISSE: It's true! …Making a big scene because I came into *my room* in a lightweight slip! *(Abruptly, nearly shouting.)* Well, what did you expect me to do, since my nightie was in my room?

VENTROUX: *(Crossing to her)* Well, I was there, you could have asked me to get it! I would have brought it to you!

CLARISSE: *(With disconcerting logic)* But that's exactly the same, you'd have seen me naked.

VENTROUX: But that's me, *me*! I'm your husband!

CLARISSE: Well, Auguste is my son!

VENTROUX: *(On the verge of tears, tearing his hair)* Oh, no, no! It's hopeless! *(To* CLARISSE.*)* So you don't see any difference?

CLARISSE: Why… he's even closer than you.

VENTROUX: Oh!

CLARISSE: Well, after all! You're a total stranger to me! Oh, you're my husband, but that's just a convention! When I married you—I can't think why –

VENTROUX: *(Bows, then:)* Thank you.

CLARISSE: *(Uninterrupted)* …I didn't know you, and bingo! all of a sudden one fine day, simply because we said I do in front of a fat man in a tricolor sash, it's quite all right! you can look at me stark naked. Well! Now, *that's* indecent!

VENTROUX: Oh, you think so?

CLARISSE: Whereas my own son, eh? He's my own flesh! My own blood! Well, if the flesh of my flesh sees my flesh, there's nothing in the least improper about it! *(Rising.)* Except for appearances.

VENTROUX: But appearances are everything! Everything!

CLARISSE: *(Crossing in front of him, haughtily)* Yes, for petty people, but thank goodness! I'm above all that!

VENTROUX: *(Collapsing into an armchair next to the fireplace)* Splendid! Wonderful! She's above all that! That takes care of everything!

CLARISSE: *(Returning to the charge, while going to sit on the sofa)* No, but really, since he was a tiny baby, hasn't he seen me dress twenty-five thousand times? And you never said a word!

VENTROUX: Nevertheless, the day comes when those practices should cease.

CLARISSE: *(Annoyingly cool)* Yes. Oh! ...I suppose so!

VENTROUX: Well then?

CLARISSE: *(Gazing at the ceiling)* I agree! ...When?

VENTROUX: What do you mean, when?

CLARISSE: *(As before)* What date? What time of day?

VENTROUX: What do you mean, what date, what time of day?

CLARISSE: It has to stop? All right, it has to happen one day, one particular hour. But why specially today? Why not yesterday? Tomorrow? So I ask you, what date? What time?

VENTROUX: *(Imitating her)* "What date? What time?" The questions she asks! ...How do I know? How do you expect me to be precise?

CLARISSE: You can't be precise! *(She gets up and bears down upon him.)* Ah, isn't that wonderful! But you still expect *me*, a mere woman! by definition not as smart as you are, -- at least that's what you keep saying, -- you expect me, *me*! to be able to do it, when you say you can't!

VENTROUX: *(Beside himself)* Good grief, what you're saying is idiotic!

CLARISSE: *(At left)* It is not! You criticize me, I just defend myself.

VENTROUX: *(Rising, crossing to her)* Just what are you trying to prove? That a mother is doing the right thing when she's exhibits herself to her son in her slip?

CLARISSE: *(Leaning against the table left)* But that's not I'm saying! If you're so disgusted by it, all right! Fine!

...You could just say so, without flying into a rage. I'd listen.

VENTROUX: *(Unconvinced)* Yes! You'd listen all right! *(Sitting down)* You know perfectly well you wouldn't! You're incapable of not sauntering around in your undergarments; the habit's too strong for you.

CLARISSE: Oh! you're exaggerating!

VENTROUX: I bring it up every day.

CLARISSE: I assure you it's not true! If you see me now and then in the morning, it's just because I haven't finished dressing, but once I'm dressed, I assure you...

VENTROUX: ...that you're no longer undressed. Exactly! Obviously! Only you never *are* dressed!

CLARISSE: *(Losing her temper)* All right then, what is it you want? That I shouldn't get dressed?

VENTROUX: No no no! Of course not! Do, do it, get dressed, by all means! But stay in your own room while you do it! And close the door! It's always wide open on such occasions! Very suitable for the servants.

CLARISSE: Oh, they don't come in.

VENTROUX: They don't *need* to come in to see you, they've only got to look.

CLARISSE: Oh, servants don't pay any attention to that!

VENTROUX: Oh no? Aren't they men like everyone else? ...Your behavior is very peculiar! You leave the door wide open while you get dressed, ...and you lock yourself in to put on your hat!

CLARISSE: *(With the little fussy and fidgety gestures madwomen make)* Yes, of course I do. Because, well, I don't like to be disturbed when I'm adjusting my hat. I don't like people hanging around, I'd never get it done.

VENTROUX: *(Rising and crossing above the sofa)* It's a great pity you aren't so particular when you wash! ...But it's not only that! You've got an even better trick: you turn on the light in your boudoir... and neglect to draw the curtains.

CLARISSE: *(With an indignant gesture)* Oh! When?

VENTROUX: Yesterday.

CLARISSE: *(Suddenly calm)* Oh. That's right, yesterday.

VENTROUX: Because you can't see out, you're like an ostrich: you imagine nobody can see in.

CLARISSE: *(Going to lean against the front of the table; casually)* Oh! Who do you think looks?

VENTROUX: Who? *(Gesturing to the window.)* Why, Clemenceau, my sweet!—Clemenceau, who lives just across the way! ...He's always at his window!

CLARISSE: Pooh, he's seen lots of women, Clemenceau has!

VENTROUX: That's as may be! ...It's quite possible that he *has* seen lots of women, but I would just as soon he did not see you. I prefer to be proper. *(He sits down on the sofa.)*

CLARISSE: What for?

VENTROUX: What for? You don't think ahead! You don't know Clemenceau! He's the worst joker in the Chamber! ...He's got a malicious wit! He's terrifying! If he were to make some silly joke about me, or if he just sticks me with some nickname, it could ruin my career!

CLARISSE: You needn't worry about that, he's in your party, isn't he?

VENTROUX: Just so! It's always in your own party that you find your enemies! If Clemenceau were a conservative, poof! I wouldn't care a rap, -- nor would he, -- but since we're on the same side, we're rivals!

Clemenceau flatters himself he might become a cabinet minister again! ...And so might I.

CLARISSE: *(Eyeing him)* You?

VENTROUX: *(Rising)* Eh? But you know very well! You know very well that in one of our last coalitions, after my speech on the farm bill, they came round to offer me the Department of...the Navy.

CLARISSE: *(Sitting right of the table)* Oh yes!

VENTROUX: Secretary of the Navy! Not bad, eh? Can't you just see it?

CLARISSE: No.

VENTROUX: *(Annoyed)* Naturally.

CLARISSE: Secretary of the Navy! You can't even swim!

VENTROUX: What does that prove, if I may ask? Does one need to know how to swim to administer affairs of state?

CLARISSE: Some affairs!

VENTROUX: *(As he speaks, he crosses up left to the back of the stage, and comes back down left of the table)* Yes, of course! I wonder why I bother arguing? No man is a prophet is his own country. Fortunately those who don't know me have a different opinion from yours. *(Sits on the chair left of the table, facing her)* Well! for pity's sake, don't jeopardize my career by committing some compromising indiscretion that could have disastrous consequences.

CLARISSE: *(Shrugs)* Disastrous!...

VENTROUX: Imagine that you're the wife of one of tomorrow's cabinet ministers. Well: when you're a ministress, are you going to gallivant around the ministry corridors in your nightie?

CLARISSE: Of course not!

VENTROUX: And when I say Minister! Well, you never know! That's the beauty of this administration: everyone can hope some day to become… President of the Republic. Well: why shouldn't it be me? *(He raises his hand to forestall her objections.)* Let's just suppose! You've have to greet kings… queens! Would you receive them in your nightie?

CLARISSE: Oh no! No!

VENTROUX: Would you let them see you like *that*?

CLARISSE: Well, of course not! … I'd put on my dressing gown.

VENTROUX: *(Rising and holding his head in both hands)* Her dressing gown! She'd put on her dressing gown!

CLARISSE: Well then, I'd wear whatever you like!

VENTROUX: *(In front of the table)* No, it's appalling, my poor creature! You've absolutely no sense of propriety.

CLARISSE: *(Rising indignantly)* Me? …I don't?

VENTROUX: *(Indulgently, taking her shoulders in his hands)* Oh, I'm not angry with you! In your case it's not a moral defect, it's merely naiveté. Although the effects are often the same. *(He crosses left.)*

CLARISSE: Oh! Name one example! Name one time when I've done something improper!

VENTROUX: Oh, we don't have far to look. No later than yesterday, as a matter of fact—when Deschanel came to see me.

CLARISSE: What about it?

VENTROUX: Not five minutes after I introduced you, you could think of nothing better to say than "My, what an odd fabric your trousers are made of! What *is* that material?" Whereupon you take to pawing his thighs! *(He joins the gesture to the word.)*

CLARISSE: Oh, his thighs, his thighs! I was just curious about the fabric.

VENTROUX: Yes, but his thighs happened to be underneath! Do you consider that a proper way to behave?

CLARISSE: Well, what did you expect me to do? I couldn't very well ask him to take his trousers off—a man I'd only just met!

VENTROUX: *(Opening his arms wide)* There! There we have it! But you might have dispensed with fingering the man's fabric! It strikes me that Deschanel has had enough of a political career that you could find some topic of conversation other than his trousers! ... accompanied by illustrative gestures.

CLARISSE: *(Crossing far left)* Oh, you see smut wherever you look.

VENTROUX: *(Shrugging)* Oh yes, of course, I see smut wherever I look.

CLARISSE: *(Abruptly turning around and going to sit left of the table, facing VENTROUX)* No, you ought to be a theatre critic, you're so hard on other people! You go on about my behavior! Well, what about yours? The other day...at the picnic? With Mademoiselle Dieumamour?

VENTROUX: What? What about Mademoiselle Dieumamour?

CLARISSE: When you sucked the back of her neck? You think *that's* decent?

VENTROUX: When I... *(Holding his forehead with both hands.)* Oh no! When women start rewriting the past...! *(He sits right of the table.)*

CLARISSE: Well? *Didn't* you suck the back of her neck?

VENTROUX: *(Forcefully)* Yes, I sucked the back of her neck! Of course I sucked the back of her neck! I sucked the back of her neck and I'm proud of it! It's all to my credit!

CLARISSE: Oh, you think so?

VENTROUX: You can't imagine that I was inspired by an attraction to her forty springtimes and her pock-marked nose?

CLARISSE: You never can tell, with men! They're so depraved!

VENTROUX: Oh, yes, of course. In point of fact Mademoiselle Dieumamour had been stung by a venomous horse-fly: the bite looked poisonous! It was already swollen. I couldn't let her die of a carbuncle merely to keep up appearances!

CLARISSE: *(Shrugging)* A carbuncle! How did you know the fly was carbuncular?

VENTROUX: *(Mordantly)* I knew *nothing* about it. But so long as there was the mere possibility, I could not hesitate. A fly bite can be deadly if it is not cauterized, or if the wound is not sucked out immediately. There was no means of cauterizing it; therefore I did my duty. I did only what simple Christian charity required... *(Big gesture)* I sucked!

CLARISSE: Oh yes, that's convenient! With that trick you can go around sucking the necks of all the women you like, on the grounds that maybe they've been stung by a carbuncular horsefly!

VENTROUX: Listen to that! What are you trying to prove? You think I did it for my own enjoyment, ha?

CLARISSE: *(Without conviction)* No, no...

VENTROUX: For two hours afterward I couldn't get the taste of old candle-wax and rancid make-up out of my mouth! If you don't think that deserves some credit!

CLARISSE: Oh yes, of course, yes! Anything other people do is scandalous, but you! Always wonderful! *(She rises.)*

VENTROUX: I did not say that!

CLARISSE: *(Above the table as she leans towards her seated husband)* All the same, well, if I'd sucked Monsieur Deschanel's neck…! Oooh my goodness! Wouldn't I have been raked over the coals? *(She moves down left.)*

VENTROUX: Well, naturally!

CLARISSE: There! You see? What did I tell you? *(She plants herself in front of him.)* And you call that fair?

VENTROUX: *(With an indulgent laugh, taking her hand and wagging his head)* Oh dear, oh dear, you have a disarming way of arguing!

CLARISSE: Really? Is that so?

VENTROUX: *(Drawing her close and loudly stressing his words)* Yes, to be sure you have: yes! You're right, you're always right. That's the last time I suck the back of Mademoiselle Dieumamour's neck!

CLARISSE: *(Quickly)* Oh, I don't mean that! If she gets stung again, poor thing, it's your duty as a gentleman!…

VENTROUX: So! Well, you see now? You agree with me.

CLARISSE: *(Up against him and speaking in a weepy tone)* But, it's only that you annoy me too sometimes! You do say hurtful things to me; and then I can't help it, I get cross.

VENTROUX: I say hurtful things to you!

CLARISSE: Yes, you do. You said I walk around stark naked and that I sucked Monsieur Deschanel's neck.

VENTROUX: I never said that!

CLARISSE: No, I mean you said I pinched Monsieur Deschanel's thighs.

VENTROUX: Well, dammit! when you do things I don't approve of, I have a right to point it out to you!

CLARISSE: (Sitting on his lap) I'm not denying that, but you could do it nicely! You know that when you talk to me gently, you can do whatever you please with me.

VENTROUX: So be it! nicely, then! I beg you pretty please not to walk around all the time in your nightie the way you do.

CLARISSE: Oh, yes, yes! Talk to me that way!

VENTROUX: All right! That's the way I like to hear *you* talk!

CLARISSE: (Her head on his shoulder) See how good I am when you're nice.

(At this moment, VICTOR walks straight in the room from the back.)

Scene Three

(The same, VICTOR)

(VICTOR, seeing CLARISSE in her nightie sitting on VENTROUX's lap and quickly wheeling around:)

VICTOR: Oh!

CLARISSE: (Turning and seeing VICTOR) Oh! (In one jump she gets to the window, almost knocking Victor over on the way because, his back turned, he blocks her way.)

VENTROUX: (Still seated but half rising on the palms of his hands): Eh? Ha? Who's that?

VICTOR: *(Without turning around)* Me, monsieur.

CLARISSE: *(In the window embrasure, pulling the bottom of the curtain around herself without unfastening the curtain-loop)* Don't look! Don't look!

VICTOR: *(In a bored voice, like a man who's seen plenty of women)* Oh!...

VENTROUX: *(Crossing the stage in a fury)* Ah! "Don't look! Don't look!" It's about time!

CLARISSE: *(Trying to calm him down)* I'm behind the curtain.

VENTROUX: *(In front of the sofa)* What's the good of that, eh? He's seen you in your nightie already, this fellow.

VICTOR: *(Far left, same bored tone)* Oh...it's not the first time in this house...

VENTROUX: *(Crossing far down right)* There you have it! You hear? It's obvious! It's not the first time he's seen you in your nightie! Oh, that's lovely!

CLARISSE: I swear to you, dear...

VENTROUX: Oh, leave me alone! Even when you know how I hate it!...

VICTOR: *(Meaning well)* Don't you get bent outta shape, monsieur! I got my own squeeze, you know...

VENTROUX: *(Lunging at him)* What's that? Aha! Is that right? You have your own squeeze! Do you imagine that Madame...

VICTOR: *(Protesting)* Monsieur! Eh!

VENTROUX: Well? Ha? What? What is it? What do you want in here?

VICTOR: I only came in to tell you there was a man here this morning. He left this card.

VENTROUX: *(Snatching the card with a curt gesture)* Who was it? *(Crossing left, fuming.)* Sticking your nose into everything! *(Reading the card.)* Oh no! It can't be...? Him? *He* came *here*? Him?...

VICTOR: Him, sure.

VENTROUX: Ha? What did you say? "Him"? What him?

VICTOR: *(Unconcerned)* That "him." That man. Said he'd come back at half past four.

VENTROUX: *(Shaking his head with an inner smile which lights up his face.)* Well! that fellow...!

(VENTROUX, turning around and noticing VICTOR right beside him, also shaking his head with an approving smile:)

VENTROUX: Will you get the hell out of here?

VICTOR: Yes, Monsieur. *(He exits.)*

Scene Four

(CLARISSE, VENTROUX)

CLARISSE: *(Coming out from behind the curtains and heaving a sigh of relief)* Ah! ...Oof!

VENTROUX: *(Crossing down to the easy-chair right)* Oh yes! You may well say "oof!"... I'm rather glad this happened, in fact!

CLARISSE: *(Who has moved along the sofa to cross down center)* You are? Oh! Well, that's all right then! I was afraid you'd be annoyed.

VENTROUX: *(Startled by this interpretation)* What? *(Angry)* Certainly I'm annoyed! It's infuriating!

CLARISSE: *(Moving towards her husband)* Well then, why did you say you were rather glad of it?

VENTROUX: I am rather glad this happened because it may serve as a lesson to you for the future. *(He sits down in a temper in the easy-chair near the fireplace.)*

CLARISSE: *(In front of the fireplace)* Ah, I didn't understand. I thought you meant something nice.

VENTROUX: Oh did you! A word of encouragement, perhaps?

CLARISSE: Well, what's so awful? It's just a little accident. *(Leaning towards her husband)* Whose card did he bring you?

VENTROUX: *(Grumbling)* "A little accident," really! That's all it meant to her!

CLARISSE: Well, do you want me to tear out my hair? *(No transition)* Who came to call?

VENTROUX: *(Enraged)* Who? What? What call?

CLARISSE: The man who left his card.

VENTROUX: *(Rising, in a temper)* What's that to do with you? *(He reaches center stage.)*

CLARISSE: *(Annoyed)* Oh! I beg your pardon. *(She sits in the seat he left vacant.)*

VENTROUX: *(Coming back to her)* All right then, if you must know, it was a gentleman in whose presence it will be *most* unfortunate if you display yourself half naked in the same room with your servants! ...Because if you did, my stock would drop with the voters!... *(So saying, he sits on the sofa.)*

CLARISSE: Why?

VENTROUX: Because if I lay myself open to his malicious gossip—*that* fellow's especially— Ugh!— *(Changing the tone)* it's the man who organized the most virulent campaign against me when I was up for election.

CLARISSE: Not Monsieur Hochepaix?

VENTROUX: The mayor of Mousillon-les-Indrets himself!

CLARISSE: What! That man who did everything he could to get your opponent elected—that Marquis de Berneville!

VENTROUX: The Consolidated Socialist! Exactly!

CLARISSE: *(Rising and crossing left)* Well! He's got a nerve! *(Leaning back against the front of the table)* The man who said you were a ping-pong?

VENTROUX: *(Looks at her in astonishment; gets up and crosses to her, then says, quizzically)* What did you say?

CLARISSE: *(Perfectly naturally)* A ping-pong!

VENTROUX: *(Laughing)* Ping-pong…! *(Correcting her)* He called me a "pinko ponce," not a ping-pong!

CLARISSE: *(As before)* Nobody said ping-pong?

VENTROUX: *(Tit for tat)* Nobody said ping-pong.

CLARISSE: Oh! I always thought it was ping-pong!

VENTROUX: *(In the same tone)* Well, you've always thought wrong.

CLARISSE: So *that's* why I didn't understand what it meant…

VENTROUX: *(Sarcastically)* Obviously that's why.

CLARISSE: Anyway, it doesn't matter! Ping pong or pinko ponce, I hope you're going to throw that gentleman out the door, with all the courtesy he's got coming to him!

VENTROUX: On the contrary, I shall be as pleasant as possible! And *please*, if *you* see him, pretend to be exceptionally polite as well.

CLARISSE: *(Surprised)* Oh!

VENTROUX: Hochepaix in my house! It's my revenge. Afterwards he can go back to being the lousiest bastard on earth…

CLARISSE: Yes he is! A bastard!

VENTROUX: But just now we must think of him as a great industrialist: that in his mills he employs five or six hundred laborers—that's how many votes he controls. It's wise to consider your constituents. You've got to be practical in this life. *(Pulling out his watch)* Meanwhile, it's nearly half past four. He won't be late. Go on, get dressed. *(He moves downstage.)*

CLARISSE: Yes, yes, I must. *(Changing her mind and crossing above the sofa)* Ah! *(She pushes the electric bell.)*

VENTROUX: *(At left)* What are you doing?

CLARISSE: Ringing for Victor.

VENTROUX: *(Sarcastically)* Don't you think he's seen enough of you?

CLARISSE: *(Slapping the air gently as if to send him a pat)* Naughty! ...It's so he'll take away your tray. *(Coming around the sofa, as she speaks, and walking in front of the coffee table)* I've told him dozens of times to clear away the cups when you've had your coffee. It's messy to see left-over cups; besides, they attract flies! and wasps! ... look! Look at that, will you? *(She lifts the front of her slip to make a kind of fly-whisk which she flaps over the coffee table.)* Shoo! Get away! Shoo, flies! Begone, wasps! Good-night, ladies! ...(To VENTROUX) I can't bear untidiness; I like my house to be neat; I do like good manners!

VENTROUX: *(Pointing at her outfit)* She likes good manners!

CLARISSE: So, now that I don't want Victor to see me in my nightie...

VENTROUX: *(Mocking)* No, really?

CLARISSE: *(Same gesture as before, sends him a pat with her hand)* Don't be a tease! *(Above the sofa, leaning on the bell button.)* When he comes, tell him to take all that away, hm?

VENTROUX: Well, don't knock yourself out: that bell doesn't work. Something must have gone wrong with the battery.

CLARISSE: Oh! It's probably dry! It's thirsty: you just have to put some water in it.

VENTROUX: Maybe so, I don't understand the thing. *(He crosses upstage.)*

CLARISSE: I'll go give it a drink.

VENTROUX: *(Accompanying her)* All right, do. Do.

CLARISSE: Yes. *(Exits through the door up right.)*

VENTROUX: *(Just as he is closing the door after her, reopens it to call out)* And put on your dressing-gown!

CLARISSE: *(Off. In her room)* Of course. You know, when you ask me nicely, you know I love to… *(Her voice fades in the distance.)*

Scene Five

(VENTROUX, then VICTOR, then HOCHEPAIX)

VENTROUX: *(Closing the door after her, he stands a moment, rolls his eyes upwards with an eloquent hand gesture and a meaningful shake of the head; puts his hand to his brow for a second; then crosses to the window whose blinds are still up. At this moment his gaze lands on a point unseen by the audience. He goes: "Ah!"and then waves.)* Good afternoon, good afternoon!… *(To the audience, with a bitter sneer)* Clemenceau! *(Furious, he closes the blinds.)* He's got nothing better to do, that man! *(Just then the front doorbell rings.)* Ah!—Now the other one! *(He crosses the stage, moves up left of the table and assumes a dignified pose.)*

VICTOR: *(Announces)* Monsieur Hochepaix!

*(*HOCHEPAIX *enters, stops on the threshold, somewhat hesitantly.)*

VENTROUX: *(Without even turning his head, indifferently)* Come in!

HOCHEPAIX: *(Stepping in)* Excuse me!

VENTROUX: *(In the same tone, to* VICTOR*)* Leave us.

*(*VICTOR*, with an astonished glance at his employer, exits.* VENTROUX *speaks in a cold, haughty voice to* HOCHEPAIX*.)*

VENTROUX: Please take a seat!

HOCHEPAIX: *(Right of the table)* My dear sir...!

VENTROUX: *(Stopping him with a gesture)* Oh! ...Your "dear" sir?

HOCHEPAIX: *(About to sit but straightening up again)* Why not?

VENTROUX: *(Tight-lipped)* After the campaign you waged against my candidacy!...

HOCHEPAIX: Oh! Oh! "The campaign!"

VENTROUX: You called me every name you could think of! Bribe-taker! Rotten egg! Stool pigeon! Putrid left-overs!

HOCHEPAIX: *(Quickly, opening his arms as if to embrace* VENTROUX*)* None of that lessens my esteem in the least, believe me!

VENTROUX: *(Sarcastically)* Oh! much appreciated!

(Seeing HOCHEPAIX *about to sit down,* VENTROUX *makes a move to do so as well, but straightens up immediately when he sees* HOCHEPAIX *stop halfway.)*

HOCHEPAIX: What did you expect? I admit it: you were not my candidate. *(About to sit)*

VENTROUX: I am well aware of that. *(He makes as if to sit, but once more straightens up when he see* HOCHEPAIX *is not sitting.)*

HOCHEPAIX: Yes1 my man was the Marquis de Berneville.

VENTROUX: *(With a pinched laugh)* That is your privilege.

HOCHEPAIX: You understand how it is: he's an old friend! and then he's a Consolidated Socialist, same as me! What's more, he held my daughter at the baptismal font.

VENTROUX: You don't say so.

HOCHEPAIX: Anyway, plenty of reasons!

*(*HOCHEPAIX *is about to sit, stands again; same business with* VENTROUX.)*

HOCHEPAIX: Not counting this one: he's a millionaire a dozen times over, and in the interests of my constituents...! Surely you understand that, don't you?

VENTROUX: Please: do me a favor, no need for excuses.

HOCHEPAIX: Especially since it was you who got elected, eh?

VENTROUX: For me, that is the most important thing.

HOCHEPAIX: Quite right!

(Same business for both HOCHEPAIX *and* VENTROUX; *about to sit and straightening up immediately.)*

HOCHEPAIX: Besides, that's all in the past! Now we are no longer candidate and voter, but the Mayor of Mousillon-les-Indrets paying a friendly call on his representative in the Chamber of Deputies, to submit a request on the part of my constituents and beg you to take the matter up with the appropriate minister. Not for one instant had I the slightest doubt of your kind reception.

VENTROUX: And you were right! *(Facing him, back to the audience.)* As a matter of fact I was just saying to my wife…

HOCHEPAIX: Oh, excuse me! I neglected to inquire after the lady. Shall I have the pleasure of an introduction?

VENTROUX: *(Turning aside, to move downstage)* Oh! Unfortunately she is just getting dressed, and you know what women are like when they're dressing! It goes on forever!

HOCHEPAIX: *(Crossing left)* Ah, what a pity!

CLARISSE: *(Offstage)* So you think you've cleared away the cups! Do you indeed! You think you took them away?

VENTROUX: *(Moving upstage when he hears CLARISSE's voice, and speaking over her)* Oh! Well, well, imagine! I've underestimated her! That's her voice! *(Coming back downstage.)* Ready so soon! It's a miracle!

HOCHEPAIX: Ah! good, I shall be delighted…!

Scene Six

(The same, CLARISSE, VICTOR)

(CLARISSE, dressed exactly as before, surges in from the hallway, followed by VICTOR; she goes straight to the coffee table:)

CLARISSE: Really? Well, come in here and just see whether you cleared the cups away!

VENTROUX: *(Turning to her as he speaks)* My dear, I… *(Seeing her half-dressed as before.)* Ah…!

CLARISSE: *(Startled by VENTROUX's voice and instinctively pivoting to escape, she bumps into the sofa and lands kneeling on it)* Ah! …Oh! You scared me.

VENTROUX: *(Flinging himself at her and stifling his displeasure)* Good grief! Will you get out? Will you get out?

CLARISSE: *(Getting to her feet, surprised)* What's the matter?

VENTROUX: Are you quite mad? Coming in here in your nightie when I have visitors?

CLARISSE: *(To* HOCHEPAIX, *over* VENTROUX's *shoulder)* Oh! I beg your pardon, monsieur! I didn't hear you ring!

HOCHEPAIX: *(Gallantly)* Madame, I'm not complaining!

VENTROUX: *(Stepping back to allow fuller rein to his outraged gesticulations)* You have no shame! Showing yourself like this, with a servant at your heels!

CLARISSE: *(Aside to* VENTROUX *in a quite natural voice)* No, it's because Victor didn't clear away these cups. *(To* VICTOR*)* Just look, my good man, see how you've cleared away the coffee things.

VENTROUX: *(Totally unhinged)* To hell with the coffee cups! *(To* VICTOR*)* Will you kindly get the hell out, you? *(Pushes Victor out.)*

VICTOR: Very good, monsieur!

*(*CLARISSE, *coming down to* HOCHEPAIX, *while* VENTROUX *is busy with* VICTOR:*)*

CLARISSE: I don't know if you're like me, monsieur? But whenever I see a dirty cup...

VENTROUX: *(Leaping at her and pushing her upstage)* Yes yes yes, fine fine fine! Out! Scoot! Scram! Get out!

CLARISSE: *(Sort of rolled up in* VENTROUX's *arms as he tries to push her upstage. Pulling loose)* Now look here, if you wouldn't mind, don't bark at me like that! I'm not a dog.

VENTROUX: *(Moving upstage, tearing his hair, back to the audience)* Ah!

CLARISSE: I mean it!

(CLARISSE, suddenly smiling and friendly, she goes to HOCHEPAIX, as VENTROUX closes the door at back:)

CLARISSE: Monsieur Hochepaix I presume?

HOCHEPAIX: *(Left of the table)* Yes, madame, yes...

VENTROUX: *(Turning, bewildered by his wife's shameless behavior)* What?

CLARISSE: *(Quite the hostess)* Delighted, Monsieur Hochepaix! Do please sit down, won't you?

(CLARISSE sits right of the table, while HOCHEPAIX sits on the left facing her.)

VENTROUX: *(Running to her)* Ah, no, no! You can't have the nerve to receive guests in that get-up?

CLARISSE: *(Not disconcerted in the least, rising)* Oh, well perhaps! It *is* a little unseemly!

VENTROUX: *(Shrugging)* Unseemly!

CLARISSE: But really, the weather is so warm!

(CLARISSE puts both her hands on top of HOCHEPAIX's hands which are resting on the table.)

CLARISSE: Here, feel my hands—do you think I'm feverish?

VENTROUX: *(Arms outspread)* There you go! There we have it! Just the way you behaved with Deschanel!

CLARISSE: *(Her hands still on HOCHEPAIX's, her breasts drooping over the table)* What you mean? Only his hands! I'm not touching his thighs!

HOCHEPAIX: How's that?

CLARISSE: Just to show how hot mine are.

HOCHEPAIX: *(Stupefied, misunderstanding)* Your th...?

CLARISSE: (*Instantly catching* HOCHEPAIX's *mistake and quickly correcting him*) My hands! My hands!

HOCHEPAIX: Oh!

VENTROUX: (*Seizing his wife's arm and propelling her upstage*) Yes, well, as if he cared! Monsieur Hochepaix doesn't give a hoot for your hands!

HOCHEPAIX: (*Quickly and very gallant*) Oh I do, I do!

CLARISSE: (*Rubbing her arm which is bruised by her husband's rough treatment*) Look! You see!

VENTROUX: (*Exploding, stalking towards her to force her farther upstage*) Yes, well, that'll do! Please just *get out!*

CLARISSE: (*Retreating upstage*) All right, all right! But why bother to tell me to be nice to him, then?

VENTROUX: (*Coming back downstage*) Huh? Who told you to be nice?

CLARISSE: What do you mean "who"? You! You did! You told me if I see Monsieur Hochepaix…

VENTROUX: (*Anticipating the blunder, in one giant bound reaches his wife and speaks intensely, in an undertone*) Yes, all right! That'll do!

CLARISSE: (*Relentlessly*) Pooh on your "All right, that'll do!" (*Carrying on*) You said "Please pretend to be particularly polite!…"

VENTROUX: (*Turns in protest to* HOCHEPAIX) Me? Me? Never in the world! Never, never, never!

CLARISSE: (*Does the same*) Oh, you're the limit! You told me to be nice to him, even if he *was* the lousiest bastard on earth!

VENTROUX: (*Wincing if he had been kicked in a sensitive spot*) Oh…

HOCHEPAIX: (*Tilting his head with a malicious smile*) Ah?

CLARISSE: *(Unrelenting)* "Even if he is a fat capitalist and employs five or six hundred workers," you said, 'it's smart to hold on to your voters!"

VENTROUX: *(Talking over her, in an effort to drown out her voice)* No no no! Never in this world! I never in my life said any such thing! Monsieur Hochepaix! you don't believe any of this, I trust...?

HOCHEPAIX: *(Indulgently)* Oh, well...even if you did!...

VENTROUX: No, no!

CLARISSE: *(Over her husband's shoulder)* Monsieur Hochepaix! I hope you have the decency to believe me!

VENTROUX: *(At the peak of exasperation, wheeling around to his wife)* Ah, you, you! You're driving me crazy! *(He points to the door.)* Leave! Get out! Get the hell out!

CLARISSE: *(On her way upstage)* Well, really! You could put it more nicely!

VENTROUX: *(Forestalling any reply)* Out! Out! Leave the room!

CLARISSE: *(Obeying but wanting to have the last word)* All right, but when you say you didn't say...

VENTROUX: *(As before)* Go on! Step on it! Scram!

CLARISSE: Don't yell at me to go away, scram! You can't even remember what you said!

VENTROUX: *(Shoving her out)* Once and for all, will you kindly go away?

CLARISSE: *(Alarmed, escaping)* Oh!

VENTROUX: *(Slamming the door and coming back downstage exasperated)* Oh!

(VENTROUX has barely come downstage when the door opens again.)

CLARISSE: *(Coming down behind* VENTROUX*'s back)* I didn't say goodbye to you, Monsieur Hochepaix! Pleased to meet you!…

HOCHEPAIX: *(Bowing)* Madame!

VENTROUX: *(Spinning around at the sound of her voice, and rushing at her as if he were going to kick her in a part of her anatomy)* Oh, for the pity's sake, will you!…

CLARISSE: *(Scampering off, scared)* Oh! …I'm just saying good-bye is all!

VENTROUX: *(Stands for a moment as if his feelings were numb, holds his head as if it were coming off, then crosses down to* HOCHEPAIX*)* I am shocked, monsieur! I am shocked!

HOCHEPAIX: *(Casually)* Oh, please!…

VENTROUX: Monsieur Hochepaix, don't give a second thought to any of it. It's a joke! "The lousiest bastard on earth!" You mustn't imagine that I ever said such a thing…!

HOCHEPAIX: Oh, don't mention it! After all, I called you a bribe-taker, a rotten egg, putrid left-overs!

VENTROUX: Yes, I know! I'd have the right! but all the same… As for my wife, I ask you to excuse her; really, the way she turned up!…

HOCHEPAIX: *(Very courtly)* But…much to her advantage!

VENTROUX: You're too kind! Nevertheless, please believe me, she does not ordinarily go around in that state; but, honestly, today, it's so warm, don't you find? It was perhaps forgivable! You did feel her hands, you could tell!…

HOCHEPAIX: Yes, of course.

VENTROUX: I too in fact! Feel mine. *(Squeezing* HOCHEPAIX's *hand between both of his own.)* My palms are all sweaty!

HOCHEPAIX: *(Pulling his hand away and wiping it on his coat)* Ah! Yes! ...Yes!

VENTROUX: It's quite unpleasant!...

HOCHEPAIX: *(Wiping his hands, emphatically)* Yes indeed! *Most* unpleasant!

VENTROUX: So naturally, my wife...feeling a bit overheated, she, ah...she felt the need of of putting on her...her...how shall I put it? ...Goodness me, there's no other word: ...her nightie.

HOCHEPAIX: Ah, how well I understand!

VENTROUX: Of course you do! *(Crossing up stage)* Of course you do!

HOCHEPAIX: If only I could do the same!

VENTROUX: *(Turning around and without thinking)* Do, do! Go right ahead, please!

HOCHEPAIX: Huh? Oh, no! No! No, really!...

VENTROUX: *(Crossing back down)* No! no! of course not! ...Well then, eh? Since she didn't hear you ring, naturally...she walked right in.

HOCHEPAIX: But of course!

VENTROUX: She thought she was alone.

HOCHEPAIX: *(Slyly, as if it were the most natural thing in the world)* Obviously! ...With the servant.

VENTROUX: *(Repeating the phrase without thinking)* With the serv... *(Realizing the implications)* Oh! yes, the... the servant... *(Trying to act unconcerned)* Ah, but that servant, that one, you understand, there... there... there was a reason.

HOCHEPAIX: No doubt!

VENTROUX: If it had been just any servant, why, clearly!…

HOCHEPAIX: Obviously, if it had been just any servant!…

VENTROUX: But! …They were brought up together.

HOCHEPAIX: You don't say so.

VENTROUX: *(Coolly)* He's…he's her foster brother. Son of her wet nurse. Suckled at the same breast. Her foster brother.

HOCHEPAIX: *(Agreeing)* Her foster brother.

VENTROUX: So, after all, a foster brother…!

HOCHEPAIX: *(Crossing up left of the table)* That hardly counts, does it?

VENTROUX: Just what I say: it doesn't count! …It doesn't… *(Eager to change the subject)* Well now, let's see, what difference does it make? Of course, all this is… nonsense! What is it you want me to do for your constituents? *(Sits right of table)*

HOCHEPAIX: *(Sitting across from him)* It's very simple! It has to do with the Paris express, eh? It stops at Morinville and then speeds past Mousillon-les-Indrets…which is an urban center at least of equal importance.

VENTROUX: *(Nodding)* Certainly! No question!

HOCHEPAIX: Well, there it is: my people have made up their minds to have the express stop at our station.

VENTROUX: *(Shaking his head)* Ah! Blast! That's difficult!

HOCHEPAIX: *(Unabashed)* Don't say that! We've twice had occasion to see that it can be done.

VENTROUX: The express has already stopped there?

HOCHEPAIX: Twice! …Once when there was a derailment, and another time when it was sabotaged.

VENTROUX: Ah?

HOCHEPAIX: Well, it didn't upset the service very much.

VENTROUX: Obviously... that is a point.

HOCHEPAIX: Only, eh? Events of that sort don't happen often enough for our commuters to count on.

VENTROUX: No! ...You would prefer a scheduled stop. Look here! I shall be delighted to look into this! If you will just draw up a brief outline of the whole matter! And in the meantime as a reminder, I'll make a note or two... *(Writes in the note pad)* Let's put down: Monsieur O-Sh-Pain!

HOCHEPAIX: *(Rises and watches* VENTROUX *write)* Just so! that's it! *(Suddenly, vigorously)* Ah, no! No! ...Pay. Not Pain. *(Spelling it out.)* P-A-I-X!

VENTROUX: *(Embarrassed)* Oh, I beg your pardon! *(Makes a correction)* Pay, not Pain! P-A-I-X! Believe me, quite an unintentional error!

HOCHEPAIX: *(Amiably)* No harm done! I'm used to it! Yours is the first spelling that comes to mind.

VENTROUX: *(Jokingly)* And the most natural!

HOCHEPAIX: *(Laughing)* Yes, yes!

(At this moment voices and the clatter of some objects behind the hall door are audible. There is a muffled exchange of dialogue offstage between CLARISSE *and* VICTOR.)

CLARISSE: There! There! Hand me that thermos!

VICTOR: Here it is, Madame.

CLARISSE: Oh! But hold me! don't let go! No foolishness now!

VICTOR: I'm holding on, Madame, I've got a good grip!

VENTROUX: *(Hearkening to this and speaking over it)* Oh good grief, what is all that racket? Can't we have a moment's peace?

(VENTROUX goes briskly to fling the double doors wide open. [A second before, the actor playing VICTOR, offstage, should draw the bolt that keeps the right door-panel stationary, so that the doors can open fully.])

VENTROUX: Well, what is it now?

(VENTROUX sees CLARISSE perched on top of a ladder, the top half of her body disappearing behind the door's archway, while VICTOR, his body leaning in, his legs straddling the lower steps of the ladder, holds her with both hands planted firmly on her rump. VENTROUX lets out a yell and springs back to right of the door.)

VENTROUX: Ah!

CLARISSE: *(At the sound of her husband's voice, bending down so that her head becomes visible; she is holding a thermos and speaks perfectly calmly to VENTROUX)* Oh! It's you!

VENTROUX: *(Almost strangled with outrage)* Aha! What in the world are you doing there?

CLARISSE: *(As before)* Well, you can see: I'm fixing the battery.

VENTROUX: *(Foaming at the mouth)* Are you trying to make a fool of me, you two? What way is that to hold the lady?

VICTOR: So's she don't fall.

VENTROUX: What?

CLARISSE: Yes, because if somebody doesn't hold on to me, I get dizzy.

VENTROUX: *(Rushing at VICTOR)* But, good lord, don't you realize you've got both your hands on her... on her... It's indecent!

that improper? Can you see any more than if I were wearing a ball gown?

HOCHEPAIX: *(Amiably)* Not at all, Madame.

VENTROUX: *(Sitting down in utter despair on the chair left of the door at back)* Ah, that's what you think, is it?

HOCHEPAIX: Why, as a matter of fact, just like that, in your nightie, with your hat on your head, you almost look as if you were paying a call.

CLARISSE: There! You hear? That's right! *(She pirouettes so she can be seen from every angle.)* What can you see? I ask you? What can you see?

HOCHEPAIX: Oh! nothing!—Ah, just there, actually, I can see you… in silhouette, just there in front of the window!

VENTROUX: *(Jumping at his wife and drawing her away from the window)* Oh!

CLARISSE: Ah, because there's a window! *(To VENTROUX)* You're awfully rough, you are. *(To HOCHEPAIX)* But if it weren't for that…!

HOCHEPAIX: Oh! without the window, nothing at all!

CLARISSE: *(Sitting on the sofa)* But you know, I don't mind! *(Giving a loud yelp and bounding to her feet)* Ouch!

HOCHEPAIX: What is it?

VENTROUX: Wha… what's the matter now?

CLARISSE: *(In pain)* I don't know! I felt something like a knife stabbing me!…

VENTROUX: A knife stabbing you?

CLARISSE: It went straight to my heart! *(As she says this she turns round, revealing a squashed wasp on the right side of her nightie, on a level with her buttocks.)*

VENTROUX: Ah, there it is. "Straight to your heart!" That's what you call your heart? *(Picks up the squashed insect by its wings and shows it to her.)* See, here's your knife stab. A wasp stung you. *(Throws it on the floor and steps on it)*

CLARISSE: *(Gasping and howling)* It stung me! Oh, my goodness! I've been stung by a wasp!

HOCHEPAIX: Poor lady!

VENTROUX: *(Vindictively delighted)* Splendid! That'll teach you to walk around in the nude! *(He crosses down left.)*

CLARISSE: *(Crossing to the coffee table)* There! It's all your fault! What did I tell you, when you leave dirty cups around…!

VENTROUX: *(As before)* Well, good! Maybe it will teach you a lesson!

CLARISSE: *(Indignant)* "Good!" He's pleased! He's delighted! *(Panicked)* For heaven's sake, a wasp! I hope it's not carbuncular!

(VENTROUX, *going to sit on the chair right of the table, while* HOCHEPAIX, *to keep out of the way, wanders upstage, pretending to study the paintings:)*

VENTROUX: No, no! certainly not!

CLARISSE: *(Crossing to him)* Oh, Julien, Julien! *(She turns around to present her backside to him and begins to lift up her nightie.)* Suck me, do, please! Suck me!

VENTROUX: Me? *(Pushing her away, rising and crossing down left.)* It's nothing to do with me.

CLARISSE: Oh! Julien! Julien! Be nice! *(At it again)* Suck me, pretty please! Suck me!

VENTROUX: *(Pushing her away again and rising to cross down left)* Oh, leave me the hell alone, will you!

CLARISSE: Oh, suck it out, please! After all! You did it for Mademoiselle Dieumamour!

VENTROUX: *(Coming back to* CLARISSE*)* In the first place Mademoiselle Dieumamour was stung in the neck, not in the... And besides, hers was a horse-fly! Not a wasp! *(He crosses up to the back.)*

CLARISSE: *(In a voice choked with emotion)* But a wasp is just as dangerous! Only two days ago, in the paper, you read that there was a man who died of a wasp sting!

VENTROUX: That has nothing to do with this! He was drinking! He choked to death.

CLARISSE: *(Beside the fireplace armchair)* Maybe I'll choke... Oh, I'm choking! I'm choking!

VENTROUX: *(Not much alarmed, sitting on the sofa)* No, no! you're not! What an idea!

CLARISSE: Yes! Yes! *(Falls into the easy chair but leaps up again with a yelp of pain)* Ouch! *(Going to her husband)* Oh! ...For pity's sake, Julien! *(Turning around as before to present her backside to him.)* Suck me, please! suck me!

VENTROUX: *(Pushing her away again)* No, I tell you! No! You're a pest!

CLARISSE: *(Panicky)* Oh, you have no heart! You're heartless! *(Not knowing where to turn.)* Oh! my goodness!

(Then CLARISSE *sees* HOCHEPAIX *wandering along the far left wall, still deep in his perusal of the curios.)*

CLARISSE: Ah! *(Crossing down to him.)* Monsieur Hochepaix!...

HOCHEPAIX: *(Turning to her)* Madame?...

CLARISSE: *(Turning round to present her backside to him)* Please, Monsieur Hochepaix! Please!

HOCHEPAIX: Me!

VENTROUX: *(Leaping at her and leading her away by the wrist)* Ye gods, are you crazy! You're going to ask Monsieur Hochepaix now?

CLARISSE: Well, what else can I do? I'd rather do that than take a chance of dying!

HOCHEPAIX: Of course, madame, you do me too much honor, but really!...

CLARISSE: *(Coming back to* HOCHEPAIX*)* Monsieur Hochepaix, in the name of Christian charity.

VENTROUX: *(Grabbing her by the arm and turning her around)* No! Now will you stop!

CLARISSE: *(Finding herself positioned so as to present the sting to* HOCHEPAIX*)* Please? ...Please?

HOCHEPAIX: I assure you, madame, really! between friends!

VENTROUX: *(Exploding, dragging her center stage)* Oh, leave us the hell alone, with your "Please, please!" Go do it yourself! *(Lets go of her and moves right.)*

CLARISSE: *(In a tearful voice)* But how can I!

VENTROUX: *(Coming back to her)* Well then! Go put a compress on it! and don't give us a hard time! "Please, please!"

CLARISSE: *(Clenching her fists in his face)* Oh, *you* go, *you* get out! I never want to see you again! And if I die it'll be all your fault!

VENTROUX: *(Sitting in the easy chair at the right)* All right, so be it! Right. I'm all for it!

CLARISSE: *(As she exits center)* That's men for you! That's the male sex! *(Exits rapidly through the door at back, calling:)* Victor! Victor! *(She shuts the door behind her.)*

Scene Seven

(VENTROUX, HOCHEPAIX)

VENTROUX: *(Slumped in his chair)* Oof! She ought to be tied up, honest to goodness! She needs a straitjacket!

HOCHEPAIX: *(Standing by the table left, after a moment's hesitation)* Monsieur Ventroux!

VENTROUX: What?

HOCHEPAIX: You will forgive me, will you not, for not thinking it my duty to...

VENTROUX: *(Can't believe his ears)* What?

HOCHEPAIX: But really, we are not sufficiently intimate as of yet...

VENTROUX: Indeed! As you say!

HOCHEPAIX: Quite so. That's what I thought.

VENTROUX: That's all I need!...

CLARISSE: *(Offstage)* All right then, I'll just tell your master! I will just tell your master!

VENTROUX: Good grief, what's she up to now?

Scene Eight

(The same, CLARISSE, VICTOR)

(CLARISSE, bursting in with her back to the audience, to VICTOR who follows her:)

CLARISSE: You're all cowards! *(Turning to HOCHEPAIX and VENTROUX.)* You're all murderers! ...And Victor's as bad as you are!

VENTROUX: Ha? What? Now what?

CLARISSE: *(Behind the sofa)* He wouldn't suck me either.

VENTROUX: *(Leaping up)* Victor!

VICTOR: *(Sheepishly, in the doorway)* Uh, monsieur, I didn't dare.

VENTROUX: Good grief, woman, are you going to go around like that asking the whole world to suck your bite?

CLARISSE: Oh! it's throbbing! it's throbbing! It must be impacted.

VENTROUX: Well, if it's impacted, go see a dentist!

CLARISSE: But it's not in my mouth!

VENTROUX: Then go to a doctor!

CLARISSE: Oh! Yes, yes! There's a doctor in the building, upstairs!…

VENTROUX: *(Surly, sitting in the easy chair he just left)* Hmmph! He's not a doctor! He's a quarantine officer! He has no right to call himself a doctor.

CLARISSE: I don't care, he must know something about medicine. Quick, Victor, go upstairs and get him!

VICTOR: Very good, madame!

CLARISSE: *(Her hand on the afflicted spot)* Oh, I'm going to put a compress on it! I'll put on a compress. *(She goes off to her room.)*

VICTOR: *(At the door, after hesitating a moment to be sure that* CLARISSE *has departed)* Monsieur, you're not going to be sore at me because I didn't …

VENTROUX: *(Leaping up)* Eh? You too? *(Shoving him out)* Will you get out! …Go fetch that quarantine officer!

VICTOR: *(Heading for the door onto the landing, without shutting the drawing-room door)* Very good, monsieur, right away!

(Just as VICTOR *is about to open the door onto the landing, the doorbell rings and he opens the door to discover* DE JAIVAL *on the threshold waiting to be admitted.)*

Scene Nine

(The same, ROMAIN DE JAIVAL*)*

DE JAIVAL: Ah! You answer the bell promptly!

VICTOR: Monsieur?

DE JAIVAL: Monsieur Ventroux, if I may!

VENTROUX: *(From the drawing room)* In here. What can I do for you, monsieur?

DE JAIVAL: Oh! excuse me! *(He comes down into the room.)* I am Romain de Jaival, of *Le Figaro.*

VENTROUX: Of course, of course, monsieur!

*(*VENTROUX, *to* VICTOR, *who lingers on the threshold.)*

VENTROUX: Well, get along with you!

VICTOR: Very good, monsieur. *(He exits, closing the door behind him.)*

VENTROUX: How can I serve you, monsieur?

DE JAIVAL: Here's the thing: my paper sent me here to get an interview with you.

VENTROUX: Aha!

DE JAIVAL: Concerning the general political situation... Your recent speeches have put you squarely in the public eye!...

VENTROUX: *(Flattered)* Oh, my dear monsieur...

DE JAIVAL: I'm only saying what everybody is thinking!
...And especially this proposed law that you and
some others are sponsoring. Labor Pains for the
Laboring Class—free delivery for all mothers, with the
government acting as midwife.

VENTROUX: Yes, oh! that's most interesting! That's a
matter I take very much to heart.

DE JAIVAL: But personally, I would prefer to write
something diverting, something colorful, no everyday
sort of thing! I make a point of doing rather sprightly
articles; if you happen to have read anything of
mine!...

VENTROUX: Oh certainly! Of course! Monsieur de...

DE JAIVAL: Jaival! ...Romain de Jaival!

VENTROUX: De Jaival, yes of course! Well! I'm at
your disposal. But first I have one small matter to
conclude with this gentleman. *(Introducing)* Monsieur
Hochepaix.

DE JAIVAL: *(Bowing)* Hochepaix?

HOCHEPAIX: *(Quickly spelling)* P-A-I-X!

VENTROUX: Mayor of Mousillon-les-Indrets.

DE JAIVAL: Oh, to be sure! I know.

HOCHEPAIX: *(Surprised and flattered)* You know me?

DE JAIVAL: I've often fished in your waters.

HOCHEPAIX: Ah! You mean Mousillon-les-... No, I
thought you meant... Oh yes, to be sure!

VENTROUX: Well! If you'll be so good as to wait a bit,
the mayor and I will step into my study; I'll be with
you in five minutes

DE JAIVAL: Oh please! Meanwhile, if you don't mind,
I'll sit down at this table and make a note or two while
I wait.

VENTROUX: *(Very affably)* Make yourself at home.

DE JAIVAL: *(Coming down and round the table to sit on the chair left)* Excuse me!

VENTROUX: Come along, my dear Mayor! ...Of Moussillon-les-Indrets!

HOCHEPAIX: After you, my dear deputy!

(They exit right.)

Scene Ten

*(*DE JAIVAL, CLARISSE, *then* VENTROUX *and* HOCHEPAIX*)*

*(*DE JAIVAL, *settling in at the table, takes out his notebook and, glancing around the room to take in the scene, jots down a few notes.)*

CLARISSE: *(Offstage)* Isn't he here yet? *(Entering from her room and coming down stage without noticing* DE JAIVAL *at the table.)* Well, for heaven's sake, what's the man doing?

DE JAIVAL: *(Unable to suppress a gasp of surprise at seeing a woman in her nightie)* Oh!

CLARISSE: *(Turning at the sound)* Ah! Here he is! *(Going to him.)* Oh, quickly! Doctor! Quickly!

DE JAIVAL: *(Stunned by his new title)* I beg your pardon?

CLARISSE: *(Taking him by the hand and pulling him towards the window)* Quick, quick, come and look.

DE JAIVAL: *(Going along)* Come and look? At what, madame?

CLARISSE: Where I was stung.

DE JAIVAL: Where you were stung?

CLARISSE: *(Raising the blinds)* Here, we'll open the blinds so you can see it better.

DE JAIVAL: *(Not understanding her drift)* Eh? ...All right, madame...

CLARISSE: You'll see, doctor!...

DE JAIVAL: *(Stopping her)* Forgive me, madame! Sorry! but I'm not a doctor!

CLARISSE: *(Behind the sofa)* Yes, I know you haven't got an M D! It doesn't matter. Here, look! *(She pulls up her nightie.)*

DE JAIVAL: *(Facing front, turns around as ordered and jumps in astonishment)* Ah!

CLARISSE: *(Nightie still raised, body bent forward, right arm propped on the back of the sofa)* Do you see?

DE JAIVAL: *(Amazed and amused)* Oh! yes! madame! ...I see clearly! ...I do indeed!

CLARISSE: Well?

DE JAIVAL: *(Enjoying this, aside)* Quite picturesque! Very smart! What a lead for my column!

CLARISSE: *(Turning her head to look at him but not changing her position)* What?

DE JAIVAL: Do you mind if I make a few notes?

CLARISSE: No, not at all! ...Here, touch!

DE JAIVAL: You want me to...

CLARISSE: Touch it! Why don't you? See what it feels like!

DE JAIVAL: *(More and more amazed)* Ah? ...Yes, madame! Yes. *(Facing front, with his reversed left hand he feels* CLARISSE's *right side. Aside)* Quite picturesque!

CLARISSE: No, not there, monsieur! It's the other side!

DE JAIVAL: *(Moving his hand to her left side)* Oh! sorry.

CLARISSE: I've been stung by a wasp!

DE JAIVAL: There? ...Oh! ...What composure!

CLARISSE: The stinger must have stuck in there.

DE JAIVAL: Could be!

CLARISSE: So look!

DE JAIVAL: *(Adapting himself to the situation)* Oh, you want me to... Yes, madame, of course! *(He puts his monocle in his eye and crouches down.)*

CLARISSE: Can you see it?

DE JAIVAL: Wait! Yes, yes! I see it!

CLARISSE: Well? well?

DE JAIVAL: Yes, yes! It's even protruding a bit, so I think that with my fingernails...

CLARISSE: Oh! try, doctor, do try!

DE JAIVAL: Of course, madame!

(Just then HOCHEPAIX, *followed by* VENTROUX, *comes out of the study.)*

HOCHEPAIX: *(Taking in the sights:)* Ah!

VENTROUX: *(In shock)* Oh!

*(*VENTROUX *flings himself on* HOCHEPAIX *and makes him turn around.)*

CLARISSE: *(Unperturbed, not moving)* Don't disturb him! Don't disturb him!

DE JAIVAL: *(Drawing out the sting and rising)* Here you are, madame! Here it is! Here it is; the little trouble-maker!

*(*VENTROUX, *leaping at* DE JAIVAL *and pushing him so that he spins to the right:)*

VENTROUX: Aha, so! How would you like a good...

CLARISSE & DE JAIVAL: *(Together)* What's the matter?

VENTROUX: You're showing off your behind to a reporter from *Le Figaro!*

CLARISSE: *Le Figaro*? From *Le Figaro*?

VENTROUX: Yes, Monsieur Romain de Jaival from *Le Figaro*!

CLARISSE: *(Stalking* DE JAIVAL *as if she were about to lay hands on him)* De Jaival! You're Monsieur de Jaival? *(Changing her tone and speaking slowly)* Oh! Monsieur! what a funny story you had in yesterday's paper! *(To* VENTROUX.*)* Wasn't it?

VENTROUX: *(Raising his arms)* There you have it! … There you have it! That's all that matters to her! *(Just then he notices that the window blinds are wide open; and he utters a piercing shriek.)* Ah! …Clemenceau!

CLARISSE: Where's Clemenceau?

VENTROUX: *(Like a drunken man.)* Clemenceau!

CLARISSE: *(Looking out the window)* Ah, look, yes, there he is! *(She waves and smiles "Good afternoon" to the invisible Clemenceau.)*

VENTROUX: He's laughing! He's sniggering! *(Collapses on the sofa.)* I'm screwed! My political career is down the tubes!

CLARISSE: *(Still waving to Clemenceau as the curtain falls)* Good afternoon, Monsieur Clemenceau! Nicely, thank you, Monsieur Clemenceau! You too, Monsieur Clemenceau? Oh, good! How nice, Monsieur Clemenceau!

(Curtain)

END OF PLAY

BLASTED EVENT

(Léonie est en avance ou Le mal joli)

CHARACTERS & SETTING

LÉONIE TOUDOUX, *the wife*
JULIEN TOUDOUX, *the husband*
CLÉMENCE, *the maid*
MME DE CHAMPRINET, *the mother-in-law*
MME VIRTUEL, *the midwife*
DE CHAMPRINET, *the father-in-law*

The TOUDOUX *dining-room. Up center, a round table with two places set; far downstage left, a card table with playing cards. Down left, door of* MME TOUDOUX's *bedroom. In the back wall at right, double-door into the vestibule. Up right, low door leading to the butler's pantry. Down right, a pedestal table; against the wall back left a dresser; chairs left and right of the dresser. In the corner between the vestibule door and the butler's pantry door a little sideboard. Right of center, about a yard from the pedestal table, an easy chair facing the audience. A lighted chandelier over the dinner table.*

Scene One

(LÉONIE, TOUDOUX, *then* CLÉMENCE)

(*As the curtain rises,* LÉONIE *in a kimono and* TOUDOUX *in pajamas are marching back and forth across the room.* TOUDOUX *is holding* LÉONIE *up by hooking his left arm around her waist as he holds each of his wife's hands clasped in each of his own. They are walking near center stage; they proceed far left, spin around to carry on their stroll far right, then up left. Once there,* LÉONIE, *nearly bent in half, stops for breath.*)

LÉONIE: Pffu!

TOUDOUX: (*Timid and hesitant*) Don't...don't you feel any better?

LÉONIE: Oh, shut up! Stop asking questions! You're wearing me out!

TOUDOUX: (*Choosing to ignore this*) Yes.

LÉONIE: (*In pain*) Squeeze my hands! Squeeze them tight! Hurt me!

TOUDOUX: (*Obediently*) Yes!

LÉONIE: Tighter still! I don't feel it!

TOUDOUX: Yes! (*Stifling a sigh*) Pffu!

LÉONIE: (*Bent in two; looking at her husband and shaking her head wearily*) Ah! You have no idea!

TOUDOUX: No!

LÉONIE: Wait! I have to sit down a while. I'm exhausted!

TOUDOUX: *(Installing her in the chair right of the card table)* Easy does it! ...There! *(He leaves his wife and crosses above the table where his already-begun dinner awaits him.)*

LÉONIE: *(Sunk in her chair, her eyes downcast, holds out her hand to the left to her husband who, she thinks, is still beside her. Not finding him, she turns around and spotting him calmly seated in front of his plate)* Ah! no! no! Squeeze my hands, don't leave me! You can finish your dinner later!

TOUDOUX: *(Submissive)* Ah? Fine, fine... *(He gets up and goes to her.)*

LÉONIE: Squeeze my hands tight! That's it! tighter! tighter!

TOUDOUX: Yes!

(LÉONIE and TOUDOUX silently face one another: he, standing, squeezing his wife's hands; she seems worn out and dejected. From time to time, he throws a glance at his waiting dinner, then finally stares at the ceiling, his thoughts elsewhere.)

LÉONIE: *(Noticing her husband's pose, almost disgusted)* You don't seem to be enjoying yourself?

TOUDOUX: Well...

LÉONIE: *(Without detaching her hands from her husband's, but using all four of them to gesture)* That's wonderful! Monsieur is not enjoying himself! Well, do you suppose that I'm enjoying *myself*?

TOUDOUX: *(Whose arms have performed all his wife's movements)* But that's not what I meant!

LÉONIE: I'm the one in pain and Monsieur decides to act like the victim!

TOUDOUX: Am I complaining? You asked me if I was enjoying myself. You wouldn't like me to say that I'm enjoying myself when I see you suffer!

LÉONIE: Oh, suffer is the right word, and all on account of you!

TOUDOUX: *(Nodding his head in contrition, but with a touch of pride)* Yes, all on account of me!

(Pause. After a while, TOUDOUX, *to* LÉONIE *whose pain seems to have subsided:)*

TOUDOUX: Well, is it better?

LÉONIE: Yes, a little.

TOUDOUX: *(Satisfied)* Ah!

CLÉMENCE: *(Enters)* Monsieur isn't eating?

TOUDOUX: Yes, yes, right away. Don't worry about it.

LÉONIE: *(Bent over, in a doleful voice)* Tell me, Clémence…

CLÉMENCE: *(Upstage)* Madame?

LÉONIE: You let Mama know?

CLÉMENCE: Over the phone, yes, madame.

LÉONIE: And the midwife?

CLÉMENCE: I sent the concierge—to the obstetrician too!

LÉONIE: Good!

*(*LÉONIE, *to* TOUDOUX, *noticing his "long-suffering victim" look:)*

LÉONIE: Oh, go and eat your dinner. Go on! That hangdog look is getting on my nerves.

*(*CLÉMENCE *exits through the butler's pantry door.)*

TOUDOUX: Me? I couldn't possibly!

LÉONIE: Yes, yes! That's to be expected! You aren't in PAIN! You can think about EATING! Go on! Take advantage of this moment of respite! Go and eat!

TOUDOUX: No, I wouldn't want to…

LÉONIE: *(Pushing him away)* Go on, I said!

TOUDOUX: *(In justification, heading towards the dinner table)* Only because you insist!

LÉONIE: Ah hah!

TOUDOUX: *(Sitting at his place on the right and spreading his napkin on his lap)* But if you need me, you know, don't worry. I'm right here.

LÉONIE: I can see you, thanks.

(Enter CLÉMENCE *with a dish.)*

TOUDOUX: Don't you want to eat a little something? Have to keep up your strength!

LÉONIE: Is that right! Me eat! No! no! I am in PAIN. To each his own!

TOUDOUX: *(Resigned)* All right then. *(To* CLÉMENCE*)* What have you got there?

CLÉMENCE: Macaroni and cheese. *(Puts it down)*

LÉONIE: *(Standing in pain and, by leaning her hands on the table, reaches the chair on the other side)* I suffer martyrdom, while you whoop it up!

TOUDOUX: *(Helping himself to the macaroni)* Whoop it up! With macaroni and cheese!

LÉONIE: *(Seated, cards in hand)* No! Here am *I* between pains, playing a game of solitaire! Just look!

TOUDOUX: How brave of you!

LÉONIE: *(Proudly)* You can tell Baby about it years from now! *(Tenderly, to the audience)* Baby!

TOUDOUX: Damn, it's got a kick to it!

LÉONIE: *(Turning to* TOUDOUX, *in the same tender tone)* The baby?

TOUDOUX: No, the macaroni!

LÉONIE: *(Scornful and pitiful)* Ah!...

TOUDOUX: *(To* CLÉMENCE) What in the world is this cheese, eh?

CLÉMENCE: Some Parmesan and some Swiss. I got 'em at the grocer's.

TOUDOUX: Ah, well... it's aggressive!

(CLÉMENCE exits through the butler's pantry.)

TOUDOUX: And there's pepper in it too.

LÉONIE: *(Pityingly)* How materialistic you are! On the day when you're going to become a *father*!

TOUDOUX: No, I said it because...

LÉONIE: Goodness, so long as he gets here in one piece!

TOUDOUX: *(Absentmindedly, nods his head. Then:)* Who?

LÉONIE: What do you mean, who? Why, Baby! I'm not like you with a head full of macaroni!

TOUDOUX: *(Eating)* Well, why shouldn't he get here in one piece?

LÉONIE: Why, because! Because he's arriving a lot sooner than we expected!

TOUDOUX: Yes, but...that proves he's ready.

LÉONIE: Oh, yes. You can arrange things to your own satisfaction, you can! *(Rising.)* Imagine... *(Painfully reaching the chair facing* TOUDOUX *at the dinner table.)* Imagine, we didn't expect him until after the twentieth of next month. *(In anguish)* A month and four days ahead of schedule.

TOUDOUX: Oh, yes, it...he's in a bit of a hurry! *(Changing his tone)* But is that so bad, after all?

LÉONIE: *(Vaguely)* Oh!

TOUDOUX: He'll always be a month and four days older than the other kids his age. What a head start!

LÉONIE: Yes, but he has to get here first! And to be born in only eight months!

TOUDOUX: It'll be all right. Why, what about, uh, Whatizname, Thingumabob! Oh—you know who—uh—Victor Hugo!

LÉONIE: Hugo? Never heard of him!

TOUDOUX: Yes, you have! Well, I read somewhere that he was also born in eight months!

LÉONIE: *(In anguish)* Ah! and he's alive?

TOUDOUX: No, he's dead.

LÉONIE: *(Already disconsolate)* There! you see!

TOUDOUX: *(Quickly)* But he did live, and for quite some time! Eighty-three years! So *you* see!

LÉONIE: Just the same I wish this were over!

TOUDOUX: So do I! Oh! This macaroni lies on my stomach like a stone! *(He takes the carafe.)*

LÉONIE: *(New attack)* Oh! …oh! It's starting again!

TOUDOUX: *(Pouring out a drink)* That's nice!

LÉONIE: *(Standing and heading right, catching hold of* TOUDOUX *on the way by grabbing his left hand)* Come on! Come on! Let's walk!

TOUDOUX: *(Who has put down the carafe, trying to pick up his glass)* Wait till I get a drink!

LÉONIE: *(Holding on to him)* Will you come on! You can drink later!

TOUDOUX: *(Compelled)* Yes, yes.

*(*LÉONIE *and* TOUDOUX *cross above the table. In passing, he tries to get his glass.)*

LÉONIE: *(Dragging him)* No! Squeeze my hands! Squeeze my hands!

TOUDOUX: *(Obediently)* Yes.

LÉONIE: *(Getting into stride)* March! March!

TOUDOUX: Yes! Yes!

(LÉONIE and TOUDOUX walk down left of the table, reach far right, then about-face and return left, up to the card table.)

LÉONIE: *(Stopping to protest the pain)* Ah no! It's too much! Too much!

TOUDOUX: Yes! Be brave, be brave!

LÉONIE: *(Sarcastic)* Oh, be brave!

TOUDOUX: It doesn't mean a thing! It doesn't mean a thing!

LÉONIE: *(With a jump)* What do you mean, it doesn't mean a thing! I certainly it will mean something!

TOUDOUX: *(Startled)* What? Ah, of course it will mean something.

LÉONIE: If I have to suffer like this for no good reason...

TOUDOUX: *(Affectionately, to her face)* Yes, of course! Ssss!

LÉONIE: *(Pushing his head away and repulsing him, but without letting go of his hands)* Ah, pooh! How disgusting!

TOUDOUX: What?

LÉONIE: You stink of cheese!

TOUDOUX: Ah! ...It's the macaroni!

LÉONIE: I don't care if it's the macaroni! You stink of cheese, that's all.

TOUDOUX: I'm heartbroken.

LÉONIE: Really, you can see I'm not well, but you don't even have the consideration not to eat macaroni!

TOUDOUX: If you'd let me take a drink! Because I'm choking a bit, you know! *(With a congested cough)* Ugh!

LÉONIE: Oh! Will you please—you're fouling the air!

TOUDOUX: 'Scuse me.

LÉONIE: You can walk perfectly well with your head turned in the other direction!

TOUDOUX: *(Submissively)* Yes.

(LÉONIE and TOUDOUX walk in silence, he turning his head away from his wife. After a couple of back-and-forths.)

TOUDOUX: I'm getting dizzy walking this way.

LÉONIE: Never mind! Squeeze me! Hurt me!

TOUDOUX: Right.

LÉONIE: *(Stopping, one hand on her hip, nearly bent in half)* Ah! What a nasty pang!

TOUDOUX: *(Taken with hiccups)* Yupp!

LÉONIE: *(Straightening up and losing her temper)* What do you mean, yupp! If I want your approval, I'll ask for it!

TOUDOUX: But I didn't say "yupp!" I have the—yupp—hiccups.

LÉONIE: Ah! now you have the hiccups! You picked a fine time for it! *(Holding it in)* Ah! I feel sick!

TOUDOUX: It's not my fault! It's the maca—yupp—roni choking me!

LÉONIE: Then don't breathe! That's no problem! It'll pass!

TOUDOUX: Don't breathe, that's no problem. Yupp! That's easy for you to say, yupp!

LÉONIE: Oh! How selfish you are!

TOUDOUX: Yupp! Me?

LÉONIE: Naturally, you're only interested in yourself.

TOUDOUX: Is that right? Yupp! Then what am I—yupp—doing now?

LÉONIE: And, once again, will you please refrain from talking with your cheese in my face all the time?

TOUDOUX: 'Scuse me! *(He turns his head away and in the same movement brings it back towards his wife just in time to hiccup)* Yupp!

LÉONIE: You're driving me crazy with your yupps!

TOUDOUX: But I have the—yupp! —Hiccups!

LÉONIE: Well, have the hiccups but don't go "yupp" all the time!

TOUDOUX: But I'm not going "yupp" on purpose! I can't help going "yupp" when I have the—yupp—hiccups, damn it!

LÉONIE: Then take a drink, if you have the hiccups! Take a drink.

TOUDOUX: *(Leaving her and rushing for his glass)* Well, that's all—yupp—I asked for—before! For an hour, I—yupp!

LÉONIE: Don't talk so much and drink.

TOUDOUX: Yupp! Yes!

LÉONIE: *(Sitting left of the card table)* Ah! what a day!

TOUDOUX: *(After drinking, comes down to his wife, above the card table; a pause)* Oh! It's gone…it's all right! Yupp! It's all right!

LÉONIE: *(Right forearm on the chairback, leaning her head on it; bitterly)* You're lucky. I wish I could say the same!

TOUDOUX: *(Affectionately taking her left hand from the table)* Are you still sick?

LÉONIE: *(Rising, losing her temper)* Of course I'm sick!

TOUDOUX: *(Gently patting her hand)* She's so sweet! My poor baby! I'm feel so sorry for you!

LÉONIE: *(Nasty)* You should!

TOUDOUX: If only I could do it for you!

LÉONIE: What? What? "If only I could do it for you!" What's that supposed to mean? You don't make much of a commitment by saying that!

TOUDOUX: I'm doing my best...

LÉONIE: *(Fresh attack)* Oh! Oh! March! March!

TOUDOUX: *(Hurriedly straddling the chair right of the table so as not to keep his wife waiting as she holds him.)* Yes! Yes!

(They reach stage right; just as they about-face to return, LÉONIE *stops.)*

LÉONIE: No! let's sit down!

*(*TOUDOUX, *who is right in front of the easy chair; sitting in it the same time as* LÉONIE:*)*

TOUDOUX: All right!

LÉONIE: *(Who has to sit on the arm)* Not you! Me!

TOUDOUX: *(Rising rapidly to give her the seat, repeating in a startled manner)* All right! Not you, me! Uh—no, not me, you!

LÉONIE: *(Sitting)* You can remain standing!

TOUDOUX: *(Far right)* I can remain standing, yes!

LÉONIE: *(Exhausted)* Ah! what agony! It makes me perspire. *(A pause. In a faint voice)* Give me something to drink, will you?

TOUDOUX: What?

LÉONIE: *(Immediately irritated)* Drink!

TOUDOUX: Drink, yes! *(He runs to the dinner table.)*

LÉONIE: Why do I always have to repeat myself?

TOUDOUX: Because I didn't hear you.

LÉONIE: Oh, you always have some smart comeback!

TOUDOUX: *(Holding out the glass)* Here!

LÉONIE: Thanks. *(Putting the glass to her lips)* Ah! pooh! This is the glass you drank out of!

TOUDOUX: Yes. So?

LÉONIE: It stinks of cheese.

TOUDOUX: Chee…? Ah, that's the macaroni! *(He takes back the glass.)*

LÉONIE: What an idiot you are, my love!

TOUDOUX: *(Returning with a different glass and the carafe)* What do you expect? It's the first time this has happened to me!

LÉONIE: *(Nervous)* Me too! And I'm not losing *my* head because of it!

TOUDOUX: *(Emptying what's left of the water in the carafe into the glass in his hand)* Well, last drop means you'll get married this year!

LÉONIE: *(Cross)* Yes, you think it's something to laugh at!

TOUDOUX: It's a joke!

LÉONIE: *(Taking the glass and shrugging)* A joke! *(She drinks.)*

TOUDOUX: *(Solicitously)* Easy, take it easy!

LÉONIE: *(After drinking, handing him the glass)* Thank you!

TOUDOUX: *(After putting back glass and carafe; returning to LÉONIE)* Well, is it better now?

LÉONIE: *(Disheartened)* Yes, for the moment.

TOUDOUX: This is awful!

LÉONIE: You have no idea! It squeezes your waist as if it were trying to cut you in half!

TOUDOUX: *(Somewhat above the easy chair, left arm leaning on the back)* Oh yes, I know!

LÉONIE: How do you know?

TOUDOUX: It sounds like what I go through in my gas attacks.

LÉONIE: *(With superb disdain)* Your gas attacks! How dare you make comparisons? Compared to my pains, your attacks are nothing! They're sheer delights!

TOUDOUX: Oh! sheer delights!

LÉONIE: *(Furious)* Yes indeed! It's quite peculiar, this vicious pleasure you take in belittling my discomfort in favor of yours.

TOUDOUX: Me?

LÉONIE: Isn't it enough that I'm in pain? At least leave me the satisfaction of my suffering?

TOUDOUX: I'll be glad to, I said so!

LÉONIE: Selfish! Always so selfish!

TOUDOUX: Selfish!

CLÉMENCE: *(Who has entered from the butler's pantry during these last lines, with a piece of Roquefort on a plate; heading towards the sideboard)* Monsieur is through with the macaroni?

TOUDOUX: Yes, I'm through! I sure am through! What have you got there?

CLÉMENCE: Cheese!

LÉONIE: What? *(Categorically.)* No! No! I'm up to here with cheese!

CLÉMENCE: Oh! such a lovely piece of Roquefort! *(She puts it on the sideboard.)*

LÉONIE: Exactly! Roquefort! No thank you! Monsieur has already imposed his macaroni on me!

TOUDOUX: Oh! I imposed!

(CLÉMENCE exits, carrying off the remains of the steak and the dish of macaroni.)

LÉONIE: But I never say a word! I never complain!

TOUDOUX: You never complain!

LÉONIE: *(Out of control)* You think I complain—me?

TOUDOUX: *(To calm her)* No, no!

LÉONIE: When I try to act to avoid complicating matters! You think I complain!

TOUDOUX: No, no!

LÉONIE: Is that so? It's easy to see you don't know what other women are like! I would love to see you married to some unreasonable woman!

TOUDOUX: But you're right, I say! You're right! I misspoke!

LÉONIE: Telling me that I complain! *(More pains)* Oh! oh! it's starting again!

TOUDOUX: Ah! you see! You're over-excited!

LÉONIE: *(Taking his hands)* Quick! March! March!

TOUDOUX: *(Stifles a weary sigh; then, resigned)* Yes.

LÉONIE: *(Walking)* Squeeze! Squeeze! *(Stage left)* Oh! the swine! This one is so sharp!

TOUDOUX: Don't think about it! Don't think about it!

LÉONIE: *(With the "hahs" of someone in pain)* Hah! you always know what to say, don't you? "Don't think about it." That's easy to say! You aren't about to give birth!

TOUDOUX: *(Instinctively screaming with her)* No.

LÉONIE: *(Screaming)* Wait! Wait! Hah! Hah!

TOUDOUX: *(Screaming)* Yes! yes!

LÉONIE: *(Screaming)* Oh, I'll never forget this!

TOUDOUX: Yes!

LÉONIE: *(Nearly bent in two, in a choked voice)* Filthy brat! I love him already...hah!

TOUDOUX: *(Ditto)* Me too! Hah!

LÉONIE: Hah! *(Abruptly)* March!

TOUDOUX: *(Ditto)* March.

(LÉONIE and TOUDOUX march.)

Scene Two

(The same, CLÉMENCE, MADAME DE CHAMPRINET)

CLÉMENCE: *(Running in upstage just as they about-face right)* Madame, Madame's mama, Madame, is here!

LÉONIE: *(Still walking)* Good, good!

(MADAME DE CHAMPRINET, entering briskly and arriving behind them just as they reach far left:)

MADAME DE CHAMPRINET: Well, my darling! What do I hear? Is it to be today?

(They both stop in place without turning around.)

TOUDOUX: *(Perpendicular parallel to and upstage of his wife in relation to the audience)* Good evening, mother-in-law!

MADAME DE CHAMPRINET: *(Already annoyed with her son-in-law)* Yes, good evening, good evening!

(CLÉMENCE exits.)

LÉONIE: *(Almost bent in two without the strength to turn to her mother)* Ah! it's horrible, mama!

MADAME DE CHAMPRINET: My poor baby!

LÉONIE: *(Holding her left hand behind her to her mother)*
Squeeze my hands, mama! Squeeze my hands!

MADAME DE CHAMPRINET: *(Tenderly)* Yes! *(Abruptly to
her son-in-law, pulling him to put herself in his place)* Get
out of the way, you!

TOUDOUX: 'Scuse me!

MADAME DE CHAMPRINET: *(To LÉONIE)* Come, darling!

TOUDOUX: *(Crossing right and sitting in the easy chair)* I
don't mind a chance to sit down for a while.

LÉONIE: March, march!

MADAME DE CHAMPRINET: Yes, yes!

(They walk right near the easy chair.)

LÉONIE: *(Stops and looks at her mother; shakes her head)*
Ah, mama! If you only knew...

MADAME DE CHAMPRINET: *(With an indulgent smile)*
Why... I do know, child, I do know.

LÉONIE: That's right. You've been through it too,
mama!

MADAME DE CHAMPRINET: Of course, darling! You
were the cause of these tender moments in my case.
It's a painful experience to go through, but, afterwards,
what's nice is that you completely forget about it! It's a
wonderful pain!

LÉONIE: That may be so, but you can't have been in as
much agony as I am!

MADAME DE CHAMPRINET: Why...every bit as much,
darling!

LÉONIE: Oh no, that's impossible! In those days...

MADAME DE CHAMPRINET: Those days and nowadays
are just the same; progress hasn't changed a thing.

LÉONIE: Just the same, how can you compare… *(Her expression changes.)* Wait! Wait! It's calming down, it's going away!

MADAME DE CHAMPRINET: Ah! you see!

LÉONIE: *(Downcast)* Only to start all over again! *(Her tone changes.)* I want to sit down!

(A pause.)

MADAME DE CHAMPRINET: *(Up against the easy chair on a level with* TOUDOUX's *knees, passing her daughter over to have her sit in the easy chair)* Yes, yes! *(Encountering* TOUDOUX *by doing so.)* Well, get out of the way, you!

TOUDOUX: *(Quickly leaping up and scurrying far right)* 'Scuse me!

MADAME DE CHAMPRINET: *(Still holding her daughter)* You see your wife in pain, trying to sit down and you hog the armchair!

TOUDOUX: I hog it?

MADAME DE CHAMPRINET: Yes, hog! *(To* LÉONIE*)* Sit down, darling!

TOUDOUX: I've never seen a hog in an armchair.

MADAME DE CHAMPRINET: Oh yes! this is a fine time to make wisecracks! I hope you're happy with what you've done?

TOUDOUX: *(Sincere)* I'll be happy when it's all over; at the moment, I'm not exactly having a ball.

MADAME DE CHAMPRINET: Really? What about my daughter, is she having a ball? You aren't having a ball, but there's still a smug, self-satisfied look about you!

TOUDOUX: Me?

LÉONIE: *(Seated half bent over and unaware of what she's saying)* Oh! don't scold him, mama! The poor boy has nothing to do with it.

MADAME DE CHAMPRINET: *(Astonished)* Ah!

TOUDOUX: What do you mean "I have nothing to do with it?"

LÉONIE: Huh? No, I mean it wasn't intentional.

TOUDOUX: *(Reassured)* Ah! that's all right!

LÉONIE: It happened because it was predestined to happen! Fate would have brought it about sooner or later!

MADAME DE CHAMPRINET: Precisely! I would have preferred later! This habit of overdoing things! It's inconvenient! What will people say? You should have known better!

TOUDOUX: I apologize for not consulting you first, mother-in-law.

MADAME DE CHAMPRINET: *(Having removed her cape and put it on the chair left of the dinner table; coming down, bringing the chair from right of the table)* Smart-aleck!

TOUDOUX: No. When I got married, you said "I hope you'll soon be presenting me with grandchildren..."

MADAME DE CHAMPRINET: I may have done. But you didn't have to get my daughter in this condition.

TOUDOUX: *(Snide)* How would you suggest I go about it?

MADAME DE CHAMPRINET: *(Sitting beside her daughter on the chair she brought over)* My poor darling, there, there!

LÉONIE: Don't pity me, mama! It's our lot.

MADAME DE CHAMPRINET: What stoicism! *(Without transition)* Did you tell them to boil some water?

LÉONIE: Yes, mama, that's taken care of. You didn't let papa know, did you?

MADAME DE CHAMPRINET: *(Unsympathetically)* What? Oh yes, as soon as I heard! I sent someone to the club to let him know.

LÉONIE: Oh! Why? It would have been better to make the announcement when it was all over. He might have been spared the emotion.

MADAME DE CHAMPRINET: Why should he be? Why shouldn't he do his share, like everyone else?

LÉONIE: Oh! poor papa!

MADAME DE CHAMPRINET: Oh, poor papa, poor papa! So I don't matter as much as he does? People always make too much fuss over men, that's why they get so selfish.

TOUDOUX: *(Between his teeth)* Thanks.

LÉONIE: *(Ingenuously)* Papa isn't a man!

MADAME DE CHAMPRINET: He is to me!

(MADAME DE CHAMPRINET, *seeing* LÉONIE's *face contract:)*

MADAME DE CHAMPRINET: Is it starting again?

LÉONIE: Yes.

MADAME DE CHAMPRINET: Do you want to walk?

TOUDOUX: Yes, that's it. Let's march.

LÉONIE: *(Flying into a rage)* No, I don't want to march.

TOUDOUX: Then let's not march!

LÉONIE: *(To her mother)* This is a mild one! I can bear it!

Scene Three

(The same, CLÉMENCE*)*

CLÉMENCE: *(Entering from the butler's pantry and coming down between* LÉONIE *and* TOUDOUX, *near the easy chair, to talk to* LÉONIE*)* They've brought the things from the store.

LÉONIE: *(Knowing what she means)* Ah, yes!

TOUDOUX: What things?

CLÉMENCE: The baby's layette, a bassinette, bottles...

LÉONIE: Yes, yes! for Monsieur Achille's room.

(Astonishment of MADAME DE CHAMPRINET *on hearing that name.)*

TOUDOUX: *(Informed)* Ah!

LÉONIE: *(To* CLÉMENCE*)* All right, bring them in here so I can see them!

CLÉMENCE: Very good, madame.

(She is about to exit.)

LÉONIE: Is everything in the room ready to receive Monsieur Achille?

CLÉMENCE: Yes, madame.

LÉONIE: You won't forget to put a ball in Monsieur Achille's crib?

CLÉMENCE: No, madame. *(She exits through the butler's pantry.)*

LÉONIE: *(To her husband)* Go help Clémence, Julien!

TOUDOUX: All right! *(On his way out.)* Hey! Clémence, I'm going to help you with Monsieur Achille's things. *(He exits.)*

Scene Four

(LÉONIE, MADAME DE CHAMPRINET)

MADAME DE CHAMPRINET: *(Facetiously)* Monsieur Achille! Monsieur Achille! So you've decided it's a boy?

LÉONIE: *(Certain)* It is a boy, yes, mama!

MADAME DE CHAMPRINET: Ah! You know in advance!

LÉONIE: *(With an irrefutable argument)* We never intended anything but a boy.

MADAME DE CHAMPRINET: *(Nodding)* Ah! in that case… And if it turns out to be a girl? What then? Send it back?

LÉONIE: *(Irritated)* It will be a boy! *(An additional proof)* In the beginning, I had almost no heart pangs, and, from what I hear, that's a definite sign!

MADAME DE CHAMPRINET: *(Pretending to be convinced)* Ah!

LÉONIE: And besides, if you take the quarters of the moon into account! People have noticed that when the moon, at the moment of gestation…

MADAME DE CHAMPRINET: No, no! if you're going to give me an astronomy lesson, I'd much rather take your word for it. *(Putting her chair back in place)* Let it be Monsieur Achille—until further notice! *(She crosses left of the dinner table.)*

Scene Five

(*The same*, TOUDOUX, CLÉMENCE)

(TOUDOUX *enters, followed by* CLÉMENCE, *carrying the bassinette containing, higgledy-piggledy, the layette, bottles and a baby's chamber pot.*)

TOUDOUX: Make way for the furnishings!

LÉONIE: *(Rising and crossing to sit painfully on the chair right of the card-table)* Show me. Oh, I feel sick!

MADAME DE CHAMPRINET: *(Gently, helping her sit)* Pay it no mind!

LÉONIE: *(To* CLÉMENCE*)* That's the bassinette, good! *(To* TOUDOUX.*)* The layette! the bottle! That all goes in his room!

*(*LÉONIE, *just as* CLÉMENCE *makes ready to carry it all off, noticing the pot at the bottom of the bassinette and picking it up:)*

LÉONIE: Oh! his chamber pot!

*(*LÉONIE, *emotionally, while* CLÉMENCE *carries off the furnishings:)*

LÉONIE: His chamber pot! When I think that soon it'll be his potty! He already seems grown-up! *(In a burst of affection, bringing the pot to her lips)* Oh! sweety-pie!

MADAME DE CHAMPRINET: *(Coming down, watching her daughter; moved, to* TOUDOUX*)* Just like me when she was born.

TOUDOUX: *(Indifferent)* Oh.

MADAME DE CHAMPRINET: *(Unable to take her eyes off her daughter)* I loved her even before she was born.

TOUDOUX: I waited till later.

LÉONIE: *(To* TOUDOUX, *holding out the pot)* Here, put it down!

*(*LÉONIE *hands it to* MADAME DE CHAMPRINET *who hands it to* TOUDOUX, *then crosses above the card table.)*

TOUDOUX: *(Obediently)* Yes. *(He looks around, not knowing where to put the pot.)*

LÉONIE: *(Watching him hold the pot any old way)* Doesn't it move you?

TOUDOUX: What?

LÉONIE: His potty.

TOUDOUX: *(Without conviction)* Oh! yes.

LÉONIE: *(Proud of herself)* Not as much as me!

TOUDOUX: Oh come on, sweetheart!

LÉONIE: Oh, darling!

TOUDOUX: What are you laughing at?

LÉONIE: *(Laughing to herself)* Nothing!

TOUDOUX: Yes you are. What is it?

MADAME DE CHAMPRINET: Tell us!

LÉONIE: No! it's just that, seeing you with that pot in your hand, I remembered a silly dream I had last night.

TOUDOUX: You dreamed about chamber pots?

LÉONIE: *(Laughing)* Yes!

MADAME DE CHAMPRINET: *(With conviction)* Ah! that's a good omen!

LÉONIE: Just imagine, the two of us were strolling at the Longchamps racetrack. I had on my gray dress and you wore your checked jacket. But instead of your top hat, you were wearing your chamber pot!

TOUDOUX: *(Who has been listening, smiling; offended)* Me!

MADAME DE CHAMPRINET: Oh, what a queer idea!

TOUDOUX: *(Annoyed)* It's idiotic! *(He crosses right.)*

LÉONIE: And you were so proud! You were tipping it to everybody. But I was upset. I said *(Slowly and emphatically)* "Julien! Julien! Take off your chamber pot. People are staring at you!" And you replied, "Leave me alone! It's all right! I'm going to launch a new fashion!"

TOUDOUX: You really have dreams like that?

LÉONIE: If you only could have seen him with it on, mama! He looked so funny!

MADAME DE CHAMPRINET: I don't doubt it.

LÉONIE: It was very becoming.

TOUDOUX: *(Trying to find a place to set down the pot)* Charming, charming!

LÉONIE: *(As naturally as can be)* Well! Put the pot on your head and show mama.

TOUDOUX: *(Turning around, dumbfounded)* Me!

LÉONIE: *(Not doubting his compliance for a minute)* You'll see, mama!

TOUDOUX: Never as long as I live! What an idea!

LÉONIE: *(Hurt)* You might have the decency to put it on your head when I ask you to.

TOUDOUX: No, but you've already seen it!

LÉONIE: *(As a peremptory argument)* It's to show mama.

TOUDOUX: I don't care if it's to show the Pope! You don't give a hoot for my feelings! Wanting me to put a chamber pot on my head. Are you out of your mind?

LÉONIE: Why not? It's brand new! It's not a used one!

TOUDOUX: New or used, it's a chamber pot all the same!

MADAME DE CHAMPRINET: *(Rising and coming downstage)* Come on, you're among friends.

TOUDOUX: That's enough! What about my dignity as a human being!

LÉONIE: *(Rising, crossing left)* There you see, he won't do anything to please me.

TOUDOUX: You have some swell suggestions!

MADAME DE CHAMPRINET: I could understand if she asked you to go to the racetrack or the club with it. But here!

TOUDOUX: Not here or anywhere else!

LÉONIE: *(Stubborn)* I want you to put that pot on your head, so there!

TOUDOUX: Really? Well, I don't want to!

LÉONIE: *(Stamping her foot)* I want you to put it on! I want you to put it on!

TOUDOUX: No! no! no! and no!

MADAME DE CHAMPRINET: *(Intervening)* Julien! Julien! If my daughter asks you to!

TOUDOUX: No, I said!

LÉONIE: I want it! I want it! I have a craving!

MADAME DE CHAMPRINET: *(Going to her daughter)* My God! There! She has a craving! She has a craving!

TOUDOUX: So what? She has a craving.

MADAME DE CHAMPRINET: *(Embracing her daughter)* Julien, I beseech you. Think of her condition! Think what a craving means!

TOUDOUX: Nuts!

LÉONIE: I want it! I have a craving!

MADAME DE CHAMPRINET: You hear her! Consider what will happen on account of your obstinacy, if your son is born with a chamber pot on his head!

TOUDOUX: Is *that* all? We can put it to use!

LÉONIE & MADAME DE CHAMPRINET: Oh!

TOUDOUX: And we can return this one, it hasn't been used!

MADAME DE CHAMPRINET: How dare he say such a thing!

LÉONIE: Unnatural father! Unnatural father!

TOUDOUX: But it's true!

LÉONIE: *(A tantrum)* You're going to put on the pot!
You're going to put on the pot!

TOUDOUX: *(In the same way)* No, I'll not put on the pot!
No, I'll not put on the pot!

LÉONIE: He won't put on the pot! Ah! ah! ah! I'm sick!

MADAME DE CHAMPRINET: There! You see what you've
done! You see what a state your wife is in!

LÉONIE: *(Dropping into the chair left of the card table)* And
he refuses to satisfy my cravings! Ah! ah!

MADAME DE CHAMPRINET: *(Exploding)* Put on that pot if
she tells you to!

TOUDOUX: Put it on yourself if you so worried about it!

MADAME DE CHAMPRINET: If my daughter asked me
to...

LÉONIE: *(Her head on her arm on the chair back)* Oh!
heartless! Heartless!

MADAME DE CHAMPRINET: *(Restraining herself with great
difficulty)* Julien, I beg you, I appeal to your feelings as
a husband and a father!

TOUDOUX: *(Starting to weaken)* But look here! Think
what you're asking me! I haven't reached the age of 38
in order to... Come on!

MADAME DE CHAMPRINET: What does age have to do
with it? *(Humbly supplicating)* Be kind. Put it on your
head!

TOUDOUX: *(Giving in more and more)* But...

LÉONIE: *(Feebly moaning)* Oh, I feel sick!

MADAME DE CHAMPRINET: *(Coaxing)* You see! She feels
sick! Julien! Put on the pot! Put on the pot!

TOUDOUX: *(As before)* It isn't my size! I can tell!

MADAME DE CHAMPRINET: *(As before)* Please put it on!

TOUDOUX: *(In a last act of resistance)* No, you know—
*(He hesitates, goes to put on the pot, again hesitates once or
twice, and then, making up his mind, puts it on his head;
infuriated)* There! There! I hope you're satisfied! I put
on the pot! Are you happy now?

MADAME DE CHAMPRINET: *(Going to her daughter, above
the card table)* Look, Léonie. He's a dear! He put it on!

LÉONIE: *(Raising her head from her arm and turning
to* TOUDOUX*)* Show me! *(Looking at him)* Oh! what a
horror!

TOUDOUX: *(Startled)* What?

LÉONIE: *(Pushing him away)* Go away! Go away! You
look ridiculous like that!

TOUDOUX: *(Recoiling)* Me!

LÉONIE: Go and hide! I'll never be able to see you again
except with that thing on your head!

TOUDOUX: This is incredible!

MADAME DE CHAMPRINET: *(Who has crossed down,
holding him by the arm in order to lead him out)* Go on!
Don't tease her! *(She crosses back above the card table.)*

TOUDOUX: *(Exasperated)* They don't give a good
goddam for my feelings!

Scene Six

(The same, CLÉMENCE, *then* MADAME VIRTUEL*)*

CLÉMENCE: *(Quickly entering upstage and going directly to
the two women)* Madame! Madame! It's the midwife.

TOUDOUX: *(Furious)* Tell her to go to hell!

LÉONIE & MADAME DE CHAMPRINET: What?

CLÉMENCE: *(Turning around at* TOUDOUX's *voice and finding herself face-to-face with him. Jumps when she sees the chamber pot on his head)* Ah! Monsieur has gone crazy!

LÉONIE: What do you mean tell her to go to hell!

MADAME DE CHAMPRINET: On the contrary, have her come in.

TOUDOUX: *(Raging)* Have her come in!

*(*TOUDOUX, *getting back to business while* CLÉMENCE *exits.)*

TOUDOUX: A great way to make an ass out of me! They ask me to put on the pot; *(He takes it off)* I put on the pot! *(He puts it on. Going to the card table and confronting his wife)* And instead of thanking me for the humiliation I've been through… *(So saying, he slams his fist on the card table.)*

LÉONIE: *(Seeing only the pot on her husband's head)* Take that thing off!

TOUDOUX: No! I won't take it off now! I've had enough of your thousand and one whims! You wanted it? *(Tapping the bottom of the pot)* I'm keeping it! You two may be a couple of flibbertigibbets, but I'm as firm as the Rock of Gibraltar! *(He crosses right.)*

LÉONIE & MADAME DE CHAMPRINET: Flibbertigibbets!

*(*MADAME VIRTUEL *enters followed by* CLÉMENCE *who carries her overnight bag; and crosses down to* LÉONIE *who stands up to meet her, helped by her mother; she moves to the chair right of the card table:)*

MADAME VIRTUEL: Good evening, ladies!

*(*MADAME VIRTUEL, *turning to* TOUDOUX *who, walking back and forth, returns to her:)*

MADAME VIRTUEL: Monsieur! *(Astonished by the pot on* TOUDOUX's *head.)* Heavens!

TOUDOUX: *(Blandly tipping his pot hat)* Good evening, madame! *(He crosses back upstage.)*

*(*MADAME VIRTUEL, *to* TOUDOUX, *while* CLÉMENCE *puts the bag on the floor left of the easy chair, then exits upstage:)*

MADAME VIRTUEL: Does that have some sort of religious significance?

TOUDOUX: *(Coming down to her; infuriated)* No, madame, but certain women have cravings!

MADAME DE CHAMPRINET: *(Quickly)* Not I!

TOUDOUX: *(Removing the pot from his head)* Let this serve as an example of the husband who put a chamber pot on his head to satisfy his wife's craving!

MADAME VIRTUEL: *(With conviction)* Ah! very good! What a good husband! Then keep it on! By all means, keep it on!

TOUDOUX: What! Keep it on! But...but... Oh! I've had enough of this! *(He goes to put the pot on the floor above the card table, then sits in the easy chair.)*

MADAME VIRTUEL: *(Who has gone to* LÉONIE, *seated on the chair right of the card table)* So, Madame, you are the mama-to-be?

LÉONIE: Yes, madame!.

MADAME DE CHAMPRINET: *(Standing, crosses above the table between her and the back of* LÉONIE's *chair)* I seriously believe it won't be much longer, seeing how the pains recur every minute.

MADAME VIRTUEL: Ah? All the better! To get it over with as soon as possible. *(To* LÉONIE*)* Right?

LÉONIE: Oh yes, madame!

MADAME VIRTUEL: *(Removing her gloves)* Just the same I didn't suppose it would be soon! When I think that you wrote the doctor yesterday to book me for a month in advance—and my first visit coincides with your delivery!

LÉONIE: How could I foresee that I would be a month ahead of schedule?

MADAME VIRTUEL: You didn't do anything reckless?

LÉONIE: Nothing!

MADAME VIRTUEL: Maybe you've figured the dates wrong?

LÉONIE: Oh! impossible! We've been married barely eight months.

MADAME DE CHAMPRINET: *(Confirming)* Yes, eight months!

MADAME VIRTUEL: And… *(Unable to refrain, with a significant wink.)* not before? Eh?

MADAME DE CHAMPRINET: *(Scandalized)* Oh! oh!

LÉONIE: *(Embarrassed)* Oh, madame, oh!

MADAME VIRTUEL: *(Candidly)* I only asked, you understand, as a point of information.

LÉONIE: *(As before)* I quite understand, yes. *(Sudden pang)* Oh! oh! here comes another one!

MADAME VIRTUEL: *(Firmly, laying stress on every word)* Ah! Very good! Very good!

LÉONIE: *(Bent in two; annoyed)* What do you mean "very good"?

MADAME VIRTUEL: It proves that labor is under way.

LÉONIE: *(Angrily)* I wish you could feel it!

MADAME VIRTUEL: Oh yes! It's no bed of roses! I know what it's like, I've been through it. I've had two children, and every time I lay in…

LÉONIE: But, madame, it's your profession! You're accustomed to it!

MADAME VIRTUEL: I am accustomed to it…but not as a patient!

LÉONIE: *(In a voice of pain)* Oh! madame, will it last much longer?

MADAME VIRTUEL: I can't tell just like that! You see, you must start preparing yourself! You and your mama go into your room and she'll help put you to bed; I'll come and see you when you're in bed. Meanwhile, I'm going to take care of a few things. *(So saying, she walks a bit upstage, as she takes off her cape.)*

LÉONIE: *(Rising)* Yes, madame.

(MADAME DE CHAMPRINET, helping LÉONIE rise and leading her off:)

MADAME DE CHAMPRINET: All right. Come on, darling.

MADAME VIRTUEL: Go on, madame.

(LÉONIE and MADAME DE CHAMPRINET make their exit, TOUDOUX rises.)

Scene Seven

(MADAME VIRTUEL, TOUDOUX, then CLÉMENCE)

(MADAME VIRTUEL, her cape over her arm and no more bothered by TOUDOUX than if he didn't exist, looks round the room, then spotting the electric-bell button left of the upstage door, she goes and rings. Next she heads towards the easy chair to pick up her overnight bag.)

(MADAME VIRTUEL, *aware of* TOUDOUX, *who has been watching her, planted in front of her bag, without looking at him:*)

MADAME VIRTUEL: Out of my way, you!

TOUDOUX: *(Retreating)* 'Scuse me!

(MADAME VIRTUEL, *after placing her cape over the back of the chair, opens her bag, removes a bed-jacket with the sleeves rolled up, a bibbed apron and a case of surgical instruments. She puts it all on the easy chair.*)

CLÉMENCE: *(Entering from the kitchen)* Monsieur rang?

TOUDOUX: This lady did.

MADAME VIRTUEL: *(Arranging her things on the chair)* Yes, I did. Have you boiled the water?

CLÉMENCE: Several basins are heating up now.

MADAME VIRTUEL: Good! And you've got all the medications?

CLÉMENCE: *(Pointing to the butler's pantry)* In there. Yes.

MADAME VIRTUEL: Good. You may bring them in.

(*As* CLÉMENCE *exits,* MADAME VIRTUEL *turns around, her empty bag in hand, and bumps into* TOUDOUX.)

MADAME VIRTUEL: Out of my way, you!

TOUDOUX: *(Retreating)* Right!

MADAME VIRTUEL: *(Believing* CLÉMENCE *is still there, as she puts her open bag on the chair right of the card table)* You can put them all on the mantelpiece.

TOUDOUX: *(Beside her)* Who do you think you're talking to?

MADAME VIRTUEL: *(Turning around)* The maid!

TOUDOUX: She left!

MADAME VIRTUEL: Oh… Oh, well, I'll tell her when she gets back! *(Finding her path blocked by* TOUDOUX.*)* Out of my way!

TOUDOUX: *(Retreating)* 'Scuse me!

*(*MADAME VIRTUEL *goes to the pedestal table and spreads out a towel which she has taken from a pile on the chair left.* TOUDOUX *has gradually moves up to her.)*

MADAME VIRTUEL: *(After spreading out the towel, turns aside and bumps into* TOUDOUX, *who is still beside her)* You again! Who are you anyway?

TOUDOUX: *(Almost an excuse)* The husband.

MADAME VIRTUEL: The hus… Ah, yes, of course, naturally…'cause you had the chamber pot. *(She takes her bag from the easy-chair and opens it on the pedestal table.)*

TOUDOUX: *(Flabbergasted)* What, because I had! *(Aside)* Oh, this is the limit! *(Trying to get into* MADAME VIRTUEL'*s good graces.)* Uh! This… this midwife business must be pretty exhausting!

MADAME VIRTUEL: *(Drily; not turning around)* Yeah.

TOUDOUX: Yes! …Do you attend many births annually?

MADAME VIRTUEL: *(As before)* Plenty. *(She crosses down to the easy chair.)*

TOUDOUX: *(Pivoting to follow her)* When you attend a birth, do you…

MADAME VIRTUEL: *(Cutting him off)* No, no, hey? I hope you don't expect me to initiate you into the mysteries of my profession?

TOUDOUX: *(Giving up)* No, no!

MADAME VIRTUEL: *(Removing her hat and holding it and her cape out to* TOUDOUX*)* Well, I still don't know where they're putting me here! So stick my hat and cape in my room, will you?

TOUDOUX: Me?

MADAME VIRTUEL: *(Dumping it all on his hands)* Yes!

TOUDOUX: *(Obediently)* Fine. *(He crosses upstage, grumbling.)* Unbelievable! Unbelievable!

*(*TOUDOUX *exits upstage.* MADAME VIRTUEL *crosses right, undoing her bodice; just as she takes it off,* CLÉMENCE *appears from the pantry, carrying the medications—big bottles of distilled water, yellow bottles of chloroform, packets of cotton wool, etc.)*

MADAME VIRTUEL: *(Surprised by* CLÉMENCE's *abrupt entrance; giving a start and modestly crossing her arms over her chest)* Who's there?

CLÉMENCE: I brought the medications.

MADAME VIRTUEL: *(Reassured; moving to the easy chair and picking up her bed-jacket)* Ah! fine, put it over there! *(She points to the pedestal table.)*

TOUDOUX: *(Breezing in upstage)* There we are!

MADAME VIRTUEL: *(Left of the easy chair, starting)* Don't come in!

TOUDOUX: *(Who has gone round the dinner table to come down left of center)* Ah! 'scuse me, I didn't know!

*(*MADAME VIRTUEL, *aided by* CLÉMENCE, *frantically getting into her bed jacket:)*

MADAME VIRTUEL: Can't you knock before you come in?

TOUDOUX: Listen, I thought a dining-room...

MADAME VIRTUEL: *(Furious)* Dining-room is beside the point! *(Opening the front of her bed jacket)* My bosom and shoulders were stark naked!

TOUDOUX: *(With a casual gesture)* Oh.

(MADAME VIRTUEL, *turning to the easy chair to get her apron; turning around again to put it on and bumping into* TOUDOUX *who has come closer*)

MADAME VIRTUEL: Hey, tell me something? Are you always going to be under foot like this?

TOUDOUX: If I have to!

MADAME VIRTUEL: I just don't like folks breathing down my neck when I work. *(So saying, she picks up her bodice from the easy chair.)*

TOUDOUX: Uh-huh.

MADAME VIRTUEL: *(Returning, holding her bodice and moving towards her bag. To* TOUDOUX*)* Out of my way!

TOUDOUX: Right. *(He moves.)*

MADAME VIRTUEL: *(Picking up the bag and holding it out to* TOUDOUX*)* Here, put this in my room!

TOUDOUX: *(Taking the bag and holding it out to* CLÉMENCE*)* Clémence!

MADAME VIRTUEL: No! No! Not Clémence! If I wanted Clémence, I would have said "Clémence." *I* need the maid!

TOUDOUX: *(Nonplussed)* Oh!

MADAME VIRTUEL: Yes!

TOUDOUX: *(Submitting)* Fine! *(He exits, grumbling.)* Oh! what a pain in the neck!

MADAME VIRTUEL: *(Adjusting the bib of her apron with safety pins)* There, that's fine, my girl! Now go and see if your water's boiling. When it's ready, bring a basinful to Madame's room, so I can have it handy. *(She crosses left.)*

CLÉMENCE: *(Finishing arranging things on the consol table)* Very good, madame.

(Just then there is a knock at the upstage door.)

MADAME VIRTUEL: Come in!

(TOUDOUX *enters and crosses down left.*)

MADAME VIRTUEL: Was it *you* knocking?

TOUDOUX: Yes, it was!

MADAME VIRTUEL: Why did you have to knock now that I'm dressed?

TOUDOUX: I didn't know that! I didn't look through the keyhole!

MADAME VIRTUEL: *(Skeptical)* Oh yeah?

TOUDOUX: *(Somewhat resentful)* You don't have anything else you want me to do, do you?

MADAME VIRTUEL: *(Waving him away)* No, no! I don't want anything from you! Out of my way there! *(She moves left.)*

CLÉMENCE: Me too, madame?

MADAME VIRTUEL: No! What time do you have dinner?

TOUDOUX: We've had dinner.

MADAME VIRTUEL: Already? *I* haven't.

TOUDOUX: Ah!

MADAME VIRTUEL: Of course not! I was about to sit down at the table, when you sent for me. So! isn't there anything to eat?

TOUDOUX: Are you hungry?

MADAME VIRTUEL: I don't eat because I'm hungry, I eat because it's time.

TOUDOUX: Oh! Well, there must be something left. *(To* CLÉMENCE*)* What about it?

CLÉMENCE: Yes, monsieur.

MADAME VIRTUEL: What kind of soup have you got?

CLÉMENCE: None.

MADAME VIRTUEL: *(Stares at her; pouts)* That's not much!

TOUDOUX: We never eat it.

MADAME VIRTUEL: *(Turning to him)* But *I* do.

TOUDOUX: *(Bowing)* Sorry.

MADAME VIRTUEL: Oh yes! I know. That's the way things are nowadays! *(Miminy-piminy)* We don't eat soup anymore! *(Energetically)* I'm old school! The good school! the one that won't have anything to do with progress!

TOUDOUX: Aha!

MADAME VIRTUEL: *(Resuming her earlier train of thought)* What next?

TOUDOUX: *(Conciliating)* Nothing!

MADAME VIRTUEL: What? First no soup! And then, no nothing!

TOUDOUX: *(Realizing his mistake)* Huh? No! Yes! yes! no! I thought you said "I'm old school, what next!"

MADAME VIRTUEL: No! What next…after the soup?

TOUDOUX: Ah! "What next after the soup", yes! Well then, after the soup…after the soup…after the soup we don't have! Round steak and macaroni.

MADAME VIRTUEL: *(Nodding)* And then?

TOUDOUX: That's all.

MADAME VIRTUEL: *(Pursing her lips)* That's pretty skimpy!

CLÉMENCE: A piece of cheese.

MADAME VIRTUEL: That doesn't count!

(MADAME VIRTUEL, *while* CLÉMENCE *goes above the table and picks up the cape left by* MADAME DE CHAMPRINET:)

MADAME VIRTUEL: You aren't big eaters here!

TOUDOUX: Really!

MADAME VIRTUEL: *(Heading for the dinner table)* All right, I'll have it, if that's all there is! *(She sits left of the table.)*

CLÉMENCE: *(Above the table, carefully folding* MADAME DE CHAMPRINET's *cape)* What would Madame like to drink? White wine? Red wine?

MADAME VIRTUEL: *(Indifferent)* Doesn't matter! I don't care... a little champagne!

TOUDOUX: *(In front of the table)* Champagne?

MADAME VIRTUEL: Yes. It's the best for my digestion!

TOUDOUX: You drink it at home?

MADAME VIRTUEL: *(Meaningfully)* When my patients send me some!

TOUDOUX: Ah.

MADAME VIRTUEL: Yes.

TOUDOUX: *(Choosing to ignore this)* Swell! *(To* CLÉMENCE *upstage right of the table)* Girl, go down to the grocer's and ask for some light stuff, you know, a...

CLÉMENCE: Maybe I won't have to! There's a bottle of Veuve Clicquot in the pantry. *(She heads for the pantry.)*

MADAME VIRTUEL: *(Good-natured)* Fine!

TOUDOUX: *(Furious, crossing down right)* No, get the other stuff!

MADAME VIRTUEL: It's all right. Veuve Clicquot's fine. What difference does it make? I'm easily pleased. I don't drink more than one bottle, you know!

TOUDOUX: *(Pretending to be sympathetic)* Really?

MADAME VIRTUEL: *(Munching a piece of bread)* Most of all, I don't want to be a nuisance.

TOUDOUX: You're so considerate.

CLÉMENCE: *(Moving to the table to remove the empty wine bottle)* When should I serve?

MADAME VIRTUEL: *(Rising and crossing downstage)* Heat it up and when it's ready, serve it!

CLÉMENCE: Might take about ten minutes.

MADAME VIRTUEL: Oh, I've got plenty of time!

(MADAME VIRTUEL, sitting right of the card table, while CLÉMENCE exits with the bottle and MADAME DE CHAMPRINET's cape)

MADAME VIRTUEL: As for Madame, it won't be a while yet.

TOUDOUX: *(Approaching)* Will it be a long while?

MADAME VIRTUEL: Well, you know, with these primiparous ones!

TOUDOUX: *(Wrinkling his brow in puzzlement)* With these...

MADAME VIRTUEL: Primiparous ones...things don't go so quickly! Madame is primiparous, I suppose?

TOUDOUX: *(Waving his arms like a man who has no answer)* Well...

MADAME VIRTUEL: Is she primiparous or multiparous? Which?

TOUDOUX: *(Hesitant, mouth agape. A pause)* Uh! *(He rotates his hand to indicate "in between," then suddenly, decisively.)* Viviparous.

MADAME VIRTUEL: *(Stunned)* What? *(Laughs)* Well, of course, viviparous! We're all viviparous!

TOUDOUX: That's right, we're all viviparous!

MADAME VIRTUEL: Not you!

TOUDOUX: Not me, no, not me!

MADAME VIRTUEL: You still haven't told me whether she's primiparous.

TOUDOUX: *(Hesitating)* Uh! *(Decisively)* No!

MADAME VIRTUEL: All the better. It'll go faster! How many children has she had?

TOUDOUX: *(Just as decisively)* None.

MADAME VIRTUEL: Then she's primiparous!

TOUDOUX: That's it, primiparous! She's primiparous!

MADAME VIRTUEL: Well, that's all I wanted to know. *(She rises.)*

TOUDOUX: I didn't catch your question.

MADAME VIRTUEL: *(Crossing up right of the table and heading towards the room left)* Well, maybe we ought to take a look at our patient!

TOUDOUX: *(Right on her heels)* Please, let's!

(MADAME VIRTUEL, turning around so abruptly that TOUDOUX bumps into her:)

MADAME VIRTUEL: No, no! Not you! You stay here. I want nobody!

TOUDOUX: Ah!

MADAME VIRTUEL: Nobody! Nobody! When I give birth, husbands and lovers aren't wanted.

TOUDOUX: Lovers! But my wife has no lovers.

MADAME VIRTUEL: I didn't say she had, I said that I don't want husbands or lovers, a fact, that's all! *(On these words, she half turns to go into the room.)*

TOUDOUX: Yes, but...

MADAME VIRTUEL: *(Turning quickly and imperatively)* Stay here!

(MADAME VIRTUEL enters LÉONIE's room. The doorbell rings.)

Scene Seven

(TOUDOUX, *then* CLÉMENCE, *then* DE CHAMPRINET)

TOUDOUX: Oh! she is maddening!

(CLÉMENCE, *coming in from the pantry with a basin full of water. At that moment, the bell keeps ringing in the vestibule; she hesitates for a moment over what to do—put down the basin or open the door. Then, to* TOUDOUX:)

CLÉMENCE: If Monsieur would please go to the door, because I'm busy with Madame?

TOUDOUX: What! Hasn't Benoit come back from his errands yet?

CLÉMENCE: No, Monsieur, and I have to bring this basin.

(*Doorbell.*)

TOUDOUX: To Madame? There's no point! They don't want anybody, not even me!

CLÉMENCE: Yes, but, I... (*Doorbell offstage; no one pays attention.*) If Monsieur would knock, because my hands are full.

TOUDOUX: (*Skeptical*) I will, but... (*He knocks at the bedroom door.*)

MADAME VIRTUEL: (*Off*) You can't come in.

TOUDOUX: (*Triumphant*) There!

(*Doorbell.*)

CLÉMENCE: (*Firm in her resolve*) It's me, the maid.

MADAME VIRTUEL: (*Off*) Ah! it's you! Come in!

CLÉMENCE: (*Triumphant in turn*) There!

(*Doorbell.* CLÉMENCE *goes into* LÉONIE's *room.*)

TOUDOUX: (*Crosses right*) Charming! Positively charming!

(Repeated doorbell offstage.)

TOUDOUX: Yes! Coming!

*(*TOUDOUX *crosses upstage and exits. The stage is empty during this offstage dialogue.)*

DE CHAMPRINET: *(Off)* Well! You certainly took your time about it!

TOUDOUX: *(Off)* Don't blame me! *I* had to come to the door!

*(*DE CHAMPRINET, *hat on head, cane in hand, entering, followed by* TOUDOUX*)*

DE CHAMPRINET: No! no! Have you any idea! No! This is it!

TOUDOUX: Well, what's wrong?

DE CHAMPRINET: *(Far left)* I have had it! Really, a man can't get five minute's peace in his life!

TOUDOUX: Tell me about it.

DE CHAMPRINET: Honestly, I don't know what you think you're playing at!

TOUDOUX: It's not my fault.

DE CHAMPRINET: *(Bowing)* It's not mine either! *(Taking off his hat)* There I was at the club after dinner quietly enjoying my usual game of whist...five louis kitty. I had a lucky streak, on top of it all! Bang, somebody runs in announcing *this* right in my face! Some fun! Naturally I threw in my hand! *(He sits left of the card table, on which he puts his hat.)* What could I do? I'm a responsible individual. But really, can't a man be left in peace at the end of the day!

TOUDOUX: *(Sitting right of the card table)* I'm ever so sorry!

DE CHAMPRINET: *(Rising and putting on his hat)* A lot of good that does! *(Heading for his daughter's room)* Now what! Can I see my daughter?

TOUDOUX: Listen, right at the moment she's under the midwife's care and she's not exactly cooperative.

DE CHAMPRINET: *(Annoyed)* Ah! *(Removes his hat and puts it and his cane on the chair left of the dinner table.)* The least you could do is offer me something to eat; I haven't had dinner, what with all of this! *(He crosses right.)*

TOUDOUX: *(Still seated)* Oh dear, if you'll be satisfied with what there is?

DE CHAMPRINET: Oh, I'm hungry enough! Do you suppose all this has taken the edge off my appetite?

(TOUDOUX, to CLÉMENCE coming out of LÉONIE's room:)

TOUDOUX: Ah! Clémence, you can set a place for Monsieur de Champrinet too.

CLÉMENCE: Very good, monsieur! *(She picks up DE CHAMPRINET's hat and cane and takes them off.)*

DE CHAMPRINET: *(His ears pricked)* Why "too"? Do you have company?

TOUDOUX: Yes.

DE CHAMPRINET: Ah?

TOUDOUX: The midwife.

DE CHAMPRINET: *(Put out)* Aha! I have to dine with a midwife.

TOUDOUX: Well...

DE CHAMPRINET: *(As before)* Splendid! Splendid!

TOUDOUX: Just this once?

DE CHAMPRINET: *(Above the card table)* Yes, yes! *(Annoyed)* The midwife indeed! *(Sitting left of the card *table, facing* TOUDOUX.*)* But how the devil did you arrange for it to be today? You didn't expect it for another month!

TOUDOUX: Leonie's ahead of schedule.

DE CHAMPRINET: *(While speaking, mechanically gathering the cards and shuffling them)* Ah, yes! A baby's a fine thing! A baby after eight months of marriage! What are people going to think? They'll never believe it.

TOUDOUX: Really?

DE CHAMPRINET: They'll insinuate, damn it, that you sampled the goods beforehand. The neighbors never did understand how a De Champrinet could have given his daughter away to a Toudoux. Obviously, they'll say it was a shotgun wedding. That's a nice kettle of fish.

TOUDOUX: *(Exasperated)* People are a month ahead of schedule every day.

DE CHAMPRINET: Of course it happens! Prove it. *(Dealing the cards for whist.)* It happens but not to everybody. Ah! you have a marvelous way of doing things! *(Picking up his hand of cards.)* Your lead!

TOUDOUX: *(Seated facing the audience, mechanically taking the cards and playing as he speaks)* If you're going to pay attention to what people *(Playing.)* say! Spades...

DE CHAMPRINET: Of course you have to pay attention! I have the king... You understand how annoying it can be...my cut...if they gossip about my daughter... trump, trump...that she had a baby after only eight months...king of diamonds, queen of hearts... The king and the vole: three points. *(Pushing the cards to* TOUDOUX*)* Your deal... You may sneer at public opinion...

TOUDOUX: *(Shuffling the cards)* Oh! that! *(He offers the deck to be cut.)*

DE CHAMPRINET: *(Cutting)* You may sneer, but just the same you have to take it into account.

TOUDOUX: *(Dealing)* Don't you realize that if you spent all your time worrying about what so-and-so said, why…

DE CHAMPRINET: *(Picking up his cards)* Of course you have to worry about it! …I have the king! *(Playing)* Hearts!

TOUDOUX: Oh yes! My cut!

DE CHAMPRINET: There we go! It's all most disagreeable.

(DE CHAMPRINET, Responding to the card TOUDOUX threw.)

DE CHAMPRINET: My cut! …Trump, trump and trump…I win! You owe me five louis.

TOUDOUX: *(Open-mouthed with his last card in the air)* What do you mean "I owe you"? I wasn't playing.

DE CHAMPRINET: You weren't playing? Well, what have you just been doing?

TOUDOUX: I played, I played! But I didn't play for five louis!

DE CHAMPRINET: That's wonderful! But you might have said so!

TOUDOUX: But it was up to you to say so!

DE CHAMPRINET: I always play for five louis! I just told you that a minute ago! If you had won, I would have paid you!

TOUDOUX: Maybe so, but that's no reason why I should give you five louis when I lose!

DE CHAMPRINET: *(Rising and crossing upstage)* This is too much! I'll never play with you again!

TOUDOUX: If you think I feel like playing!

DE CHAMPRINET: Eh? *(Energetically)* Well, neither do I! It's purely automatic! Not when my poor child is undergoing such a painful ordeal!

(TOUDOUX, rising and crossing to the door left, as does DE CHAMPRINET)

TOUDOUX: And a long one! What can they be doing in there?

(DE CHAMPRINET and TOUDOUX put their ears to the door.)

DE CHAMPRINET: Yes! I should very much like to give my daughter a kiss.

(At that moment, MADAME VIRTUEL abruptly exits from the room holding a basin of water; coming in backwards, she turns around in the doorway and as she moves pours her basin over TOUDOUX who is downstage of her and half-drowns him. DE CHAMPRINET, by a backward movement, has avoided being drenched.)

TOUDOUX: *(Leaping backward)* Oh!

Scene Nine

(The same, MADAME VIRTUEL)

MADAME VIRTUEL: *(Crossing center stage)* Well, would you look at that!

TOUDOUX: No, that does it! Not only do you drown me...

MADAME VIRTUEL: Tough luck! If you weren't always under foot!

TOUDOUX: *(Coming down far left)* I'm drenched!

MADAME VIRTUEL: That'll teach you to peep through keyholes, the two of you.

DE CHAMPRINET: *(Not believing his ears)* What?

TOUDOUX: *(Protesting)* Keyholes!

DE CHAMPRINET: See here!…

TOUDOUX: *(Moving center)* We're not in the habit of peeping through keyholes!

MADAME VIRTUEL: *(Skeptical)* Oh no!

TOUDOUX: I have to change now, on account of this.

MADAME VIRTUEL: *(Who has been looking for somewhere to put down the basin; turning around at this.)* Yes! Well, make yourself useful for once! Put this basin in the kitchen on your way out. *(She puts the basin in his hands.)*

TOUDOUX: Me!

MADAME VIRTUEL: Get along, get along!

TOUDOUX: *(As he exits with the basin; furious)* What a pest! *(He exits.)*

(DE CHAMPRINET, to MADAME VIRTUEL, who has taken stage:)

DE CHAMPRINET: Say, Madame, I'd like to see my daughter.

MADAME VIRTUEL: Yes. Well, you'll have to wait 'cause I don't need any strangers right now. *(She sits in the easy chair.)*

DE CHAMPRINET: What strangers? You think I'm a stranger, I, her father?

MADAME VIRTUEL: You're a stranger to giving birth.

DE CHAMPRINET: *(Nodding)* Ah! that!

MADAME VIRTUEL: All right. I can permit you to kiss your little missy in a while.

DE CHAMPRINET: "My little missy!" She's a married lady!

MADAME VIRTUEL: I didn't say she wasn't! But to you she'll always be your little missy. You may kiss her,

but just go in and come right out! In the meantime I'll
tell your missus you're here if she feels like seeing you.
Out of my way! *(She crosses in front of* DE CHAMPRINET
and heads for the room left.)

DE CHAMPRINET: See here, madame, you're not
particularly polite!

MADAME VIRTUEL: *(Coming back to him)* Polite! Polite!
I'll have you know I'm not one of your floozies!

DE CHAMPRINET: What?

MADAME VIRTUEL: I'm past the age of hanky-panky
with men!

DE CHAMPRINET: Pardon me, I didn't ask you for
hanky-panky.

MADAME VIRTUEL: You all but did. When I'm at work, I
am serious. I'm willing to have a laugh any other time.

DE CHAMPRINET: *(Jeering)* Ah!

MADAME VIRTUEL: But when duty calls *(Slapping her
chest)* I'm at my post!

DE CHAMPRINET: Good! Go to it!

MADAME VIRTUEL: Right! *(She pivots and heads towards
the bedroom.)*

DE CHAMPRINET: *(Theatrically)* "Once more into the
breach, dear friends!"

MADAME VIRTUEL: *(Turning quickly, with dignity)* Did
you say "breech"?

DE CHAMPRINET: No! It's a quotation!

MADAME VIRTUEL: *(As before)* Ah! I hope so! ...I'll send
you your missus.

DE CHAMPRINET: *(Going to sit right of the card table)* All
right!

(MADAME VIRTUEL *exits.)*

Scene Ten

*(*DE CHAMPRINET *and* MADAME DE CHAMPRINET*)*

DE CHAMPRINET: *(Gathering the cards together)* Oh
my! My my! Oh! my, my, my, my, my, my, my, my!
*(Dealing the cards as if playing whist with an imaginary
partner.)* "I'm not one of your floozies." Ah! I'll say
you're not! *(Turning up trumps)* Spades. *(He puts down
the deck of cards, turns over his hand and studies it for a
minute; next, he puts it on the table, picks up his opponent's
hand, studies the cards, then puts them back down with a
disappointed laugh.)* He's got the king. *(He picks up his
hand, is about to play, changes his mind, again turns over
his opponent's hand, takes the king, puts it in his hand, from
which he removes a low card which he exchanges for it; then
picking up his own cards.)* His lead!

MADAME DE CHAMPRINET: *(Coming out of her daughter's
room)* What, you're on your own!

DE CHAMPRINET: Monsieur Toudoux wants to change
his trousers!

MADAME DE CHAMPRINET: He worries about his
wardrobe while his wife lies on a bed of pain!

DE CHAMPRINET: He thought it amusing to be watered
by the midwife! How is she?

MADAME DE CHAMPRINET: *(Sitting left of the card table)*
Who? The midwife?

DE CHAMPRINET: No, Léonie! I don't give a damn about
the midwife!

MADAME DE CHAMPRINET: As well as can be expected.

DE CHAMPRINET: Ah! I really need all this nonsense.
I've been out of sorts for the past hour! Having a
baby…after eight months of marriage! *(He rises.)*

MADAME DE CHAMPRINET: Ah yes! It's most annoying!

DE CHAMPRINET: That's your Toudoux for you! That's how your Toudoux arranges things!

MADAME DE CHAMPRINET: My Toudoux! He's not my Toudoux!

DE CHAMPRINET: *(Moving right of center)* You were the one who urged on the marriage. I didn't want any part of it!

MADAME DE CHAMPRINET: But you, you, you didn't approve of any husband! Toudoux or anybody else, you hated him in advance!

DE CHAMPRINET: *(Above the card table)* Put yourself in my place, I can't help it. He disgusts me, this— gentleman! When I think that a man has only one daughter, that he sacrifices everything to raise her properly, that he avoids speaking one word louder than another or making an unseemly gesture so as not to sully her mind, and bingo! one fine day there comes a gentleman, a gentleman we don't even know! *(Moving down a bit)* And there you are! He carries off your daughter and has sex with her! *(Pounding the table with his fist for emphasis)* And we know about it, and all we can do is say "Amen!" *(Sitting right of the card table)* Doesn't that turn your stomach?

MADAME DE CHAMPRINET: What can we do? That's marriage!

DE CHAMPRINET: *(Facing the audience, left arm on the chair back)* Well yes, there's no denying that! *(Glancing at the door through which* TOUDOUX *made his exit.)* Her Toudoux! Her Toudoux! *(Turning his head to his wife.)* Do you like that man?

MADAME DE CHAMPRINET: For goodness' sake!

DE CHAMPRINET: *(Still staring at the door)* If I had to have sex with him, I couldn't do it!

MADAME DE CHAMPRINET: *(Mocking)* But then, he didn't ask you to marry him!

DE CHAMPRINET: Oh! he's capable of it!

MADAME DE CHAMPRINET: Anyway, he's making your daughter happy.

DE CHAMPRINET: *(Rising)* He had better!

MADAME DE CHAMPRINET: He's ever so kind! I might as well give him his due, so long as he isn't here! He complies with his wife's whims with such a good grace! Just now I could have proved it. Didn't Leonie have a craving! a pregnant woman's craving!

DE CHAMPRINET: He satisfied it? He merely did his duty.

MADAME DE CHAMPRINET: Even so, I know some men who…! She absolutely insisted that he put a chamber pot on his head!

DE CHAMPRINET: *(Not daring to believe such a thing; sitting right the card table)* And…he put it on?

MADAME DE CHAMPRINET: *(Stringing out her words)* He put it on!

DE CHAMPRINET: *(Delighted)* Oh! that's rich! I'm delighted! My son-in-law with a chamber pot on his head! I'm overjoyed!

MADAME DE CHAMPRINET: Malicious creature!

DE CHAMPRINET: *(As before, gathering the cards)* What do you expect? I'll never be able to look that fellow in the face again! Your lead!

MADAME DE CHAMPRINET: What?

DE CHAMPRINET: *(Looking up at the ceiling)* I have the king.

MADAME DE CHAMPRINET: What do you mean "I have the king"? I'm not playing cards!

DE CHAMPRINET: *(Baffled)* Huh? *(Shouting)* Neither
am I, I'm not playing cards, I said "I have the king"
because I have the king! It's sheer distraction! I'm
otherwise engaged!

MADAME DE CHAMPRINET: So am I, I assure you.

Scene Eleven

(The same, TOUDOUX, *then* MADAME VIRTUEL*)*

TOUDOUX: *(Entering from the vestibule)* I had to change
everything, because of that nonsense!

DE CHAMPRINET: Ah, there you are!

TOUDOUX: Yes, here I am!

MADAME VIRTUEL: *(Bounding out of the room left)* The
young lady's calling for her papa and mama.

DE CHAMPRINET: Ah!

(Simultaneously DE CHAMPRINET *and his wife rise to go to*
LÉONIE.*)*

*(*MADAME VIRTUEL, *quickly barring the way of* DE
CHAMPRINET *who is ahead in the rush:)*

MADAME VIRTUEL: But…not for long, you know! Not
for long!

*(*DE CHAMPRINET, *sending her left with a shove, up right of
the card table)*

DE CHAMPRINET: Yes, yes!

MADAME VIRTUEL: *(Rubbing her right shoulder)* Oh!
Why, he pushed me!

DE CHAMPRINET: *(About to enter* LÉONIE's *room; whisper
to his wife)* Ah! that old bat gets on my nerves!

MADAME VIRTUEL: *(Sulking)* I don't like to be bullied!

MADAME DE CHAMPRINET: Here's papa, sweetheart!

DE CHAMPRINET: *(Entering his daughter's room)* How are you feeling, darling?

(The door closes.)

*(*TOUDOUX, *approaching* MADAME VIRTUEL *who is seated right of the card table and is automatically starting to shuffle the cards:)*

TOUDOUX: Madame, is it making any progress?

MADAME VIRTUEL: *(Not turning around, making two stacks of cards and cutting the bottom one; bleating)* Heuheuheu!

TOUDOUX: Not much yet?

MADAME VIRTUEL: Pffu! She's a quarter. *(Meanwhile she makes a gesture with her hand to express her meaning, index and thumb joining to produce an opening about the size of a quarter.)*

TOUDOUX: *(Not understanding)* She's…

MADAME VIRTUEL: And when I say a quarter, I exaggerate!

TOUDOUX: Ah!

MADAME VIRTUEL: She's more between five cents and a quarter.

TOUDOUX: *(Who wants to seem as if he understands)* Yes… she's a dime.

MADAME VIRTUEL: *(Rounding on him)* What! "A dime"? What's a dime supposed to mean? A dime's a coin, not a size!

TOUDOUX: *(Intimidated)* Ah! yes, yes…that's right, it's… it's a coin!

MADAME VIRTUEL: No. Like this. *(So saying, she joins her index and thumb to demonstrate the size she means.)*

TOUDOUX: *(No better off)* Like that! Yes! It's… it's not serious?

MADAME VIRTUEL: No, no! Anyway it'll be a while yet.

TOUDOUX: Ah! yes! but it doesn't mean anything bad?

MADAME VIRTUEL: Not at all! *(Rising.)* Although there are some things I can't explain!

TOUDOUX: Ah!

MADAME VIRTUEL: I laid hands on the mother-to-be, and couldn't exactly locate it.

TOUDOUX: Aha!

MADAME VIRTUEL: *(Detached)* Perhaps it's due to a little uterine hydropsy.

TOUDOUX: *(Without a clue, but tries to seem in the know)* I wouldn't be at all surprised!

MADAME VIRTUEL: And yet, when I pressed on that side, there seemed to be perhaps three points of resistance. *(She lends support to her statement by poking* TOUDOUX's *abdomen in three places—right, left and right.)*

TOUDOUX: So?

MADAME VIRTUEL: Well, I don't know! Maybe it's a gemellary pregnancy!

TOUDOUX: *(Leaning toward her, scowling like a man who has not heard right)* Gemel…

MADAME VIRTUEL: …lary. *(Back to the table, left arm on the chair back.)* You don't happen to know if there's already been a case in your family or the lady's of gemellary birth?

TOUDOUX: *(Slowly, spreads his arms and shrugs, in ignorance).*

MADAME VIRTUEL: You don't remember? No?

TOUDOUX: Well…

MADAME VIRTUEL: Yes, you don't remember.

TOUDOUX: No, I don't… But what could come of it?

MADAME VIRTUEL: What do you mean, "what"? *(Standing.)* Why… twins!

TOUDOUX: *(Jumping)* Tw…twins! *(Crossing right)* Good grief! Two layettes! Two cribs!

MADAME VIRTUEL: *(Crossing left)* Well, I only say it might be! Without a stethoscope, you understand. *(Sitting left of the card table)* Do you know if anyone used a stethoscope?

TOUDOUX: *(Right of the card table)* A stetho…?

MADAME VIRTUEL: …scope

TOUDOUX: *(Hesitant)* Ah…no…no! *(Sitting down.)* But I do know she took a bath this morning.

MADAME VIRTUEL: That's beside the point! It's as if I were to ask you, "Do you catch cold?" and you answer "No, but I wear suspenders!" *(Rising)* It's as stupid as that!

TOUDOUX: Sorry.

MADAME VIRTUEL: *(Above the table)* I asked if anybody used a stethoscope, because it would detect the heartbeats.

TOUDOUX: Yes, yes.

MADAME VIRTUEL: *(Indifferently, as if she were speaking of the most obvious thing)* Now it is possible that it's simply a left posterior sacro-anterior breech presentation.

TOUDOUX: Breech presentation?

MADAME VIRTUEL: Yes indeed. *(So saying, she goes up to the dinner table to find a piece of bread to nibble.)*

TOUDOUX: *(His right hand grabbing her by the rump and pulling her back)* And, tell me…uh, Madame What'syername!

MADAME VIRTUEL: *(Caught)* Oh!

TOUDOUX: Breech presentation, is that good?

MADAME VIRTUEL: *(Above the card table, nibbling her bread)* Well, I would have preferred a cranial!

TOUDOUX: A cranial! Ah! yes, of course, a cranial! Naturally.

MADAME VIRTUEL: It's obvious that a right or left occipitoiliac, anterior or posterior...

TOUDOUX: Yes, yes! Never mind!

MADAME VIRTUEL: *(Crossing up to the easy chair as she speaks)* Ah! we see such odd things in our profession! *(Sitting)* Why, just the other day didn't I have me a patient with a hydatiform mole?

TOUDOUX: You don't say!

MADAME VIRTUEL: *(With a graphic gesture)* Looks like a bunch of grapes, you know?

TOUDOUX: *(Imitating her gesture)* Grapes! My goodness, grapes!

MADAME VIRTUEL: *(Bunching up in the easy chair)* I'll bet that's something you don't often come across?

TOUDOUX: No, I can't recall! *(Aside)* Oh! She's driving me crazy with these technical terms!

MADAME VIRTUEL: Hydatidiform moles are very curious, very curious.

TOUDOUX: Yes, yes indeed. *(Rising and going to her.)* Well now, I never saw a...hydatidiform mole, but what I have seen like that was...a case of...I don't know if you're familiar with it!

MADAME VIRTUEL: *(Without hesitating, self-importantly)* Of course I'm familiar with it!

TOUDOUX: *(His hand on the chair back)* A case of... *(Very slowly)* constantinopolitis.

MADAME VIRTUEL: *(Stiffening, leaning forward)* Of what?

TOUDOUX: *(Categorically)* Constantinopolitis.

MADAME VIRTUEL: *(Seems to scan her brain for a moment; then, sinking back in her chair)* Ah! yes, yes, that's been known to happen!

TOUDOUX: *(Startled)* You've seen it!

MADAME VIRTUEL: Many times!

TOUDOUX: *(Crossing left of center)* Well! she's got a nerve!

MADAME VIRTUEL: *(Changing the subject)* But aren't we going to have dinner?

TOUDOUX: *(Starting for the pantry door)* Yes, I think so.

MADAME VIRTUEL: *(Rising and moving up to the dinner table)* I could eat a horse!

TOUDOUX: *(Who has opened the pantry door; speaking into the wings)* You may serve, Clémence!

Scene Twelve

(The same, DE CHAMPRINET, *then* CLÉMENCE*)*

*(*MADAME VIRTUEL *notices* DE CHAMPRINET *leaving his daughter's room)*

MADAME VIRTUEL: Ah, there you are, *you*!

DE CHAMPRINET: Yes!

MADAME VIRTUEL: *(Scolding him)* I said "Go in and come out". You paid me no mind!

DE CHAMPRINET: Oh!…

MADAME VIRTUEL: No mind!

DE CHAMPRINET: *(One knee on the chair right of the card table)* Well, yes, of course. The poor little thing, I saw her, she's being brave. Will it still be a while?

MADAME VIRTUEL: *(With a vague gesture)* Who knows? *(She moves up to the dinner table.)*

TOUDOUX: *(Happy to display his knowledge; in a detached tone)* She is a quarter!

DE CHAMPRINET: *(Looks at him in astonishment)* What's that mean?

(TOUDOUX, with a sudden shout of triumph, slapping on the back MADAME VIRTUEL who is standing, back to the audience, busy fussing about the dinner table:)

TOUDOUX: Ah! ah! ah!

MADAME VIRTUEL: *(Jumping to face him)* Oh!

TOUDOUX: You don't know either! I'm delighted to hear it! Well, ask Madame Whosis!

MADAME VIRTUEL: *(Shocked)* Whosis!

TOUDOUX: Madame Virtuel.

DE CHAMPRINET: *(To MADAME VIRTUEL)* What's the meaning of "She's a quarter"?

MADAME VIRTUEL: Eh? …Well! you see, it' s when the… *(She vaguely sketches an explanatory gesture and then, changing her mind.)* No! these things aren't for children's ears! *(Chucking him under the chin like a baby)* Kitchy kitchy koo! *(She moves left, pushes the chair right of the card table under the table to get it out of the way for the next scenes—for the dinner table must be visible—then comes down past the card table and crosses far left.)*

DE CHAMPRINET: *(Nonplussed for a moment, then crossing to Toudoux who is in front of the easy chair; arms akimbo)* That midwife doesn't give a hoot who I am!

TOUDOUX: She's a character!

CLÉMENCE: *(Bringing the leftover steak and casserole of macaroni, as well as the bottle of Veuve Clicquot. Placing the bottle on the table)* Dinner is served! *(She places the macaroni and the steak on the breakfront.)*

MADAME VIRTUEL: Ah!

(MADAME VIRTUEL quickly goes to DE CHAMPRINET, who is still standing arms akimbo and slips her arm into his.)

DE CHAMPRINET: *(Surprised, turning towards her)* What is this?

MADAME VIRTUEL: Dinner is served, so I'm taking your arm.

DE CHAMPRINET: *(With ironically exaggerated courtesy)* Oh! I beg your pardon!

MADAME VIRTUEL: *(Snapping her fingers)* Now we're cooking!

DE CHAMPRINET: *(Bowing, mocking)* As you say, "now we're cooking."

(They cross upstage, while TOUDOUX sits in the easy chair.)

MADAME VIRTUEL: What seat are you taking?

DE CHAMPRINET: *(Most chivalrous)* Whichever one you don't take!

MADAME VIRTUEL: *(Moving left, indicating the seat left of the dinner table)* Then I take this one, because over there you get a draft from the door on your back. And I don't care much for that.

DE CHAMPRINET: *(Bowing, moved)* Thank you!

(They sit at the table, facing one another.)

(MADAME VIRTUEL, to CLÉMENCE, who, during the preceding, has changed the place settings, taking fresh ones from the dresser:)

MADAME VIRTUEL: Well, my girl, while I'm having dinner, you stay with Madame! In case she needs somebody while I'm eating!

CLÉMENCE: What about serving?

MADAME VIRTUEL: We'll take care of it. If necessary *(Pointing to TOUDOUX, still seated.)* Monsieur's already had dinner, so he can hand us the plates.

TOUDOUX: Me?

MADAME VIRTUEL: Besides, there aren't that many! Just put them on the table.

DE CHAMPRINET: Yes, no need to stand on ceremony.

CLÉMENCE: *(Placing the steak and macaroni on the table)* Very good, madame.

(MADAME VIRTUEL, while CLÉMENCE heads for LÉONIE's room; graciously to TOUDOUX)

MADAME VIRTUEL: Men make the best waiters.

TOUDOUX: *(Bowing; sarcastic)* Too kind of you!

(CLÉMENCE knocks on Léonie's door.)

MADAME DE CHAMPRINET: *(Off)* Come in!

(CLÉMENCE exits.)

MADAME VIRTUEL: *(Throwing herself back in her chair and, smugly, to DE CHAMPRINET)* Ah! this is nice!

DE CHAMPRINET: *(Helping himself to steak)* What is?

MADAME VIRTUEL: This! The two of us!

DE CHAMPRINET: *(Mocking)* Ah! Really?

MADAME VIRTUEL: *(Helping herself to macaroni)* I remember we had a little party like this with the Duke de Cussinge… *(Passing the casserole to DE CHAMPRINET)* Here, help yourself!

DE CHAMPRINET: Thanks! *(He serves himself.)*

MADAME VIRTUEL: …while the Duchess was lying in.

DE CHAMPRINET: Ah! so you were the one who…?

MADAME VIRTUEL: *(Swallowing a mouthful of macaroni)* Yes, that was me! It all came about through my intermittence!

DE CHAMPRINET: *(Repeating deliberately)* Through your intermittence! Ah! You don't say!

MADAME VIRTUEL: We dined in private like this, the Duke and me. *(Most exhilarated)* Aha! He's a rascal!

DE CHAMPRINET: Would you believe it!

MADAME VIRTUEL: Just like tonight, although there we had a heap of flunkeys.

TOUDOUX: *(Kidding, from his position)* I'm so sorry.

MADAME VIRTUEL: Oh, it's not a reproach! I got no flunkeys at home myself. *(She eats.)*

TOUDOUX: Ah!

MADAME VIRTUEL: *(Holding out the bottle of champagne)* Here, uncork the champagne!

TOUDOUX: Me?

MADAME VIRTUEL: Of course, you!

TOUDOUX: *(Rising)* Fine! Fine! Fine! *(He takes the bottle and sits on the chair against the wall, right of* LÉONIE's *bedroom door.)*

MADAME VIRTUEL: *(Considering* DE CHAMPRINET*)* As a matter of fact, "De Cussinge" and "De Champrinet" are two peas in a pod! Are you high society too?

DE CHAMPRINET: *(Modestly)* Goodness me!

MADAME VIRTUEL: What are you? Marquis? Viscount? Commander? What?

DE CHAMPRINET: *(Modestly)* Count.

MADAME VIRTUEL: *(Appreciatively)* Ah! Count! That's swell! But if you're a count, how come you have a son-in-law *(Turning towards* TOUDOUX, *still busy trying to uncork the bottle)* who's nothing?

DE CHAMPRINET: Well…I had no choice!

MADAME VIRTUEL: *(Mouth full)* Like you say…a person got no choice!

TOUDOUX: They're charming!

MADAME VIRTUEL: *(Choking)* Oof! Goodness me! This macaroni is heavy stuff! Don't you think so?

DE CHAMPRINET: *(Also choking)* I was just about to say the same thing!

MADAME VIRTUEL: *(Taken with hiccups)* Yoop! ...Oh, it's given me the "kickups", yoop! How about you?

DE CHAMPRINET: No, I never get hiccups.

MADAME VIRTUEL: You're lucky! Yoop! *(Turning to* TOUDOUX*)* Hurry up and uncork that bottle... yoop... you!

TOUDOUX: I can't get the cork out, it's stuck!

MADAME VIRTUEL: *(Turning over the empty carafe)* That's great! There isn't—yoop—a thing to drink—yoop!

DE CHAMPRINET: As a matter of fact I've—yoop—got a thirst on me! See here—yoop—I've got the hiccups too!

MADAME VIRTUEL: Find a cork—yoop—screw!

DE CHAMPRINET: *(Rising)* Wait! Give that—yoop—to me!

TOUDOUX: *(Crossing to him)* Gladly! If you can pull it out!

MADAME VIRTUEL: *(Coming downstage)* Hurry up! Yoop!

DE CHAMPRINET: All right, all right, yoop!

(Wordless scene. TOUDOUX *is center stage between* DE CHAMPRINET *who attempts to uncork the bottle and* MADAME VIRTUEL *eager to see the bottle uncorked. Alternately and as if antiphonally* MADAME VIRTUEL *and* DE CHAMPRINET *hiccup.)*

MADAME VIRTUEL: Yoop!

(Pause)

DE CHAMPRINET: Yoop!

(Pause)

MADAME VIRTUEL: Yoop!

(Pause)

DE CHAMPRINET: Yoop!

(Pause)

MADAME VIRTUEL: Yoop!..Oh!

(Pause)

DE CHAMPRINET: Yoop!

(Pause)

MADAME VIRTUEL &: DE CHAMPRINET: *(Together)* Yoop!

TOUDOUX: *(Crossing down left)* No, it's really true—people who have hiccups are a pain in the neck to people who don't!

DE CHAMPRINET: What's the matter with this—yoop—bottle?

MADAME VIRTUEL: Water! Liquid! Anything!

DE CHAMPRINET: *(Putting the bottle on the dinner table)* Where's the corkscrew? Yoop!

MADAME VIRTUEL: *(Abruptly)* Over there! *(Pointing to the pedestal table.)* Distilled water! Yoop!

DE CHAMPRINET: Ah! yes! distilled water...yoop! *(He runs to the pedestal table and quickly takes one of the bottles.)*

MADAME VIRTUEL: Be careful! Yoop! Don't take the chloroform! Yoop!

DE CHAMPRINET: *(Snapping the cap off a bottle)* No, this is it! "Distilled water", yoop!

(DE CHAMPRINET *quickly returns to the table and half fills* MADAME VIRTUEL's *glass. She swallows the contents while he pours himself a drink.)*

MADAME VIRTUEL: *(After drinking)* More! More! Yoop! Even more!

(They pour out drinks.)

MADAME VIRTUEL: *(With a sigh of satisfaction; sitting down)* Ah! That's better!

DE CHAMPRINET: *(Drinking; shaking his finger for emphasis on what he's about to say)* Ah, yes!

Scene Thirteen

(The same, MADAME DE CHAMPRINET*)*

MADAME DE CHAMPRINET: *(Hurrying from her daughter's room)* Madame Midwife, if you don't mind. Would you please come in here?

MADAME VIRTUEL: *(Rising in her chair)* What's the trouble?

MADAME DE CHAMPRINET: I don't know! You'd better take a look! It's something I can't explain!

MADAME VIRTUEL: *(Making haste)* Ah!

TOUDOUX: *(Up right of the card table)* What? What is it?

DE CHAMPRINET: *(Approaching)* Is she all right?

MADAME DE CHAMPRINET: It's nothing! Never mind! Madame Midwife had better…

*(*MADAME VIRTUEL, *passing in front of* MADAME DE CHAMPRINET *who follows her out:)*

MADAME VIRTUEL: I'm coming! *(About to leave, she turns around abruptly, bumping against* MADAME DE CHAMPRINET.*)* Oops! Sorry. *(To* TOUDOUX.*)* Make me some coffee!

TOUDOUX: What?

MADAME VIRTUEL: *(Repeating)* Coffee! *(About to exit, one last hiccup.)* Yoop! Oh, there it goes again!

(MADAME VIRTUEL *exits, followed by* MADAME DE CHAMPRINET.)

TOUDOUX: *(Annoyed; heading towards* DE CHAMPRINET*)* "Make me some coffee!" *(To* DE CHAMPRINET.*)* She must think I'm her servant!

DE CHAMPRINET: Fine, make me some coffee too! *(He sits in the easy chair.)*

TOUDOUX: *(Dumbfounded)* Perfect! Anything else?

DE CHAMPRINET: Nothing else, thanks.

Scene Fourteen

(DE CHAMPRINET, TOUDOUX, CLÉMENCE)

*(*TOUDOUX, *to* CLÉMENCE *who leaves the bedroom and busily crosses the dining-room:)*

TOUDOUX: Clémence!

CLÉMENCE: *(Without stopping)* Monsieur?

TOUDOUX: Some coffee and make it snappy!

CLÉMENCE: *(Waving him away in order to get by)* I ain't got time! *(She exits right.)*

TOUDOUX: *(Nonplussed)* Ah! ah! I beg your pardon! *(To* DE CHAMPRINET:*)* A thousand pardons! She hasn't time! It'll have to wait. *(He goes up to the dinner table.)*

DE CHAMPRINET: *(Peeved, taking a cigarette from his cigarette case)* Charming! What a day! A wretched dinner! My daughter having a baby! Hiccups! No coffee! It's perfect! *(He lights the cigarette.)*

TOUDOUX: *(Backed up, almost sitting, against the dinner table)* I am deeply sorry!

DE CHAMPRINET: *(Rising and crossing left)* Oh, yes! You are deeply sorry… *(He crosses nervously upstage, then*

stations himself, back to the audience, facing TOUDOUX.)
So?

TOUDOUX: So what?

DE CHAMPRINET: Who's going to suckle the baby?

TOUDOUX: *(Bitterly)* So far as I know, its mother—not
me!

DE CHAMPRINET: *(Startled)* Its mother! You have the
audacity to make a wet nurse of my daughter?

TOUDOUX: Why not? Lots of women do it!

DE CHAMPRINET: Lower-class women, yes! but not
people of our standing.

TOUDOUX: *("I don't give a damn")* Oh!

DE CHAMPRINET: *(Crossing left)* I didn't hand over my
daughter so you could turn her into a canteen! Or
convert her into a seltzer-bottle! A De Champrinet!

TOUDOUX: 'Scuse me, a Toudoux!

DE CHAMPRINET: *(Disdainfully over his shoulder)* Oh yes!
Get that! "A Toudoux," how elegant! *(Sitting left of the
card table)* And all because you're too cheap to pay for a
wet nurse or bottle feeding!

TOUDOUX: *(Shrugging)* Bottle feeding is for scrawny
runts.

DE CHAMPRINET: *(Rising and bowing)* Thank you very
much! I was nursed that way! *(He sits down again.)*

TOUDOUX: *(Tit for tat)* Well, look! How am I supposed
to know?

DE CHAMPRINET: Turning Léonie into a wet nurse!

TOUDOUX: *(Nerves on edge)* No, listen! The baby isn't
even born yet! At least wait till he gets here!

DE CHAMPRINET: *(Bantering)* Why don't you ask her to
provide the cream for your coffee, while you're at it!

TOUDOUX: Oh, stop exaggerating!

DE CHAMPRINET: I mean it!

Scene Fifteen

(The same, MADAME VIRTUEL, *then* CLÉMENCE*)*

MADAME VIRTUEL: *(Bursting in)* The maid? Where's the maid?

DE CHAMPRINET & TOUDOUX: What's wrong?

MADAME VIRTUEL: *(Not stopping, going to the pantry door)* I want the maid. *(Calling through the half-opened door)* Adèle!

TOUDOUX: What "Adele"? Don't bother calling "Adèle," her name is Clémence!

MADAME VIRTUEL: Right, I'm confusing her with the last house. *(Calling)* Clémence!

CLÉMENCE: *(Off)* Coming!

TOUDOUX: She's making coffee for my father-in-law!

MADAME VIRTUEL: *(Crossing)* He can wait!

TOUDOUX: And for you.

MADAME VIRTUEL: *(Changing her tone)* Ah! good.

CLÉMENCE: *(Appearing at the pantry door)* Madame called?

MADAME VIRTUEL: Bring a bowl of hot water to Madame's room! Quick! *(She finishes her sentence as she starts to move back to* LÉONIE's *room.)*

CLÉMENCE: Very good! *(She disappears.)*

TOUDOUX: *(Grabbing* MADAME VIRTUEL *by the arm)* Madame Virtuel! Madame Virtuel! *(Leading her down to the forestage.)* I can see you're busy! Has something new happened?

MADAME VIRTUEL: Yes, something new, certainly something new!

DE CHAMPRINET & TOUDOUX: Ah?

(DE CHAMPRINET *rises and crosses to* MADAME VIRTUEL.)

MADAME VIRTUEL: No need to see any more. I've decided. It's happened!

TOUDOUX: *(Beaming)* It's happened?

DE CHAMPRINET: Already?

TOUDOUX: Then you know what it is?

MADAME VIRTUEL: Oh yes!

DE CHAMPRINET & TOUDOUX: Ah!

TOUDOUX: *(Affirmatively)* It's a boy!

MADAME VIRTUEL: No!

DE CHAMPRINET: A girl?

MADAME VIRTUEL: No!

DE CHAMPRINET: Neither a boy nor a girl?

TOUDOUX: *(In agony)* What then?

MADAME VIRTUEL: Nothing at all!

DE CHAMPRINET: Nothing?

TOUDOUX: What do you mean, nothing at all?

MADAME VIRTUEL: *(Flapping her hand over her head to imitate something flying by)* Ffut! Nervous pregnancy!

DE CHAMPRINET: Nervous pregnancy!

TOUDOUX: *(Aghast)* What in the world is that?

MADAME VIRTUEL: Something that happens! It even fooled me!

DE CHAMPRINET & TOUDOUX: *(Dumbfounded)* Oh!

MADAME VIRTUEL: I once knew a woman who carried for twenty-five months. People started to wonder. They

said, "It can't possibly be an elephant!" Mme Toudoux
is at present acting out the fable of the mountain that
gave birth to a mouse!

TOUDOUX: A mouse came out!

DE CHAMPRINET: Huh?

MADAME VIRTUEL: What? No. You'll have to start all
over again from scratch, my poor sir! This one was a
misdeal.

TOUDOUX: *(Sinking into the easy chair)* Misdeal! It was a
misdeal!

DE CHAMPRINET: *(Infuriated)* Ah, you do some fine
work! Congratulations!

TOUDOUX: What?

DE CHAMPRINET: Not even capable of producing a
child! The next time you decide to be a father, we'll
probably end up with a rabbit!

TOUDOUX: Listen here! Is it my fault?

MADAME VIRTUEL: *(Intervening)* Come, come,
gentlemen, gentlemen!

(DE CHAMPRINET, *spinning* MADAME VIRTUEL *around and
sending her stage left:)*

DE CHAMPRINET: Go fly a kite, you!

MADAME VIRTUEL: Oh! what a roughneck!

Scene Sixteen

(The same, MADAME DE CHAMPRINET*)*

MADAME DE CHAMPRINET: *(At her wits' end, running to
her husband)* A nervous pregnancy!

TOUDOUX: Ah! here's the other one!

DE CHAMPRINET: Yes, that's your Toudoux for you! That's what your Toudoux does to us.

MADAME DE CHAMPRINET: Ah! If I had had any idea!

TOUDOUX: But...

DE CHAMPRINET: After I told you time and time again we ought to have taken a son-in-law from our own crowd!

TOUDOUX: You're starting to get on my nerves... "From your own crowd, from your own crowd!" After all, it's your daughter who got pregnant, not me! Well, she's from your crowd.

(MADAME VIRTUEL, *to* TOUDOUX *who has come near her as he finishes his line*)

MADAME VIRTUEL: There, there, calm down. Not so much noise!

(TOUDOUX, *to* MADAME VIRTUEL, *setting her spinning:*)

TOUDOUX: Shut your trap!

MADAME VIRTUEL: But there are sick people here!

TOUDOUX: *(To the others, while passing before them)* Just now you chewed me out because I was going to have a baby! Now it's because I don't have one! You don't know what you want! *(He has reached far right.)*

DE CHAMPRINET: *(Truculent)* What?

MADAME DE CHAMPRINET: *(Crossing right)* Keep still, monsieur, you are being positively ridiculous.

DE CHAMPRINET: *(Sitting right of the card table)* Yes, ridiculous!

TOUDOUX: All right! I'm ridiculous. That suits me fine!

MADAME DE CHAMPRINET: I'm not surprised! Any gentleman who agrees to put chamber pots on his head!

TOUDOUX: What did you say?

MADAME DE CHAMPRINET: You heard me!

TOUDOUX: *(Violent)* I've got to get out of here! *(He heads up to the door.)*

MADAME DE CHAMPRINET: *(Quickly picking up the chamber pot and presenting it to* TOUDOUX's *back, while making a deep bow, which brings her left)* All right! Here, monsieur, here's your hat!

TOUDOUX: *(Snatching the pot for her hands)* Ah, my hat!

*(*TOUDOUX's *about to fling it to the ground and break it, but stops when* DE CHAMPRINET *says:)*

DE CHAMPRINET: *(Quickly)* Oh! no! no!

TOUDOUX: Huh? *(He moodily throws the pot on the dinner table.)*

DE CHAMPRINET: Oh, put it on! So I can say I saw you in it!

MADAME VIRTUEL: Yes, yes!

TOUDOUX: What?

DE CHAMPRINET: You must be the first person I ever saw with a chamber pot on his head!

TOUDOUX: Really?

DE CHAMPRINET: You can be sure!

TOUDOUX: Is that right? Well, now you can say you're the second.

*(*TOUDOUX *puts the pot on* DE CHAMPRINET's *head.)*

ALL: Oh!

(General tumult. They rush to DE CHAMPRINET *to remove it.)*

CLÉMENCE: *(Entering with a bowl of water)* I've got the b...oh!

TOUDOUX: Get the hell out, the lot of you!
(Curtain)

END OF PLAY

THE AWFUL TOOTH
(Hortense a dit "Je m'en fous!")

CHARACTERS & SETTING

FOLLBRAGUET, *a dentist*
MARCELLE FOLLBRAGUET, *his wife*
MONSIEUR JEAN, *his assistant*
VILDAMOUR, *a patient*
LEBOUCQ, *a patient*
MADAME DINGUE, *a patient*
ADRIEN, *a servant*
HORTENSE, *the maid*
THE COOK

FOLLEBRAGUET's *dental office. At back, doors right and left. Between the doors, in the center of the party wall, a wash basin.*

Upstage right, a door covered by wall-paper. Downstage, against the wall, on a little table, an autoclave (sterilizer) At left, the fireplace. Above it, a door opening into MME FOLLBRAGUET's *rooms.*

As to furniture, at right, a desk perpendicular to the footlights. Between the wall and the desk, the office chair. Pieces of furniture here and there. Dead center, before the prompter's box and facing the audience, the operating chair. Left of the chair, a little chest of drawers, on high legs, which holds the instruments and medications. Nearby, the dentist's drill on a wheel operated by a treadle. Right of the chair, the spitoon with its glass tube to pump out the patients' saliva.

Scene One

(FOLLBRAGUET, VILDAMOUR, *then* ADRIEN, *then*
MARCELLE, *then* MONSIEUR JEAN)

(*As the curtain rises,* VILDAMOUR *is sitting in the operating
chair, a bib around his neck, his mouth gagged by a block
of black rubber, which allows only the tooth to be treated to
emerge at its center. This piece of rubber is fixed to either
side of the mouth by a clamp attached to a kind of rubber
garter which goes around the neck. To complete this torture
device, in the left corner of the mouth, the aforementioned
saliva pump.*)

(FOLLBRAGUET *is right of* VILDAMOUR *working on his
mouth with the drill.*)

VILDAMOUR: (*Biting down on the rubber block*) Oooooon-
on-on!

FOLLBRAGUET: (*Hard at work*) Patience! It won't be
much longer! Open your mouth!

VILDAMOUR: (*In pain*) Oon-on-on!

FOLLBRAGUET: (*Working on*) Pay it no mind! Think of
something fun!

VILDAMOUR: (*Incomprehensible behind his gag*) Ah! …
eh…ih…ee-aw-oo-ah-ay! (*Which means, so far as we can
tell: "Ah! yes, it's easy for you to say!"*)

FOLLBRAGUET: Don't move, please! Open your mouth
wider…I am not hurting you, I tell you, I'm not hurting
you.

VILDAMOUR: *(Moaning)* Ooon-on-on!

FOLLBRAGUET: Not at all, not at all: when I'll have to hurt you, I'll let you know.

VILDAMOUR: *(In anguish)* Oha!

FOLLBRAGUET: Take it easy! *(He stops to change his instrument.)*

VILDAMOUR: Oo-uh-eh-aw-ess! *("You're full of promises.")*

FOLLBRAGUET: *(Who has taken up another instrument)* There! ...Open your mouth! ...Good! ...Take care!

VILDAMOUR: *(Turning pale)* Aw? *("What?")*

FOLLBRAGUET: Don't worry...now this may hurt just a little bit...

VILDAMOUR: *(Worried)* Ah? *(Suddenly)* Ow!...

FOLLBRAGUET: There! ...I did tell you beforehand! No, no, don't turn your head...oh!

VILDAMOUR: *(Exhausted)* Ay!...ay-uh-oh-eh. *("Wait! Wait a moment.")* Ah! uh-ee-eh! Uh-ee-eh! *("Ah! bloody hell! Bloody hell!")*

FOLLBRAGUET: There, all done! All done.

VILDAMOUR: Ah! uh-ee-eh, oo-oh-oh-ah-ih-ay! Ih-aw-ih-eh...ay ih-ih ih-oh ay eh! Uh-uh! Ay-oo-uh-er...aw-ih-eh!... *("Ah! bloody hell, you don't know what it's like! It's horrible... it's like drilling into my brain. Whirr, whirr! It goes right to my heart...it's awful!")*

FOLLBRAGUET: *(Automatically)* Yes, yes, monsieur, yes.

VILDAMOUR: Ay uh oh oo eh-eh-eh oo-ay, uh ee uh ah ee-ee ih! *("I don't know who invented toothache, but he was a stinking pig.")* Oo ih ah-oh ay ah ah ay-oh-eh oo-eh, uh ih ay. *("Two years ago I had a violent toothache, but nothing like this.")*

FOLLBRAGUET: *(Attaching his instrument to the end of the drill)* There! Open your mouth.

VILDAMOUR: Oh! uh ih ah-eh! *("Oh! the drill again!")*

FOLLBRAGUET: A mere trifle! ...a joke!... *(He operates.)* There! I'm not hurting you.

VILDAMOUR: *(With conviction)* Eh-oo-ah! *("Yes you are!")*

FOLLBRAGUET: It's for your own good...there...there...you see, you're getting accustomed to it; open your mouth! If you did that for a week running, you wouldn't want to do without it.

VILDAMOUR: *(Moaning)* Oon! Oon! Oon!

FOLLBRAGUET: No, no, don't be silly. There, it's done! *(Carrying on all the same.)* It's all over...

VILDAMOUR: Oon! Oon!

FOLLBRAGUET: It's over now! *(He stops.)*

VILDAMOUR: *(Standing up)* Ah!

FOLLBRAGUET: Wait! Wait! I haven't finished!

VILDAMOUR: *(Sitting down again)* Oo ee ay ee "ih uh eh" ay oo aw ih-ih! *("You keep saying it's over and you don't finish!")*

FOLLBRAGUET: *(During this has lighted a little alcohol lamp to heat his hot-air bulb)* Nothing to it now. Don't be afraid! Open your mouth!

VILDAMOUR: *(At every puff squeezed from the bulb)* Hha! hha! hha! hha!

FOLLBRAGUET: There!

VILDAMOUR: Oh! ih ih oh uh eh eh. *("Oh! this is so unpleasant.")*

FOLLBRAGUET: *(Quickly)* Don't close your mouth! ... Keep it wide open. *(He has wound a piece of cotton around a steel rod, and after soaking it in a little bottle of pharmaceutical, he introduces it into the tooth he has just treated.)* There! It wasn't as bad as all that! *(He undoes the rubber, removes the saliva pump, and holding out a glass a quarter full of a mixture of dentifrice and water.)* Spit!

VILDAMOUR: *(Obeys and having rinsed out his mouth)* Thanks...most kind of you...to torture me like that!

FOLLBRAGUET: *(Heading towards his desk)* Not at all! Not at all! That sort of talk is what makes it hurt! Now, look: you're going to keep this dressing on it for a day or two, and after that come back here so I can put in a gold filling. *(Leafing through his date-book)* Let's see, what appointments do I have? Wait...day after tomorrow, five o'clock, are you free?

VILDAMOUR: Five o'clock day after tomorrow? ...No, I have an appointment.

FOLLBRAGUET: Aha! *(He's already looking for another day.)* Let's see...

VILDAMOUR: Oh! that'll do just fine! It's a creditor! There'll be nobody home! It's a stroke of luck!

FOLLBRAGUET: Perfect. Then *(Writing it down)* February eleventh, five o'clock, Monsieur Vildamour. Don't forget!

VILDAMOUR: You can see I never forget, if I can remember a meeting with a creditor. *(Pause)* Ouch! *(Pause)* It still hurts, you know.

FOLLBRAGUET: *(Indifferent)* Yes, yes.

VILDAMOUR: You don't seem to care much.

FOLLBRAGUET: I don't, because it's all perfectly normal. You will be in pain like this for another fifteen minutes, and then it will start to subside. I've just hollowed out the orifice, it takes time for it to disengage.

VILDAMOUR: Aha!

FOLLBRAGUET: *(As he speaks, he goes to push an electric-bell button)* However, if you continue to feel pain, then come back. I'll fit you in between two appointments.

VILDAMOUR: Yes, oh! you are the most painless of dentists. Except for today. Whenever I recommend you, you know...you can ask...I always say: ah, my dentist, he's a gem! Such a touch! It's a pleasure, you never feel a thing!

FOLLBRAGUET: *(Flattered)* Ah! and what do they say to that?

VILDAMOUR: They reply, "So is mine!"

FOLLBRAGUET: *(Cool)* Ah!

ADRIEN: *(Appears at back)* Monsieur?

FOLLBRAGUET: You may show the gentleman out! Then, you will tell Monsieur Jean to come in... *(To* VILDAMOUR*)* Day after tomorrow at five o'clock, right?

VILDAMOUR: Absolutely.

FOLLBRAGUET: And be sure to cover your mouth. Be careful not to expose your tooth to the cold. But you're making off with my bib!

VILDAMOUR: Oh! sorry!

(He puts the bib on the back of the operating chair. Since ADRIEN *has opened the door to let* VILDAMOUR *out, in the waiting room we can glimpse* MARCELLE *bickering with* HORTENSE. *They are both speaking at the same time.)*

MARCELLE: That'll be enough of that! If I give you an order, you mustn't talk back!

FOLLBRAGUET: Why, what's the matter?

*(*VILDAMOUR, *followed by* ADRIEN, *crossing in front of* MARCELLE:*)*

VILDAMOUR: Excuse me, madame!

MARCELLE: *(Quickly and curtly)* Good afternoon, monsieur.

FOLLBRAGUET: The waiting room is no place to argue with servants, especially during my consulting hours.

MARCELLE: *(Erupting into* FOLLBRAGUET's *office and holding out a muff she has in hand)* My dear, please touch that!

FOLLBRAGUET: I say that the waiting room...

MARCELLE: Well! I'm not in the waiting room! I'm in your office. Will you please touch that?

FOLLBRAGUET: *(Automatically touching it)* What for? ... Ah! what's this? It's wet.

MARCELLE: *(Triumphant)* Ah! you think it's wet too.

HORTENSE: *(On the threshold)* I never said it wasn't.

FOLLBRAGUET: *(Automatically sniffing his fingers)* What of it? ...Oh! it's water.

MARCELLE: Water! Oh! so you think it's water.

FOLLBRAGUET: Well, since it's wet!

HORTENSE: There!

MARCELLE: It's cat pee!

FOLLBRAGUET: *(Furious)* Oh! how disgusting!

MARCELLE: You can't be such an expert.

FOLLBRAGUET: *(Rinsing his hands at the wash basin)* And you made me touch it!

HORTENSE: No, no, monsieur! Madame insists that my pussy forgot herself on her muff. Now, since everyone knows that my pussy never goes into your rooms, I ask you how she could have done it.

MARCELLE: But, for heaven's sake, you only have to smell it! *(To* FOLLBRAGUET*)* Go ahead, smell it!

FOLLBRAGUET: Certainly not!

MONSIEUR JEAN: *(Appearing right, he is in work clothes, white linen jacket)* You called for me, Monsieur Follbraguet.

FOLLBRAGUET: *(Wiping his hands)* Yes!

MARCELLE: *(Holding out her muff to him)* Monsieur Jean, will you please tell me what this smells like?

FOLLBRAGUET: Oh no, I beg of you.

MARCELLE: I beg of you too, don't influence him.

MONSIEUR JEAN: *(Sniffing obligingly)* I don't care much for this perfume.

MARCELLE: That's not what I asked you. What does it smell like?

(FOLLBRAGUET, *while* MONSIEUR JEAN *smells at length)*

FOLLBRAGUET: She's crazy!

MONSIEUR JEAN: It's eucalyptus.

MARCELLE: *(Quickly pulling away her muff which brushes* MONSIEUR JEAN'*s nose)* No, monsieur, it's cat pee.

MONSIEUR JEAN: *(Wiping off his nose)* Not my favorite perfume.

MARCELLE: *(To* HORTENSE*)* You see everyone is in agreement. You can't go on telling me...

FOLLBRAGUET: *(Pushing them out)* Yes, well, pee or not, I would be obliged if you'd carried on your quarrel somewhere other than my office. I have to see patients, and they don't need to be privy to your business!

MARCELLE: *(Arguing as she lets herself be pushed out, along with* HORTENSE*)* You can't go on telling me that it isn't your cat...

HORTENSE: I beg your pardon, madame! Madame mustn't make me say anything that isn't the truth.

MARCELLE: Will you please keep your mouth shut! I won't allow you to talk back when I make a statement...

FOLLBRAGUET: Get out and leave me in peace, blast it!

(FOLLBRAGUET *pushes them out and closes the door on them. We can hear the argument going on behind the door as it fades in the distance.*)

FOLLBRAGUET: Oh! it's appalling that a man can never have any peace! *(To Monsieur Jean.)* What was I going to say? ...Yes... Are there many patients out there?

MONSIEUR JEAN: Not a soul. I had Sarah Bernhardt just now; a wisdom tooth was obtruding.

FOLLBRAGUET: Well, well!

MONSIEUR JEAN: I made an incision in the gum to facilitate the extrusion.

FOLLBRAGUET: Perfect! Still has her looks?

MONSIEUR JEAN: I'll say!

FOLLBRAGUET: Why didn't you tell me? ...I would have loved to see her.

MONSIEUR JEAN: You were busy with a patient, so I took her.

FOLLBRAGUET: So self-sacrificing!

MONSIEUR JEAN: Oh! Monsieur Follbraguet, Madame Bernhardt and I would never... neither of us.

FOLLBRAGUET: *(Ironically)* Oh!

MONSIEUR JEAN: *(Solemnly)* I swear it!

FOLLBRAGUET: That's all right...I wanted to tell you! You have to stop by What'sizname...the one who supplies us with amalgam compound...

MONSIEUR JEAN: Bringuet.

FOLLBRAGUET: Yes, tell him that his last shipment was no good. All of my latest fillings disintegrated and fell apart; it isn't serious, but I'll have to change them.

MONSIEUR JEAN: All right, monsieur.

FOLLBRAGUET: That's all.

MONSIEUR JEAN: Very good, monsieur.

Scene Two

(The same, MARCELLE, *then* HORTENSE*)*

MARCELLE: My dear, please...

FOLLBRAGUET: Oh! you again!

MARCELLE: Why! There's nobody here...

FOLLBRAGUET: I beg your pardon, people are waiting.

MARCELLE: Well! let them wait! If you've got a toothache you wait. I insist that you dismiss Hortense, this very minute.

FOLLBRAGUET: Oh, now what?

MARCELLE: I'm making a remark to her and she says, "I don't give a good goddam!"

FOLLBRAGUET: Well! say it back to her.

MARCELLE: You admit it! You admit she contradicted me by saying "I don't give a good goddam!"

FOLLBRAGUET: Which proves she's philosophical.

(Stifled little laugh from MONSIEUR JEAN*)*

MARCELLE: What have *you* got to laugh about?

MONSIEUR JEAN: Oh! nothing, madame.

MARCELLE: *(To her husband)* Oh! very witty! Anyway, it's no surprise! Everybody knows you don't care if I'm insulted! It's just because they know that I have no one to stand up for me that people dare to...

FOLLBRAGUET: Don't be silly, what's your point? If you didn't keep pestering that girl.

MARCELLE: I pester her, I pester! That's incredible!

MONSIEUR JEAN: May I go, monsieur?

FOLLBRAGUET: Yes, Monsieur Jean. I realize that this conversation is of no interest to you!

MONSIEUR JEAN: Oh! it's not that!

FOLLBRAGUET: No excuses...go on, Monsieur Jean, go on.

(MONSIEUR JEAN *exits.*)

MARCELLE: There you have it! There's a perfect example! How do you expect him to respect me, if you make fun of me when he's around.

FOLLBRAGUET: What, he didn't disrespect you!

MARCELLE: No, but he will! Go on defending that girl!

FOLLBRAGUET: But I'm not defending her.

MARCELLE: All right, I know that from now on my muffs are to be used as urinals for my maid's pussy. *(He goes upstage.)*

FOLLBRAGUET: Ah! for pity's sake! Enough with that pussy business! Turn it into a rabbit stew, and stop talking about it.

MARCELLE: Will you fire her, yes or no?

FOLLBRAGUET: Oh, you are such a nuisance!

MARCELLE: *(Going upstage and calling)* Hortense! Hortense!

FOLLBRAGUET: For pity's sake! For pity's sake!

MARCELLE: Hortense!

HORTENSE: *(Off)* Madame?

FOLLBRAGUET: What a life!

(MARCELLE, *to* HORTENSE *who appears:*)

MARCELLE: Come in! so that the master can fire you!

FOLLBRAGUET: Certainly not!

MARCELLE: Yes indeed!

FOLLBRAGUET: Oh!

MARCELLE: I just told the master the way you dare to speak to me. He is outraged!

FOLLBRAGUET: *(At the end of his rope)* No, this is exasperating!

MARCELLE: There! You hear him! The master says it's exasperating!

HORTENSE: Was the master saying that about me?

MARCELLE: You aren't suggesting that it's about me?

HORTENSE: I don't know.

MARCELLE: You hear! You hear the way she talks to me! Well, say something, won't you! Be brave enough to talk to people to their face!

FOLLBRAGUET: But what in the world do you want me to say?

MARCELLE: This girl here replies to a remark with "I don't give a good goddam!", you'll grant that?

FOLLBRAGUET: *(Unpersuaded)* No.

MARCELLE: Well, if you won't grant it, prove it by firing her! *(Pause)* Well?

FOLLBRAGUET: Well! wait...what!

HORTENSE: Of course I'd be very sorry to leave this house because Monsieur has always been good to me, but if Monsieur insists.

FOLLBRAGUET: Now, my girl, how did you say "I don't give a good goddam" to the mistress?

MARCELLE: What difference does it make how she said it! There aren't a lot of ways to say "I don't give a good goddam!" I will not allow a lady's maid to swear like a trooper in my presence! She said "I don't give a good goddam!" Well! fire her! Plain and simple.

FOLLBRAGUET: *(To* HORTENSE*)* Well? what can I do, my girl, since the mistress absolutely insists that I fire you.

HORTENSE: Very good, monsieur. *(Pause)* I'll miss Monsieur who has always been so good to the staff.

MARCELLE: Never mind that! Go get your account book, so we can settle up.

*(*HORTENSE *exits.)*

Scene Three

*(*FOLLBRAGUET, MARCELLE, *then* ADRIEN, *the* MADAME DINGUE*)*

FOLLBRAGUET: *(Back against the desk)* Why be so hard on the girl just because she has a good word for me?

MARCELLE: Oh yes! of course! You let her take you in and don't see it's another insult meant for me...I can tell...

FOLLBRAGUET: Oh! you're always seeing conspiracies in everything!

MARCELLE: And you're too spineless! Spineless! Ah! what a dishrag!

FOLLBRAGUET: Naturally! if someone doesn't agree with you, he's a dishrag! *(A knock at the door)* Come in!

ADRIEN: Has the master forgot that there's still someone in the waiting room.

FOLLBRAGUET: All right! What do you expect? The mistress won't leave me alone for a minute.

MARCELLE: Such tact! Such tact!

FOLLBRAGUET: It's the truth! *(To* ADRIEN*)* Show him in.

MARCELLE: What a dishrag! *(She exits left.)*

FOLLBRAGUET: Yes, yes, that's old news.

(As MADAME DINGUE *enters.)*

FOLLBRAGUET: Come in, madame!

*(*MADAME DINGUE, *to* ADRIEN *who is slipping away)*

MADAME DINGUE: Sorry!

*(*ADRIEN *exits.)*

FOLLBRAGUET: You didn't make an appointment?

MADAME DINGUE: No, Doctor. This is the first time I've been here. My regular dentist has unfortunately passed away. Actually I have no luck with dentists, this is the third one I've lost!

FOLLBRAGUET: Ah! that's not very encouraging.

MADAME DINGUE: Oh! it proves nothing! Though we shall see.

FOLLBRAGUET: Thank you, madame.

MADAME DINGUE: I know that you are the dentist of one of my good friends. He's the one who recommended you, Monsieur Bienassis.

FOLLBRAGUET: Aha!

MADAME DINGUE: You know him well?

FOLLBRAGUET: Certainly, I sued him.

MADAME DINGUE: Ah! he didn't tell me.

FOLLBRAGUET: Oh! he owes me money, that's all!

MADAME DINGUE: Oh! then it isn't serious! Money doesn't make for happiness.

FOLLBRAGUET: Yes, still it makes you wonder why the rich hold on it so tight!

MADAME DINGUE: Ah! here we are chatting away, and I'm taking up your time! Here's my problem, Doctor. Just a little accident, when I was eating lentils, the servants are so inattentive in their chores. They left in a pebble, and I broke a tooth.

FOLLBRAGUET: Ah! that's a shame! If you will kindly sit down.

MADAME DINGUE: Of course. *(She sits in the dental chair.)*

FOLLBRAGUET: *(Preparing to examine her)* Which tooth is the broken one? *(He steps on to the chair.)*

MADAME DINGUE: I'll show you. *(Pulling a set of dentures out of her handbag)*

FOLLBRAGUET: Aha!

MADAME DINGUE: Of course, this is between us!

FOLLBRAGUET: Oh! professional confidentiality!

MADAME DINGUE: *(Contemplating her dentures)* They're pretty, aren't they?

(FOLLBRAGUET nods in agreement.)

MADAME DINGUE: It's the last creation of the poor departed.

FOLLBRAGUET: Ah, yes! the last dentist…before me.

MADAME DINGUE: Yes. I asked him for something special, because—I don't know if you agree—but I think a woman's main attraction is pearly teeth.

FOLLBRAGUET: They are worth whatever you pay.

MADAME DINGUE: That's so true.

FOLLBRAGUET: There's not a dentist who would disagree with you. *(He lowers the chair.)*

MADAME DINGUE: Oh! where am I going?

FOLLBRAGUET: Don't worry, madame. You are there.

MADAME DINGUE: Delightful!

FOLLBRAGUET: Dear me, madame, one tooth has to be reset. But it will take a few days. Are you in a hurry?

MADAME DINGUE: Oh! I have my backup set, the everyday ones, so in the meantime…

FOLLBRAGUET: Ah, so these are the Sunday teeth.

MADAME DINGUE: Oh! no, I have a horror of dressing up on Sundays, but if there's a dance or a dinner party on the cards.

FOLLBRAGUET: That's fine! *(Opening the door behind the curtain.)* Monsieur Jean, if you will.

MONSIEUR JEAN: *(Off)* Coming, monsieur, right away.

FOLLBRAGUET: *(Behind his desk, opening his appointment book)* If you'll give me your name and your address.

MADAME DINGUE: Madame Dingue…Iza…Iza Dingue…8, rue Bugeaud.

FOLLBRAGUET: Mme Iza Dingue…8, rue Bugeaud… repair "yum, yum, yum".

MADAME DINGUE: What do you mean repair "yum, yum, yum"?

FOLLBRAGUET: I put that in for me: I'll understand. You don't want someone to open the book by chance and read "Mme Dingue, repair false teeth".

MADAME DINGUE: Oh no!

FOLLBRAGUET: So, "yum, yum, yum" I know what it means, and the uninformed will not.

MADAME DINGUE: Most ingenious.

FOLLBRAGUET: Yes, always in such cases! …You aren't the only one… *(Flipping through his appointment book.)*

Look here… Madame Rethel-Pajon. "Yum yum"…
insert an incisor.

MADAME DINGUE: Mme Armand Rethel-Pajon?

FOLLBRAGUET: Yes.

MADAME DINGUE: Oh! but I know her very well. What,
she wears dentures?

FOLLBRAGUET: *(Rattled)* Yes…eh? No! no!

MADAME DINGUE: But what about "yum, yum, yum"?

FOLLBRAGUET: *(Quickly)* It's a mistake, it isn't her.

MADAME DINGUE: Oh, don't worry, I'll be discreet.

FOLLBRAGUET: Oh! please don't take advantage of a
slip-up. Anyway, one discretion for another… you
understand.

MADAME DINGUE: Yes, yes! well, I never would have
thought it, I always admired her teeth!…

FOLLBRAGUET: *(Bowing)* You really are too kind.

MADAME DINGUE: Ah? they're yours?

FOLLBRAGUET: They are mine.

MADAME DINGUE: What an artist!

MONSIEUR JEAN: You were asking for me, Monsieur
Follbraguet?

FOLLBRAGUET: *(Pushing the electric-bell button)* Yes, it's
for this lady, where did I put them?

MADAME DINGUE: What?

FOLLBRAGUET: Your teeth… *(He looks in his pockets.)*
Ah! they're in my pocket. *(Handing the dentures to*
MONSIEUR JEAN*)* Here they are!

MONSIEUR JEAN: *(Innocently)* Aha?

MADAME DINGUE: What do you mean "aha"?

FOLLBRAGUET: Second molar upper left to be replaced…

MONSIEUR JEAN: Fine!

FOLLBRAGUET: And something elegant, eh? This is the fancy set.

MONSIEUR JEAN: Very good, monsieur. Does Madame have a date set for her bridge?

MADAME DINGUE: My bridge! What bridge? …I don't play bridge…

MONSIEUR JEAN: No, it's for the …

FOLLBRAGUET: *(To* MADAME DINGUE*)* Yes, it's also called a bridge.

MADAME DINGUE: Ah, I didn't know.

FOLLBRAGUET: *(Sending him away)* All right, Monsieur Jean…I'll set a date for this lady…

*(*MONSIEUR JEAN *exits with the dentures.)*

ADRIEN: *(Entering)* Monsieur rang?

*(*FOLLBRAGUET, *to* ADRIEN, *who appears at the door left)*

FOLLBRAGUET: See this lady out.

ADRIEN: Very good, monsieur.

MADAME DINGUE: Thank you, doctor. *(She goes to take her muff from the desk.)*

FOLLBRAGUET: Anyone else out there?

ADRIEN: No one at the moment, but Hortense is waiting in the hall to speak to Monsieur.

FOLLBRAGUET: *(With an angry gesture)* Ah!… *(After a pause)* All right, after your mistress goes out.

MADAME DINGUE: Now, Doctor, when will I get it?

FOLLBRAGUET: What's that, Madame?

MADAME DINGUE: My "yum, yum, yum."

FOLLBRAGUET: *(Understanding)* Ah!

ADRIEN: *(Teeth clenched, sarcastically)* Well!

FOLLBRAGUET: Oh! it'll take seven or eight days, I'll send them to you.

MADAME DINGUE: All right, doctor, good-bye.

FOLLBRAGUET: My respects, madame. *(On the threshold)* Come in, you!

Scene Four

*(*FOLLBRAGUET, HORTENSE*)*

HORTENSE: I've brought the master my book.

FOLLBRAGUET: All right, hand it over! *(He takes the book and goes to sit at his desk.)*

HORTENSE: The master will see. It stopped at January 30, so there's the account from the first to the ninth.

FOLLBRAGUET: *(While thumbing through the book)* Fine, fine!

HORTENSE: Plus my month which starts on the sixteenth, makes a month minus seven days, plus my two weeks' notice that I have a right to, that makes a month and one day, sixty-two francs in all...

FOLLBRAGUET: It's dreadful, all these irrelevant items in here.

HORTENSE: *(Primly)* After all! those are expenses for the mistress.

FOLLBRAGUET: Oh yes! I'm well aware...

HORTENSE: Oh! I'm well aware that the master is well aware!

FOLLBRAGUET: Look at that! Muslin, muslin, tulle, muslin, muslin, muslin, tulle, muslin, muslin. What can you make with all that muslin?

HORTENSE: Frills!

FOLLBRAGUET: What's this here?

HORTENSE: *(Coming close to* FOLLBRAGUET) Sorry... *(Reading) Sodanum.*

FOLLBRAGUET: *(Somewhat ironically)* Ah!

HORTENSE: My handwriting's not very good.

FOLLBRAGUET: That's not what I meant!

HORTENSE: In my station in life, after all?

FOLLBRAGUET: Laudanum, yes, yes. Why buy it, when we have it here?

HORTENSE: One night when Monsieur had gone out, Madame had to make a poultice, so, since she didn't have any *sodanum,* she sent me to the drugstore.

FOLLBRAGUET: Got it. *(Reading)* Lavender, 75 centimes; starch, 80; uh, what? ...What did you put there? Curling what?

HORTENSE: *(Checking it)* Curling tongs.

FOLLBRAGUET: Tongs is spelled with a t, not a d!

HORTENSE: Ah? ...That's possible.

FOLLBRAGUET: The total comes to eight-six francs twenty plus sixty-two, one hundred and forty-eight francs twenty. Write: "Received in full settlement of all demands one hundred and forty-eight francs twenty" and your signature.

HORTENSE: Oh! oh! If the master would write it himself, what with those all foreign words... I'd never get through it.

FOLLBRAGUET: All right... *(He writes.)*

HORTENSE: Would the master write me my character?

FOLLBRAGUET: *(While writing)* Oh! not today, you can get it tomorrow. *(Finishing writing)* ...One hundred and forty-eight francs twenty! February ninth 1915. There, write at the bottom, in receipt, and sign it.

HORTENSE: *(Taking the pen)* Yes, monsieur.

FOLLBRAGUET: No, no, "in receipt" isn't three words, it's not a title. *(Spelling.)* I-n, then...r-e-c-e-i-p-t!...

HORTENSE: I forgot to put in any *punk shoo-action.*

FOLLBRAGUET: There's no need. Sign it.

HORTENSE: *(Signs)* There.

FOLLBRAGUET: *(Rising)* I'll get you what you're owed.

HORTENSE: I hope the master won't hold it against me.

FOLLBRAGUET: No... Ah! you had to bring me into this mess!

HORTENSE: I'm very sorry, but if the mistress hadn't said to me...

FOLLBRAGUET: Hadn't said what to you?

HORTENSE: That it was my pussy that went...

FOLLBRAGUET: Ah! your pussy. What difference does your pussy make? You're not going to take your pussy personally! It isn't your mother or your sister. You're not going to make a federal case out of this!

HORTENSE: What does Monsieur expect! Just because a person is a servant, she can't allow a person to say whatever a person wants to her!

FOLLBRAGUET: A fine kettle of fish! But no, you can't help it! You always have to answer back.

HORTENSE: Anyway, the master knows what the mistress is like. She always talks to a person in a tone of voice.

FOLLBRAGUET: I'm not saying…

HORTENSE: You'd think the master didn't know what I'm talking about. When I see the way she often treats the master…

FOLLBRAGUET: Yes, oh! well, for my part…

HORTENSE: And in front of us too, honestly, we get so embarrassed.

FOLLBRAGUET: Well, yes, I'm well aware…

HORTENSE: We were just talking about it in the servant's hall: Adrien was outraged.

FOLLBRAGUET: Ah!

HORTENSE: He was saying—because Adrien is a man who doesn't just like to hear himself talk, he's got common sense—he was saying, "Really, I admire the master. If I had a wife like the mistress, I wouldn't have stayed twenty-four hours."

FOLLBRAGUET: What do you expect…

HORTENSE: That habit, just yesterday, when we were waiting at table, of calling the master all sorts of names…calling him a eunuch…

FOLLBRAGUET: And it isn't true!

HORTENSE: How do I know, monsieur, I've got no way of knowing!

FOLLBRAGUET: Ah! yes, but…

HORTENSE: Euncuh! Is that the kind of thing to say in front of servants?

FOLLBRAGUET: That…!

HORTENSE: How can Monsieur expect the servants to respect him after that! "Eunuch!"

FOLLBRAGUET: Yes, fine…

HORTENSE: Ah! if masters only knew how wrong they are to act that way! ...Do servants go and talk about their private affairs in front of their employers? ...Oh no! not so dumb as all that!

FOLLBRAGUET: Yes. Ah! it's unfortunate that you didn't say that to my wife.

HORTENSE: It isn't easy!

FOLLBRAGUET: I've gone blue in the face trying to tell her... But she can't help it... As soon as there's an audience, she'll say whatever's on her mind... If I have the bad luck to say something she doesn't like, —I don't know, —that I don't care for her dress or her hair style. Oh dear, oh dear, the things she can come out with about me or mine: "Ah! naturally, you'd prefer me to look like a floozy, like your sister!"

HORTENSE: And heaven knows that the master's sister...

FOLLBRAGUET: Why, you were there, the other day, when she made that scene... *(Without transition)* Do sit down.

HORTENSE: Yes, monsieur.

FOLLBRAGUET: About her wardrobe...I never give her enough money for her clothes, she doesn't have anything to wear.

HORTENSE: It's crazy!

FOLLBRAGUET: After all, you know something about it. You know all I've had to pay, all the time, all those bills...and why? ...For trifles, for frills and furbelows, like in your book.

HORTENSE: Muslin, muslin, muslin, tulle, muslin, muslin, muslin.

FOLLBRAGUET: Yes.

HORTENSE: But why does the master let her do it?

FOLLBRAGUET: What do you want me to do?

HORTENSE: Say once and for all: "That'll be enough of that! I'm giving you this much for your dresses, and not a penny more!"

FOLLBRAGUET: That's all very well, but when the bills arrive, the things have already been bought.

HORTENSE: Well! then say: "I'm sorry but I won't pay". The next time the mistress will take it for granted.

FOLLBRAGUET: *(Dreamily)* Obviously...

HORTENSE: The master is too good, so he gets run over!

FOLLBRAGUET: What can you do? To keep the peace it's better to give in a little...

HORTENSE: Ah! when it comes to that!...

FOLLBRAGUET: Well, that's what you should have done too... instead of insisting on an argument.

HORTENSE: Obviously, the master has a sweeter temper than I do.

FOLLBRAGUET: The fact is, your mistress has a very short fuse, but if you don't put up any resistance... I am convinced that tomorrow...she'll see you here doing your job...she won't even remember that she dismissed you.

HORTENSE: Yes, but the master must understand... serving in such conditions...

FOLLBRAGUET: No! listen! Listen! You're wrong there! At this moment you're the one who's being unreasonable!

HORTENSE: When you feel that no one appreciates you! For instance, Monsieur: when I started to work for the mistress, I asked for seventy francs... The mistress said: "No, sixty and if, after six months, I'm satisfied

with you, I'll raise it ten francs." To avoid an argument,
I accepted.

FOLLBRAGUET: Well then?

HORTENSE: Well, I've been here eight months and the
mistress hasn't given me the raise.

FOLLBRAGUET: Maybe she forgot.

HORTENSE: No, no! I reminded her, and she said, "Fine,
fine, we've got plenty of time to talk about it!"

FOLLBRAGUET: Oh! if it's only a matter of ten francs.

HORTENSE: Oh! I know it's not the master who would
refuse me!

FOLLBRAGUET: Of course not. Ten francs isn't worth
talking about.

HORTENSE: Thank you very much, monsieur.

FOLLBRAGUET: What for?

HORTENSE: For the ten francs.

FOLLBRAGUET: Ah! yes…after all… Only, please, be
very careful! …Avoid scenes, it drives me frantic, and
I'd prefer anything but that!

HORTENSE: Yes, monsieur!

FOLLBRAGUET: I'll go and get your money, since you've
checked your book…

HORTENSE: If the master will…

(Knock at the door)

FOLLBRAGUET: *(About to exit)* Come in!

Scene Five

(The same, THE COOK*)*

THE COOK: It's me, monsieur.

FOLLBRAGUET: What in the world are you doing in the office? Why aren't you in the kitchen?

THE COOK: Because I'm coming to dress the mistress since she got nobody to do it. The mistress sent me here...

FOLLBRAGUET: Yes, all right, right away. *(He exits through the door behind the curtain, right.)*

THE COOK: *(Once FOLLBRAGUET is gone)* So?

HORTENSE: What?

THE COOK: You're leaving on the spot!

HORTENSE: No.

THE COOK: I thought they fired you.

HORTENSE: Yes.

THE COOK: For saying to the mistress "I don't give a good goddam."

HORTENSE: Yes.

THE COOK: Well then?

HORTENSE: The master raised my wages ten francs.

THE COOK: *(Amazed)* Wow!

FOLLBRAGUET: *(Enters)* Well, are you still here?

THE COOK: The mistress told me to ask the master...

FOLLBRAGUET: Now what?

THE COOK: To ask him if "he had done it?"

FOLLBRAGUET: *(Looking at HORTENSE with a bob of the head as if to say: "Can you believe it?", then to THE COOK)* It's all right. Tell Madame that I'll give her the answer in person.

THE COOK: Very good, monsieur. *(She exits.)*

Scene Six

(HORTENSE, FOLLBRAGUET, *then* MARCELLE)

FOLLBRAGUET: *(With a sour grin)* She never lets up!

(HORTENSE *makes the gesture of a woman who's known that for a long time.*)

FOLLBRAGUET: Listen, my girl…let's say a hundred and forty-eight francs twenty… First here's the twenty centimes…and then a hundred and forty-eight; 48 out of 60… Can you change 60 francs?

HORTENSE: Sure, monsieur. *(Pulling out a change-purse and extracting two francs)* Here are two francs, monsieur.

FOLLBRAGUET: No, no! sixty minus forty-eight is twelve francs.

HORTENSE: But you gave me a ten-franc raise.

FOLLBRAGUET: Ah! that…yes…yes…that's right, the…

HORTENSE: Thank you, monsieur.

(MARCELLE *bursts in and sees the seated* HORTENSE, *who rises when she enters:*)

MARCELLE: Ah? …What's all this? You're holding court now?

FOLLBRAGUET: Eh? …No! …I was just in the middle of lecturing her.

MARCELLE: And you let her sit down for that?

FOLLBRAGUET: Because it was going to take a long time… After all, you know, she's a good girl…and her heart's in the right place…

MARCELLE: Never mind about that…did you give her her wages?

FOLLBRAGUET: *(Worried)* Yes…yes, I gave her her wages…I settled with her… *(To* HORTENSE*)* Didn't I?

HORTENSE: Yes, monsieur.

MARCELLE: Well, why is she taking so long in leaving…

FOLLBRAGUET: She's waiting…yes, yes, of course: what is she waiting for? Just now we were talking…she was saying great things about you…that you were a very elegant lady.

MARCELLE: How good of her. Who asked her opinion?

FOLLBRAGUET: No, nobody…that's not why she said that … Only you've got to admit that you can be a little abrupt.

MARCELLE: What?

FOLLBRAGUET: With me, for instance. Obviously, when all's said and done, you're not ill-tempered… But as she was telling me: there are some things that shouldn't be said in front of the servants.

MARCELLE: Huh? You're asking the servants their opinion of me?

FOLLBRAGUET: No, no, it just came up, in the course of the conversation… It's…it's like this, you see? You promised her a ten-franc raise… So since you made a promise…

MARCELLE: What about it?

FOLLBRAGUET: Well, I told her I'd let her have it.

MARCELLE: (With a start) Huh?

FOLLBRAGUET: I thought you'd approve…

MARCELLE: No! this is incredible! I tell you to fire her, and you give her a raise!

FOLLBRAGUET: Listen!…

MARCELLE: No, no, that'll do! Since I'm no longer mistress in my own house! …Since when it comes to my maid and me, you take the maid's side…very well, I know what I have to do.

FOLLBRAGUET: Now don't fly off the handle like that, for heaven's sake! Ah!

MARCELLE: Oh! I'm not flying off the handle... However, I am making the decision demanded by my dignity, I am leaving this house.

FOLLBRAGUET: See here, Marcelle...

MARCELLE: No, no, don't even try! I'm leaving...

FOLLBRAGUET: Ah! then go on, after all, I'm not holding you back...

MARCELLE: *(Crossing upstage)* Don't worry, you don't have to tell me twice! Ah, no, honestly!

FOLLBRAGUET: *(To* HORTENSE*)* What a temper!

*(*HORTENSE *approves by casting her glance skyward.)*

HORTENSE: The master is a saint!

MARCELLE: *(Coming back downstage)* And I'm even leaving you my bedroom. You can install Hortense in there, it'll make it easier for you to sleep with the maid!

FOLLBRAGUET: What!

HORTENSE: What did the mistress say?

MARCELLE: Good-bye! *(She exits left.)*

FOLLBRAGUET: She's insane! She is stark staring mad!

HORTENSE: Oh no! Oh no! I won't allow anybody to talk to me like that.

FOLLBRAGUET: Pay her no mind...

HORTENSE: Just because a person is a lady's maid doesn't mean a person has the right to say anything to her.

FOLLBRAGUET: Yes! ...And that's what my life is like, my girl, what my life is like!

HORTENSE: It may be what the master's life is like, but it isn't going to be mine! I'm leaving, monsieur! I'm leaving!

FOLLBRAGUET: What hell on earth, my God! hell on earth!

(A knock at the door.)

FOLLBRAGUET: Come in!

Scene Seven

(The same, ADRIEN, LEBOUCQ, then MONSIEUR JEAN)

ADRIEN: Monsieur, a gentleman has come about an inflamed gum.

FOLLBRAGUET: Ah! what a nuisance!

(ADRIEN sees HORTENSE going upstage. Snivelling:)

ADRIEN: What's wrong with you?

HORTENSE: *(Gently but angrily pushing him away, as she passes in front of him to exit)* Nothing, leave me alone!

ADRIEN: But what is it?

HORTENSE: *(Off)* Nothing…

FOLLBRAGUET: Oh! oh! oh! *(He crosses up to the door at back, which is open.)* What do you want, monsieur?

LEBOUCQ: *(His face wrapped in a bandage)* Monsieur, I'm in pain…I have an inflamed gum!

FOLLBRAGUET: *(Enraged)* All right, I can see that ! …Sit down over there! …And take off your bandage… *(He goes up to the wash basin and fills the glass with a mixture of dentifrice and water.)*

LEBOUCQ: *(Obeying)* Yes, monsieur! *(He sits. After a pause)* I think I caught it yesterday at the theatre, there was a draft.

FOLLBRAGUET: *(Putting the glass on the tray next to the chair)* Open your mouth!

(FOLLBRAGUET, at the end of his tether, as LEBOUCQ obeys:)

FOLLBRAGUET: Oh! I've had just about enough! It's high time it came to an end!

LEBOUCQ: What?

FOLLBRAGUET: Nothing! Open your mouth!

LEBOUCQ: *(Pointing to the tooth)* It's that one!

FOLLBRAGUET: Well, yes, it's a rotten tooth!

LEBOUCQ: *(In anguish)* Ah! then…

FOLLBRAGUET: I'll have to pull it.

LEBOUCQ: Wouldn't you care to keep it?

FOLLBRAGUET: Why? I don't collect them.

LEBOUCQ: Keep it for me.

FOLLBRAGUET: Oh! if you insist, you can keep it!

LEBOUCQ: Oh! you're really very rude!

FOLLBRAGUET: *(Looking for an instrument in his drawer)* Ah! if you were in my shoes! …Open your mouth!… *(He inserts the instrument into his mouth.)*

(LEBOUCQ, while FOLLBRAGUET pulls the tooth:)

LEBOUCQ: Ah! ah! ah!

FOLLBRAGUET: *(While pulling)* Stop shouting! My nerves are frayed enough without that!

LEBOUCQ: Oh!

FOLLBRAGUET: That's one tough stump you've got! I suggest you hold on to it. *(He puts the tooth in a tiny box like a pillbox.)*

LEBOUCQ: *(Panting)* Oh! good lord! Oh! good lord!

FOLLBRAGUET: Here! rinse out your mouth!

LEBOUCQ: *(Almost fainting)* Ah! *(He swallows the contents of the glass.)*

FOLLBRAGUET: Don't drink it!

LEBOUCQ: *(As before)* Leave me be! ...Leave me be!

FOLLBRAGUET: Come, come! You're not going to be sick?

LEBOUCQ: Ah! I feel that I'm going to...

FOLLBRAGUET: Don't leave... Here, you can lie down for a minute! *(Going to the upstage right door.)* Monsieur Jean! Monsieur Jean!

MONSIEUR JEAN: *(Appearing)* Monsieur!

FOLLBRAGUET: *(Who has come down to* LEBOUCQ*)* Here, take the gentleman to rest on the divan.

MONSIEUR JEAN: Yes, Monsieur.

*(*FOLLBRAGUET *passes* LEBOUCQ *to* MONSIEUR JEAN, *who takes him.)*

MONSIEUR JEAN: Come along, monsieur.

FOLLBRAGUET: Wait!

LEBOUCQ: *(In a faint voice)* What?

FOLLBRAGUET: *(Holding out the little box containing the tooth)* Here's your tooth, monsieur! You wanted to keep it...

LEBOUCQ: *(Taking the box conscientiously)* Oh! I don't want to any more! I'm going to! ...I feel that I'm going to.

FOLLBRAGUET: All right, go on!

*(*MONSIEUR JEAN, *leading* LEBOUCQ:*)*

MONSIEUR JEAN: This way, monsieur, this way.

*(*LEBOUCQ *to* MONSIEUR JEAN *exit right.)*

FOLLBRAGUET: *(Going to sit at his desk)* What a day, good God! what a day!

(A knock at the door)

FOLLBRAGUET: Come in!

Scene Eight

(The same, ADRIEN, *then* HORTENSE, *then* MARCELLE*)*

ADRIEN: *(Cold and dignified, stopping on the threshold)* It's me, monsieur.

FOLLBRAGUET: What do you mean, it's you?

ADRIEN: I would like to have a word with the master.

FOLLBRAGUET: What? What? What now?

ADRIEN: I was waiting until the master was through with his patient. When I heard Monsieur Jean take him away, I knocked.

FOLLBRAGUET: All right, talk!

ADRIEN: *(Crossing downstage)* Very well! The master is not unaware that the mistress has just seriously insulted Hortense?

FOLLBRAGUET: Oh! no! no! you're not going to start bothering me with that all over again!

ADRIEN: I am sorry to bother the master all over again, but I'm not doing it for fun. The master knows no doubt that I am dating Hortense?

FOLLBRAGUET: What?

ADRIEN: She finally gave in.

FOLLBRAGUET: Ah!

ADRIEN: Oh! with good intentions, for, even so, I plan to marry her.

FOLLBRAGUET: Ah! ...Well?

ADRIEN: Well! in my capacity as her husband, I cannot allow the mistress to say that Hortense is sleeping with the master, that would be degrading!

FOLLBRAGUET: Degrading! Degrading! First of all, I don't suppose you believe it!

ADRIEN: Oh no! I know my Hortense.

FOLLBRAGUET: Thanks on my behalf.

ADRIEN: And then I remember the way the mistress called the master a eunuch.

FOLLBRAGUET: Now listen here!

ADRIEN: I'm not trying to hurt the master's feelings, I just want to point out the illogicality of women.

FOLLBRAGUET: I didn't say you were, but...

ADRIEN: In short, Monsieur, things being what they are, I regret to announce that I shall be obliged to leave Monsieur's service.

FOLLBRAGUET: Well then, leave it! What do you want me to say?

ADRIEN: *(Dignified)* Very well, monsieur. From this point on I shall resume my place in society and speak man to man.

FOLLBRAGUET: What?

ADRIEN: I am a husband who is defending the honor of his wife. Either the mistress takes back what she said and apologizes to Hortense...

FOLLBRAGUET: *(Nervously bursts out laughing)* Hortense!...

ADRIEN: Or else, I haven't forgotten that I am an ex-regimental fencing coach, and I shall have the honor of sending my seconds to Monsieur.

FOLLBRAGUET: Your seconds! Ah! you must be kidding! You think I'm going to fight a duel with my servant?

ADRIEN: I am no longer a servant.

FOLLBRAGUET: *(Going to him)* Why, I'll throw your seconds out the door.

ADRIEN: In that case, after insulting those men, it will be shown that...Monsieur refuses to fight, and he will be declared incompetent.

FOLLBRAGUET: *(Bursting with angry laughter)* I'll be declared incompetent...incompetent...that's incredible! All right! Declare me incompetent! What the hell do I care?

ADRIEN: That's the master's business!

FOLLBRAGUET: *(Tearing out his hair)* Good lord! Good lord! Why is everybody giving me a hard time, what have I got to do with all this?

ADRIEN: Oh! I know it's not the master's fault. But since that the husband is responsible for his wife...I shall wait for the master's decision until tonight... Either the mistress apologizes...

FOLLBRAGUET: First of all, if you think the mistress will consent...

ADRIEN: Oh! because the master wishes it, because after all the master is legally head of the household, all the master has to do is declare his authority and say, "That's enough of that! I am the master and I insist!"

FOLLBRAGUET: Ah! yes... Easy for you to talk.

ADRIEN: Anyway, the master has until tonight before I send him my seconds.

HORTENSE: *(Who has been leaning in the doorway listening for a moment, bursting in and rushing to* ADRIEN*)* What are you saying? Seconds? You're going to fight?

ADRIEN: *(Pulling loose from her embrace)* Ah! please, this is men's business: keep quiet!

HORTENSE: Ah! no, you're not going to fight with these people!

ADRIEN: That's enough of that, I tell you! I am the master! And I insist!

(HORTENSE *takes it as settled. At that moment, there's ringing in the hallway.* ADRIEN, *in another tone, to* FOLLBRAGUET:)

ADRIEN: Until tonight, I shall do my job. I shall go and open the door.

MARCELLE: (*Leaving her room like a whirlwind*) Here's m...

(MARCELLE, *encountering* HORTENSE, *stops, looks the servants up and down; they make a dignified exit. Once they are gone, she throws a key on the table.*)

MARCELLE: Here's my key! ...My room is free, you may dispose of it!

FOLLBRAGUET: Is that so! Well, here's what I think of your key, I throw it in the fire!... (*He sends it flying into the fireplace.*)

MARCELLE: As you please!...

FOLLBRAGUET: You know what you've driven me to with your carrying-on?

MARCELLE: I don't care to know.

FOLLBRAGUET: I'm having a duel with my servant!

MARCELLE: (*Sarcastically*) Imagine that!

FOLLBRAGUET: Imagination nothing! ...Since Adrien is engaged to Hortense and you insulted her, he wants to take it out on me.

MARCELLE: Excellent! That's excellent! That proves that he's not like some people. When his wife is insulted, he takes up her cause! He's not a poltroon!

FOLLBRAGUET: Yes, well! meanwhile, you insulted Hortense, you're going to do me the pleasure of apologizing to her.

MARCELLE: Me! Indeed!

FOLLBRAGUET: And this very minute.

MARCELLE: Why? Are you scared?

FOLLBRAGUET: What are you saying, you idiot? Anyway, that'll be enough of that. I am the master and I insist.

(ADRIEN *appears and stops on the threshold.*)

MARCELLE: Ah! "you insist"! Take that! *(She slaps him.)*

FOLLBRAGUET: Oh!

MARCELLE: The master insists! *(She exits left.)*

FOLLBRAGUET: *(To* ADRIEN*)* Well! that's what happens, my good man, when I show authority. That's what happens!

ADRIEN: Ah! Of course... if you try to beat the odds...

FOLLBRAGUET: *(Exasperated)* Oh! no! no!

ADRIEN: Oh! but the master has all day ahead of him...

FOLLBRAGUET: Ah! leave me the hell alone!...

ADRIEN: The gentleman that the master treated earlier today is back.

FOLLBRAGUET: What gentleman?

ADRIEN: The one who was here just before the lady who came for her "yum, yum, yum."

FOLLBRAGUET: Ah!

ADRIEN: It seems he's still in pain.

FOLLBRAGUET: Fine! Good!...

Scene Nine

(The same, MARCELLE, THE COOK*)*

MARCELLE: *(Entering back left)* And now I bring you the cook.

FOLLBRAGUET: What? Why the cook?

*(*MARCELLE, *to* THE COOK *who, in the waiting room, is visible through the door:)*

MARCELLE: Come in, come in, my good woman!

*(*MARCELLE, *to* FOLLBRAGUET, *as* THE COOK *enters.)*

MARCELLE: Since it is clear that I mean nothing in this house...

FOLLBRAGUET: *(At the end of his tether)* Oh!

MARCELLE: That the servants mean more than I do...

FOLLBRAGUET: No, no.

MARCELLE: Yes, yes. Well, I abdicate my authority! From now on, you can take charge of the cook, her accounts and her menus! *(To* THE COOK*)* From now on, you can deal with Monsieur. I resign! Good-bye! *(She storms out.)*

FOLLBRAGUET: *(Runs after her)* Marcelle! Marcelle!

MARCELLE: *(Off)* Go to hell!

THE COOK: So what would the master like for dinner?

FOLLBRAGUET: *(Furious)* I don't give a good goddam!

THE COOK: *(Matching him in loudness)* Neither do I!

FOLLBRAGUET: What did you say? Are you telling me you don't give a good goddam?

THE COOK: *(Losing her cool)* But, Monsieur...

FOLLBRAGUET: Get out! Get out! You're fired. Go pack your bags. You'll leave here this very minute...

THE COOK: Oh, but, Monsieur, I didn't say it to offend Monsieur…

FOLLBRAGUET: Go on, scram! You'll go nevertheless!

THE COOK: It was to get a raise…like Hortense.

FOLLBRAGUET: Go on! Go on! On the double! *(He pushes her out and slams the door.)* Ah! everyone in the world is on my case around here!

ADRIEN: *(Who has been present during this, unnoticed in a corner)* Should I show the patient in?

FOLLBRAGUET: Yes! …No! …Who cares! Yes!…

Scene Ten

(FOLLBRAGUET, VILDAMOUR, ADRIEN)

ADRIEN: *(Opening the door at back right)* If Monsieur will step in!

VILDAMOUR: *(Coming downstage)* Oh! yes!

(VILDAMOUR, *to* FOLLBRAGUET, *while* ADRIEN *exits.)*

VILDAMOUR: Oh! I couldn't take it…I'm in worse pain than before…

FOLLBRAGUET: *(Indicating the dental chair)* All right, take a seat!

VILDAMOUR: Yes, monsieur!

FOLLBRAGUET: *(His mind elsewhere, elbows at his side, convulsively waving his fists and in a tone of muffled threat)* Oh! oh! oh! oh! oh!

VILDAMOUR: What?

FOLLBRAGUET: No, nothing, I'm talking to myself. *(He attaches a bib around his neck.)*

VILDAMOUR: Careful, you've caught my chin!

(FOLLBRAGUET *disengages* VILDAMOUR's *chin.)*

FOLLBRAGUET: You ought to pay attention!

(VILDAMOUR, *seeing* FOLLBRAGUET *prepare the rubber:*)

VILDAMOUR: Are you going to put a grand piano in my mouth again?

FOLLBRAGUET: I'm doing what has to be done.

VILDAMOUR: Oh! I'm going to have a fit...

FOLLBRAGUET: *(Thinking of himself)* Ah! ...If you think you're the only one!

VILDAMOUR: Yes, but I don't care about the others.

FOLLBRAGUET: Yes...oh! naturally...an egotist! Open your mouth!

VILDAMOUR: You're not going to hurt me.

FOLLBRAGUET: Of course not! Open up! *(He places the rubber on the tooth and fastens it behind, then inserts the saliva pump into the mouth. Then, he goes up to fill his glass at the wash basin: dentifrice and water.)*

VILDAMOUR: *(Incomprehensible under his gag, only the vowels decipherable)* Actually, this tooth should have been dealt with a long time ago, but I always held off, as long as it didn't hurt.

FOLLBRAGUET: *(Coming back with his glass)* Yes! Yes! Yes!

VILDAMOUR: *(As before)* But last night, the pain I suffered...

FOLLBRAGUET: *(An instrument in hand to hollow the tooth)* Yes, open your mouth!

(VILDAMOUR *obeys.* FOLLBRAGUET *pulls out the cotton and throws it away.)*

VILDAMOUR: *(As before)* I couldn't get a second of shut-eye, I felt like someone was drilling into my skull!

FOLLBRAGUET: *(Enervated)* Ah! please, don't keep talking...you're preventing me from working.

VILDAMOUR: *(Nonplussed, no sooner said than done)* Ah!

FOLLBRAGUET: *(His mind elsewhere, as he works)* And when I think I was stupid enough to get married!

(VILDAMOUR, startled, turns toward FOLLBRAGUET with eyes wide open.)

FOLLBRAGUET: Open your mouth!

(FOLLBRAGUET starts to operate the drill, which makes VILDAMOUR grimace.)

FOLLBRAGUET: Open up! *(He works on the tooth.)*

Scene Eleven

(The same, MARCELLE)

MARCELLE: *(Storming in)* The cook tells me you fired her?

FOLLBRAGUET: *(Exasperated)* Ah! You can go to hell!… *(Noticing that in his movement he has grazed VILDAMOUR's tooth with his rotating drill.)* Sorry! *(To his wife.)* I'm busy, please let me work.

MARCELLE: Yes, well! I won't allow you to fire Noémie, because I never had anything but praise for her.

FOLLBRAGUET: And when the cook is rude to me, I throw her the hell out! And anyway, that's enough of that! I'm with a patient, please leave me alone.

MARCELLE: All right!… *(To VILDAMOUR)* Sorry, Monsieur. *(To FOLLBRAGUET)* We'll discuss this presently. *(She exits at the back left.)*

FOLLBRAGUET: This is ridiculous! …Ridiculous, monsieur! Ever since this morning, monsieur, it's been like this!…Oh! …Open your mouth! *(He goes back to work.)*

MARCELLE: *(Offstage)* There's no need to fret so, my girl, the master isn't in his right mind, there's no need to pay him any attention.

(FOLLBRAGUET, *who hears everything, can hardly contain himself.*)

MARCELLE: *(Offstage)* He won't take offense on behalf of his wife, but he will take offense for his own sake.

(FOLLBRAGUET *as before*)

MARCELLE: *(Offstage)* Anyway, I'm telling you you can stay! I assume that I'm the mistress here! If anyone is in charge, it's me.

FOLLBRAGUET: *(Slamming his instrument down on the tray, and rushing into the waiting room, closing the door behind him, which doesn't prevent us from hearing everything.)* Excuse me, but I'm in charge of you!

MARCELLE: You! Ha ha ha!

FOLLBRAGUET: There's no ha ha ha about it! The only authority you have around here is what I've let you take, but you forget that I'm the one and only master, and the proof is that I fired the cook and she's going to make tracks this very minute.

THE COOK: But, monsieur, it ain't my fault.

FOLLBRAGUET: Well, you're leaving all the same!

MARCELLE: Never mind him…he's crazy!

FOLLBRAGUET: That's highly possible, but I expect to be obeyed! And that's that! Ah! really! *(He enters slamming the door; and comes down to VILDAMOUR.)* Open your mouth! …She's driving me berserk… *(Automatically holding out the glass to VILDAMOUR.)* Take it!

(Hearing the dialogue that carries on behind the door, FOLLBRAGUET *dashes to the door and opens it.*)

FOLLBRAGUET: And I repeat that you had better get out of here! I've had enough of your arguments! Get out!

MARCELLE: *(Offstage)* Is that so!

FOLLBRAGUET: I have spoken! Obey! *(He closes the door on her and comes back down.)* How dare she... *(No transition, to* VILDAMOUR.*)* Spit!...

*(*VILDAMOUR *obeys.)*

MARCELLE: *(Offstage)* Oh! I've had enough of this! I shall leave the house!

FOLLBRAGUET: *(Opening the door)* Do leave the house. You keep saying you will, but you never do! Leave it!

MARCELLE: *(Offstage)* Perfect, I shall leave it!

FOLLBRAGUET: What a blessing! *(Closing the door on her)* Oh! what a plague!

MARCELLE: *(Quickly opening the door)* What did you say?

FOLLBRAGUET: *(Spinning her around and pushing her out)* Go to hell! *(He closes the door and shoots the bolt.)*

MARCELLE: *(Behind the door, shaking it)* Open up! Open up!

FOLLBRAGUET: Drat!... *(To* VILDAMOUR*)* I beg your pardon for this grotesque interlude.

VILDAMOUR: *(Indulgently)* Oh!

MARCELLE: *(Bursting through the door at back right and crossing down to* VILDAMOUR*)* Monsieur! You are my witness! ...You are my witness that he called me a plague!

VILDAMOUR: *(Gagged)* But, madame!...

MARCELLE: You are my witness that he is throwing me out of his house! That he told me to leave the house.

FOLLBRAGUET: Yes, I did! Yes, I did!

MARCELLE: Did you? Well, I won't go! You forget that you put the lease in my name...because of your creditors... This is my house! You have to get out!

FOLLBRAGUET: Is that so? All right, I'll take you at your word! I'll leave your house! It's idiotic to work myself to death for your sake! You want to have all the benefits? Fine! You can also have all the expenses! Here, these are my instruments, this is my patient, I hand in my resignation. Go on! go on! work in my place!...

MARCELLE: Me?

VILDAMOUR: *(Terrified by the prospect)* Oh! no.

MARCELLE: Not if I know it! That's all right for you! Poking your finger in anybody's disgusting mouth, it would turn my stomach!

FOLLBRAGUET: *(Furiously removing his lab coat which he replaces with a suit jacket unhooked from a cupboard along with his hat)* Yes, which doesn't prevent that, thanks to those disgusting mouths *(Instinctively indicating* VILDAMOUR*)* in which I poke my fingers, I can pay for your dresses and "muslin, muslin, muslin." From now on, you can figure out a way to earn it yourself, as for me, I take my leave!

MARCELLE: Easy for you to talk! Only I warn you, tonight you won't find me in the house!

FOLLBRAGUET: Or me either! Good-bye! *(He exits out the back.)*

MARCELLE: Good-bye! *(She exits left.)*

VILDAMOUR: *(Who has followed this bit of dialogue in agony, rising and terrified at being abandoned with this contraption in his mouth.)* Hey! ...Hey! ...Hey!

(Curtain)

END OF PLAY

CPSIA information can be obtained
at www.ICGtesting.com
Printed in the USA
FSOW02n1842290817
38116FS